DANIEL
THE
PROPHET

Pilkington & Sons
Toll Free 1-888-316-8608
www.pilkingtonandsons.com

M. R. De Haan Classic Library

DANIEL THE PROPHET

M. R. DE HAAN

kregel
PUBLICATIONS

Grand Rapids, MI 49501

Daniel the Prophet by M. R. De Haan © 1995 by the M. R. De Haan Trust and published by Kregel Publications, P.O. Box 2607, Grand Rapids, Michigan 49501. All rights reserved.

Cover photo: Copyright © 1995 Kregel, Inc.
Cover design: Art Jacobs

Library of Congress Cataloging-in-Publication Data

De Haan, M. R. (Martin Ralph), 1891–1964.
    Daniel the prophet: thirty-five simple studies in the book of Daniel / M. R. De Haan.
        p.   cm.
    Originally published: Grand Rapids, Mich.: Zondervan, 1947.
        1. Bible. O.T. Daniel—Devotional literature. I. Title.
BS1555.4.D44   1995   224'.506—dc20   95-24911
                                                                                    CIP

ISBN 0-8254-2475-5

2 3 4 5 printing/year 99 98 97

Printed in the United States of America

Contents

Introduction

The messages which follow in this volume were first prepared for broadcasting purposes, and then later slightly corrected for publication in book form. We mention this fact at the very beginning because it will explain why much detail has been eliminated due to the limitations of radio time. No attempt, therefore, has been made to cover the book in great detail, but rather to give the mountain peaks, the more important truths, and to give a general working outline for the average believer to be used in further and more intensive study. There are two primary reasons for publishing a volume on the book of Daniel at this particular time. We fully realize that many splendid books on Daniel are on the market today, and that more able writers have set forth expositions of this marvelous prophetic book. Nevertheless, we felt very definitely led to add to the many books already in circulation this volume on this most up-to-date prophetic work given by the Holy Spirit.

The reasons were, first, the continual and insistent demand by the great number of our radio listeners for a volume on the book of Daniel as a companion book to our former volume on the book of the Revelation of Jesus Christ. Second, because we are living in the very days of which we believe Daniel wrote, the days of the end time and the end of this age; and because of the present-day developments and events, especially in Europe, we felt that a book on Daniel would be of

not only great interest but great blessing in explaining
the many things which are being fulfilled before our
very eyes. The unusual activity in the countries surrounding the Mediterranean, the Palestinian crisis, the
rapid development of the king of the north as exempli-
fied by Russia and its satellites, and the growing tension
and rift between the Anglo-Saxon and the Russian
peoples have led us to feel that a new interest might be
created by adding one more volume to the many others
already on the market.

One of the first rules in the study of the book of Daniel
is to remember that this book is primarily and first of
all a prophecy, dealing with things which still lie in the
future, and that Daniel was primarily a prophet. The
Lord Jesus Christ Himself in Matthew 24 tells us that
Daniel was a prophet. By this we mean a prophet, not
only in the broad sense of the term as a "forthteller"
of the good news, but particularly in the narrow sense
of the meaning of that word, a "foreteller" of things
which were to come in the days ahead.

Daniel should, therefore, be read and studied in connection with the last book of the Bible, the Revelation
of Jesus Christ, given by the Holy Spirit to John.
Daniel occupies the same office among the Old Testament
writers as John the Seer, the writer of the Apocalypse,
does in the New Testament. Both deal with the events
of this age in which we live and the end time which in
the broad sense covers this entire dispensation and in
the narrower sense refers to the end of this dispensation
and particularly the days preceding and during the
Tribulation. Daniel in his dealing with the end time
gives most of his attention to the "times of the Gentiles"
and the history of the Gentile nations during this present age and then the Tribulation as a secondary subject.

John, on the contrary, while he covers the same period of time, places his emphasis more particularly upon the Church during this present dispensation, and then gives more time to the Tribulation Period which is to follow. In Revelation 1 to 3 we have the history of the Church outlined under the seven churches of Asia Minor. As we said, Daniel gives the most space and time to the "times of the Gentiles," while John gives most of his space and time to the Tribulation Period. Both present to us a very graphic description of the chief actor of the end-time Tribulation, the "man of sin." And so we repeat that if one is to obtain a thorough understanding of the book of Daniel, he should read it in connection with Revelation and by the same reasoning the book of the Revelation should always be studied in connection with the book of Daniel.

OUTLINE OF DANIEL'S PROPHECY

In preparing a consecutive series of expository messages on the book of Daniel we find that this prophecy is not as easy to follow chronologically as the book of Revelation in which we can begin with the first chapter and follow through to the twenty-second and find that the events follow very generally in their proper chronological order, although there are some repetitions and explanations. However, in the book of Daniel, we have an accounting of a series of apparently separate events given in its twelve chapters, yet all of them interrelated and interlaced, and bearing on the same subject, the same object and the same purpose.

TWO MAIN DIVISIONS OF DANIEL

The prophecy of Daniel divides itself naturally into two parts of six chapters each. The first six chapters

of the prophecy of Daniel record for us the personal
history of Daniel, the man, of his own personal separated
and dedicated life, and his ministry in the court of the
king of Babylon where he interpreted the dreams of the
king in regard to the image as well as the tree vision of
Nebuchadnezzar. In addition to these incidents we have
the history of the four Hebrews, the three Hebrew children in the fiery furnace and Daniel in the lions' den, all
of which, as we shall see, have a very definite bearing
upon the purpose of Daniel in setting before us the
history of God's ancient people Israel during the time
of the Gentiles.

The second division of Daniel, chapters 7 to 12, is a
series of visions which Daniel himself received at various
times during his captivity in the land of Babylon, and
contains for us one of the most complete of all the revelations in the Scriptures concerning the course of this age
and particularly the time of the Tribulation Period.

It will greatly assist the Bible student who wishes
to master the prophecy of Daniel to summarize first of
all the contents of the twelve chapters of Daniel, bearing
in mind the two main divisions. It will greatly help in
understanding this prophecy if he has clearly in mind
just what each chapter relates and its relationship to
the other chapters which precede and follow it. The
harmony of the whole, and especially the progression of
the revelation in Daniel, will be appreciated. To assist
in grasping the teaching of Daniel we give the brief outline which follows and suggest that this outline, at least
the main features giving the content of each one of the
chapters, be memorized. This is not nearly so difficult
as it would seem at first. The best way to memorize it is,
first of all, to read through the book in one sitting if
possible; then to mark each chapter with your own de-

scription of its content and then memorize them in their order. To assist in this we suggest the following enumeration of chapter contents:

Chapter 1: God's Requisites for Divine Revelation
   A. A Separated Life of the Believer
   B. An All-Consuming Conviction of Truth

Chapter 2: The Image of Nebuchadnezzar
   A. A picture of the "Times of the Gentiles"
   B. History from Daniel to the Second Coming of Christ.

Chapter 3: Three Hebrews in the Fiery Furnace
   A. God's Reward for Faithfulness
   B. A Prophetic Picture of Israel in the Tribulation

Chapter 4: The Tree Vision of Nebuchadnezzar
   A. The End of Gentile Government upon the Earth
   B. The Conversion of the Nations in the Millennium.

Chapter 5: The Fall of Babylon
   A. The Writing on the Wall Today
   B. The End of Gentile Governmental Confusion

Chapter 6: Daniel in the Lions' Den
   A. An Encouragement to All Who Are Called Upon to Suffer for Their Faithfulness to the Cause of Christ
   B. A Picture of Israel's Preservation during the Time of Gentile World Dominion and the Great Tribulation

We feel that the little time spent in memorizing the twelve chapters and their contents will richly repay in a more thorough understanding of the book of Daniel and in facilitating not only grasping the content of each chapter but seeing the relationship between each one of these chapters to the total and whole of the purpose of the book of Daniel. Each reader should be encouraged to make his own outline. This will make it easier to remember and will be more of a personal matter. We give a number of rules of Bible study in the chapters of this book which will greatly assist not only in understanding the book of Daniel but in understanding all of the Word of God as well, especially prophetic truth. There is one rule of interpretation which is mentioned in one of the following chapters which is of such great importance that we want to insert it in the introduction at this time. It is this:

1. All Scripture has one primary interpretation.
2. All Scripture has several practical applications.
3. Most Scripture passages have also a prophetic revelation.

Bearing this rule in mind will prevent the Bible student from becoming unbalanced and bigoted and narrow-minded. To insist only upon the primary interpretation without regard to its practical implications and applications is to give way to a bigoted orthodoxy without warmth and without life. On the other hand, to ignore the primary interpretation and to be occupied only with its practical applications may result in fanaticism and losing the real purpose for which the revelation is given. It may be a practical blessing, and yet we may miss the greatest benefit by overlooking its primary interpretation. In the same way a great mistake is often made by ignoring the prophetic revelation by being occupied with the primary interpretation and its practical application, all of which may be exceedingly profitable, but if the man of God is to be thoroughly furnished unto every good work, he must not overlook the fact of prophetic revelation in the Scriptures. The warning, however, must be given in this connection that one can also be so occupied with the prophetic revelation of Scripture that the primary interpretation and the highly necessary practical applications are lost sight of so that one becomes a narrow-minded and bigoted eschatologist, sound in doctrine and efficient in prophecy, but fruitless in practice and cold in experience and as a result useless to his fellow men.

We send this volume forth with the prayer that the Holy Spirit who alone can bless the Word to the hearts of men may see fit to take these feeble efforts and apply them unto the hearts of God's people, creating in them a deeper interest in the study of the Word which we believe to be the greatest need of this age today. And then we also pray that it may awaken those who are still without Christ, should they read these pages, to a realization of the certainty of coming judgment and the certainty of salvation by grace, that they may turn and flee from the wrath to come. We pray God that these messages may be blessed in even a greater way in printed form than they were blessed as they were given over the air. It will be highly profitable to those who are interested in the study of this book, to first of all read through the twelve chapters of Daniel and then with a thorough knowledge of its contents read this volume, realizing that no exposition of the Scripture can ever take the place of the Scripture itself. With this hope and desire and with a prayer for God's blessing in the heart of each and every reader, we send forth this message, "looking for that blessed hope, and the glorious appearing of the great God and our Saviour Jesus Christ."

Grand Rapids, Michigan   M. R. DE HAAN

DANIEL
THE
PROPHET

CHAPTER ONE

The Scriptures Cannot Be Broken

Of all the beloved characters found in the Scriptures there is none more interesting, none more appealing and none more lovable and pure than the man Daniel. Together with Joseph he stands among the heroes of the Old Testament as one of whom practically no evil is recorded. And yet Daniel was a sinner and needed the grace of God as much as any other, as he himself so clearly acknowledges and admits in his prayer of repentance as recorded in the ninth chapter. And what is true of the man Daniel is true of the book which he wrote and which bears his illustrious name. The book of Daniel is a most remarkable book in many, many ways. It records for us the course of the history of the nations from Daniel's time even until the end, with an accuracy which has made the higher critics and skeptics groan in despair. No other book in the Bible has been vindicated by history more than the book of Daniel. All of the predictions and prophecies which it records have up until this time been meticulously and accurately fulfilled in every detail.

Target of the Critics

For this very reason the book of Daniel has been assailed by unbelievers and critics almost from the time of its writing. Those who reject the supernatural inspiration and infallible dictation of the Scriptures must somehow do away with the Prophet Daniel in order to disprove the Bible, for Daniel wrote concerning things of the future which would occur *after* the days of Daniel. Since all the things recorded in Daniel concerning the kingdom of Nebuchadnezzar and the kingdoms of Persia, Greece and Rome, all came true just as Daniel had predicted, the enemies of the Bible have put forward the explanation that Daniel was not an actual historic character at all, that he was not a prophet and that the book of Daniel was written long after the events prophesied had already happened. And so, they say, it is a history and not a prophecy, and was written by someone who just gave it the name and the setting of Daniel and dated it several hundred years back to make it appear as though it were written before the events actually transpired. But this denial of the inspiration and authenticity of Daniel is more serious than it at first appears, for it is more than an attack upon Daniel; it is a satanic attack upon the whole body of the Scriptures, and more especially an attack upon the truthfulness and veracity of the Lord Jesus Christ Himself.

Scriptures Verify Daniel

If Daniel was not real then the prophet Ezekiel also was mistaken, or an impostor, for in Ezekiel 14, the prophet enumerates and classes Daniel together with Noah and Job. And our Lord Jesus Christ Himself, when He was here upon the earth, took occasion to place His stamp of authenticity both upon the man and the book of Daniel, leaving absolutely no room for doubt as to Daniel's person and mission. Here are the words of the Lord Jesus speaking in Matthew concerning the end days, of which Daniel also wrote so much,

> When ye therefore shall see the abomination of desolation, spoken of by Daniel the prophet (Matthew 24:15).

Jesus calls Daniel *"the prophet."* To deny therefore the book of Daniel is to deny the Lord Jesus Christ. We have gone to this length in dealing with the authority of Daniel because there is no sense in studying the book unless we accept its genuineness and authority. If the Bible is no more than a book of fiction, there are other works of fiction easier to read and more pleasant to contemplate. If the Bible is merely a book of ancient history, there are other historic books as interesting and pleasant to read. But when we accept the Bible as the expression of the very mind of God, the infallible revelation through the Spirit of God, of His will, His purpose, His program and His plan of salvation, then the Bible becomes alive and real and the most intensely interesting and profitable book in all the world. Unless we realize that in the Bible *God* is speaking, and not man, it will mean little or nothing. Man, in the Scriptures, is only the channel and the instrument, God is the infallible Author. This, of course, presupposes faith, and the subjugation of reason and understanding to faith in God, but it is the only approach to the truth of God. Unless our faith in God, in His Word, and in His infallibility is greater than our own reason and understanding we shall never know the truth,

> . . . for he that cometh to God must believe that he is, and that he is a rewarder of them that diligently seek him (Hebrews 11:6).

And so the question comes down to this: Do you
believe this Bible to be the Word of God, the perfect
and complete expression of His divine will and the
revelation of His program and plan for the world and
the nations, and the lives of men and women? Your
answer can be either *yes* or *no*. There is no other al-
ternative. If your answer is *yes,* then you are prepared to go on with us as we study this first chapter
of Daniel and have your heart blessed and warmed by
its sweet and blessed truth, because you have faith to
believe in Him who made the worlds and the atoms,
who made you and who wrote this book of divine revelations for your instruction and profit, blessing and salvation. If your answer is *no!* and you say that you
do not believe the Bible to be infallibly true, then I
fear that this book will not mean much to you. It will
seem very dull and dry, unless the Lord opens your
eyes to the truth of His Word, for the unbeliever is
blind to the truth and the Word, and

> the natural man receiveth not the things of the Spirit
> of God,

and Satan

> hath blinded the eyes of them which believe not,

and Jesus says,

> Except a man be born again, he cannot see.

And so the rest of this book will be directed to you
who *believe God,* with a prayer that others of you
may be pierced by the two-edged, sharp sword of the
Word, until you too shall believe and enter into the
glorious experience of salvation and have your eyes
spiritually opened to see the wondrous things in the

Word of God. And so before we study Daniel let me suggest these five rules to guide us:

I. Daniel is a historic character who actually lived in the days of Nebuchadnezzar, king of Babylon (Ezekiel 14:20).

II. Daniel was a *prophet* who predicted things to happen in the future (Matthew 24:15).

III. Daniel deals with the things which will happen during this present Gentile age and the Tribulation Period to follow (Daniel 2:28).

IV. Daniel and his godly companions were a type of the nation of Israel to which they belonged. Their experience in the fiery furnace and Daniel's in the lions' den, are typical pictures of the history of Daniel's nation during the "times of the Gentiles" of which the reign of Nebuchadnezzar was a type and shadow. The deliverance of the three young men from the furnace and Daniel's safe-keeping and final deliverance from the lions are pictures of Israel's present protection by Jehovah and their ultimate deliverance and restoration in the land of Palestine.

V. In studying Daniel we must observe one of the primary rules of Bible study, a rule that every one who would know more of the Scriptures should memorize and bear in mind constantly. Here is the rule:

A. All Scripture has but one *primary interpretation.*

B. All Scripture may have several practical *applications.*

C. Many Scriptures have also a *prophetic revelation.*

I cannot emphasize too strongly the necessity of observing this rule. It will prevent us from becoming bigoted and narrow and conceited. To insist upon our *primary* interpretation and reject the practical applications results in a cold, dead, lifeless orthodoxy. To take only the practical applications of Scripture without regard to the primary doctrinal interpretation leads to fanaticism. To ignore the *prophetic revelation* is to close our eyes to the future, but to take only the prophetic in the Word of God without regard to the interpretation and application makes one a top-heavy, one-sided, unbalanced eschatologist.

Much of the Scripture by *interpretation* refers to the nation of Israel, such as almost the entire Old Testament. The tabernacle, the sacrifices, the feast days, the special laws of diet and dress and worship and the law and the ceremonies are not for us to observe. By primary interpretation they are for *Israel* during the age of the *law*. But they *do* have an application for us today and are part of that Scripture which is given for our profit and admonition.

As we study Daniel we shall further illustrate this point. The first chapter of Daniel carries some of the most needed practical lessons for this day of apostasy and compromise, although it is primarily a book of prophecies concerning the nations.

DANIEL THE MAN

Daniel lived before and during the captivity of the kingdom of Judah. The first two verses of the book tell us the setting and how Daniel came to Babylon.

In the third year of the reign of Jehoiakim king of Judah came Nebuchadnezzar king of Babylon unto Jerusalem,

and besieged it. And the Lord gave Jehoiakim king of
Judah into his hand (Daniel 1:1-2).

Now the opening record seems unimportant, telling
us that the king of Babylon came and captured the kingdom of Judah. That is history as we all know, but one
phrase in verse 2 is most significant. It is this:

And the Lord gave Jehoiakim . . . into his hand.

Why this record? Because God had prophesied this
very thing many, many years before it came to pass and
He reminds us here that God always keeps His word,
whether it be in the promise of blessing or of judgment.
Many years before, Hezekiah king of Judah had ex-
hibited the holy vessels of the Temple to a heathen king
in his pride and eagerness to strike a worldly alliance
and as a result God sent the prophet Isaiah to him as
recorded in II Kings 20:17-18:

Behold, the days come, that all that is in thine house . . .
shall be carried into Babylon . . . saith the Lord. And
of thy sons . . . shall they take away; and they shall be
eunuchs in the palace of the king of Babylon.

The same prophecy is recorded also in Isaiah 39. Now
the events in Daniel occurred over one hundred years
after these words were spoken by Isaiah but even
though delayed for a century or more, God never fails
to do what He promises, *whether* in blessing or in
judgment. Notice how accurately and in every detail
the prophecy was fulfilled. In addition to the spoiling
of the Temple, Isaiah had said that of Hezekiah's descendants the royal princes would be taken to be made
slaves, serfs and eunuchs in the house of the king of
Babylon.

This was literally fulfilled in Daniel 1:3:

And the king spake unto Ashpenaz the master of his
eunuchs, that he should bring certain of the children of
Israel, and of the king's seed, and of the princes.

Yes, God keeps His word, for among the captives were
the royal seed of which four are specifically mentioned
in Daniel 1:6:

Now among these were of the children of Judah, Daniel,
Hananiah, Mishael, and Azariah.

Many, many are the lessons here. God does visit evil
with judgment, for although He forgave Hezekiah his
sin, he had to pay the price. God delayed the judgment
one hundred years but it came. Significantly Daniel
was among those who suffered for the sins of his ancestor Hezekiah. Significantly, too, his name is *Daniel*
from the word *dan,* "to judge," and the fragment *el,*
meaning God. Daniel means *"God will judge."*

God Will Judge

This, then, is one of the first lessons in Daniel: God
will judge sin and evil. And that is true today. You too,
my friend, are under the judgment of God because your
ancestor sinned. Adam's sin lives on in you unless
blotted out by the blood of Calvary. You had no part
in Adam's sin but you are a sinner because of it and
under the sentence of death. Daniel too had no part in
the sins of his forefather Hezekiah, but he suffered
for them just the same. That is a truth, unpleasant
though it be. You may rebel against it all you wish, it
cannot change the fact that we do suffer for others' sins
and our children have to pay for and suffer for our
mistakes and sins. But that is not all. There is more.
God is also a God of mercy. In the midst of judgment
He remembers mercy. And although Daniel suffered

because of the sins of his fathers, God not only forgave but exalted Daniel and his three friends because they acknowledged their sin, believed God and were willing to serve Him. We shall take up the noble conduct of these four, Daniel and his friends, in the next chapter. Read Daniel 1 in the interim and refresh your memory with the beautiful story of these three Hebrews who refused to disobey God and because of it were *saved* from judgment.

APPLICATION TO THE SINNER

You have, I am sure, already grasped the lesson for us. Adam fell and God who had promised judgment must keep His word. Hence we, Adam's seed, are all under judgment and the sentence of death. Adam too was a king and we are the seed royal, like Daniel and his friends, but our father sinned and we are under judgment. There is no use denying it. But there is also a plan of mercy. And God today, in Jesus Christ who died and was buried and rose again from the grave, offers mercy and forgiveness and salvation and victory to all who like Daniel will *trust His promise* and believe His Word. Trust Him now and flee from the wrath to come.

> Verily, verily, I say unto you, He that heareth my word, and believeth on him that sent me, hath everlasting life, and shall not come into condemnation; but is passed from death unto life.

CHAPTER TWO

The Sins of the Fathers

"The mills of God grind slowly, yet they grind exceeding small." Thus runs the ancient proverb, setting forth the great but oft-forgotten truth that God, in spite of all that is said about His love and compassion and mercy, is still a God of righteousness, justice and truth, and will in no wise clear the guilty. The book of Daniel emphatically illustrates the truth of God's justice, for in Daniel we find God's own covenant people, Israel, in bondage to a heathen king in Babylon. God's people, to whom pertained the promises and the covenants and the law and the inheritance, reduced to slaves and vassals in a Gentile land. Because of Israel's idolatry and disobedience, the Lord had sent upon them the captivity of Judah. In the previous chapter, we pointed out the sad but patent fact that God does visit upon the children the iniquities of the fathers. God sees humanity as one race in Adam, and what Adam did must affect his children and posterity. This is an inviolate rule of creation. The whole tree is wrapped up in the seed and the whole forest lies hidden in the one tree. What the seed is, the tree will be and what the tree is, the forest which lies within it will also be.

ADAM'S SIN

As a result of this law of federal headship, God saw in Adam the whole human race, and when Adam fell the whole race fell and when the sentence of death was pronounced upon Adam, it fell upon all who were to spring from Adam's loins. This is ever true, and was true in Daniel's day. Because Hezekiah many years before had desecrated the holy Temple and its holy vessels by exhibiting them to a Gentile king to gain his favor, God had pronounced judgment upon King Hezekiah's seed. Isaiah the prophet had predicted in II Kings 14 and again in Isaiah 39, that of the royal seed eunuchs and slaves would be made in the palace of the Babylonian monarch. Years passed by and the pronouncement of judgment was forgotten by many, but finally the Word of the Lord came true and Nebuchadnezzar did come and did lead Israel captive, and of the royal seed were taken the choicest of the young men to become vassals, slaves and eunuchs in the palace of a wicked king. We repeat this fact again because it is one which is so often overlooked in the study of Daniel. For among this royal seed, so terribly and ignominiously disgraced by their involuntary subjection to a heathen king, were Daniel and his three friends, Shadrach, Meshach and Abed-nego. The record is given in Daniel 1:6:

> Now among these [that is among those who were to become eunuchs in the king's house] were of the children of Judah, Daniel, Hananiah, Mishael, and Azariah: unto whom the prince of the eunuchs gave names: for he gave unto Daniel the name of Belteshazzar; and to Hananiah, of Shadrach; and to Mishael, of Meshach; and to Azariah, of Abed-nego.

Here are three excellent and pure young men, suffering because of a judgment pronounced upon their

fathers before they were even born. The law of federal
headship works uninterruptedly, just as Adam's sin is
transmitted to all his offspring. Paul states this important truth again and again as illustrated in Romans
5:12:

> Wherefore, as by one man sin entered into the world, and
> death by sin; and so death passed upon all men, for that
> all have sinned.

Now the natural reaction to such a doctrine, in the
natural unregenerate human heart, is to rebel against
this fact and to accuse God of being unjust and unfair
in punishing the children for the sins of the fathers.
But rebelling will not help or change the fact. It is
a stark, inescapable *fact* which we face. The rather
we should acknowledge the righteousness of a sovereign
God and accept His remedy which He has provided for
the condition of our inherited sinful heart. It is not
only a *fact* that Adam's curse is passed on to us, but
it is a far greater and more glorious fact also, that
God in infinite wisdom has devised a plan whereby the
righteousness of another, even Jesus Christ the Son
of God, the Second Man and the Last Adam, can be
imputed to us freely and fully by faith in accepting
God's promise of salvation and righteousness.

ONLY TWO MEN

There are only two men in God's sight. The first man
Adam, the sinner, is the representative head of all
humanity. He is the head of a fallen race and "in
Adam all die." You are a sinner first of all, not by
choice, but by natural birth. If you have been born but
once you are lost with all of Adam's seed. But there is
another man, the *man* Christ Jesus. He is the head

of a redeemed race. Those who believe God's Word, repent, believe and receive this Man Christ Jesus as Saviour and Lord are born again and become members of a new race, the "general assembly and church of the firstborn, which are written in heaven" (Hebrews 12:23).

No Use Rebelling

The natural man rebels against the truth of inherited sin and the fact that we suffer for others' sins, but in rebelling he closes his eyes to the God-given remedy He has provided. The path of sanity lies in another direction. It is not in rebelling, but in facing the fact, and accepting God's provision, whereby our judgment may be removed. How beautifully it is all illustrated in the simple story of Daniel and his companions as seen in this first chapter of Daniel. Let me remind you again that *Daniel* means *God will judge*. And the presence of Daniel as a slave in Babylon was the evidence that God will judge the sins of the fathers. Now Daniel and his friends might have become cynical and rebellious and kicked against God's dealing with them, but it would only have meant tragedy and could not have helped them. How refreshing therefore to note the reaction of these four Hebrew youths in Babylon. Instead of finding fault with God's sovereign dealings and hopelessly resigning to a fatalistic philosophy of life, we read these tremendously informative words. *Note them carefully.*

But

But Daniel purposed in his heart that he would not defile himself with the portion of the king's meat, nor with the wine which he drank: therefore he requested of the prince of the eunuchs that he might not defile himself (Daniel 1:8).

In this verse we have another of those important *"but's"* of the Scriptures. Daniel had been made a eunuch because his fathers had sinned. He had been made a slave, he was being forced to eat unclean food, and drink the soul-damning and body-wrecking concoction of hell, intoxicating drink. Daniel might have become discouraged and bitter and blamed God and his fathers for his sad plight and either meekly submitted to his seemingly hopeless fate or become fatalistically despondent and say, "What's the use, I might as well get the most of this; eat, drink and be merry, for tomorrow I die."

But—but—but Daniel did no such thing. He did not lose faith in the righteousness and wisdom and justice of God. He did not lose heart for he knew God's promises. He knew that God had made a provision whereby guilty sinners could be forgiven, that God receives our repentance and will save. He knew that obeying God rather than men, and living a life of faith and separation would be rewarded by God's free grace. And so we read,

> But Daniel purposed in his heart that he would not defile himself with the king's meat.

He purposed to obey God. Daniel was a Hebrew of the royal seed and knew the restrictions concerning clean and unclean foods imposed upon the covenant nation and he would not defile himself, even upon pain of death. In a succeeding chapter, we shall see how his faith and obedience were rewarded by the Lord.

Ah, my friend, how I wish that I could press this lesson upon *your* heart, too! The book of Daniel is rich beyond all comprehension in lessons and instructions, but none more important than this great truth which lies here right on the surface in chapter 1. In God's dealings it is a law that "like produces like" and that everything brings forth after its kind. You are a sinner first because you were born of sinful parents, but you are a sinner also because you have chosen to reject God's only remedy. We have a most striking record of this same truth in the prophet Ezekiel who was for a time at least a contemporary of Daniel. In the eighteenth chapter of Ezekiel, we have the record of a dialogue between Jehovah and some of the captives of the nation of Israel who, unlike Daniel, did not accept God's remedy but insisted upon rebelling and finding fault with God's sovereign dealings.

SOUR GRAPES

God is speaking through His prophet and addressing the captives in exile.

> The word of the Lord came unto me again, saying, What mean ye, that ye use this proverb concerning the land of Israel, saying, The fathers have eaten sour grapes, and the children's teeth are set on edge? (Ezekiel 18: 1-2).

This was Israel's charge against Jehovah. They were suffering because of the sins of the fathers. The fact was recognized but they did not understand God's *entire* plan. For while God does visit the sins of the fathers upon the children, He *does not hold them responsible* for the sins of the fathers, but rather for their own sins of *rejecting God's remedy for sin*. This is the plain teaching of the verses which follow.

> As I live, saith the Lord God, ye shall not have occasion any more to use this proverb in Israel. Behold, all souls are mine; as the soul of the father, so also the soul of the son is mine: the soul that sinneth it shall die (Ezekiel 18:3-4).

Yes, the children suffer for the sins of the parents. That is an inexorable law. Like father, like son. But the individual will not be condemned finally for the sin of another. Christ died for Adam's sin and the only sin, the one and only sin, which can now condemn one is the *sin of unbelief in God's Word and in His Son.* God has taken care of Adam's sin; *you must receive His remedy.* But still they rebelled and we read in Ezekiel 18:25, as Israel still argues,

> Yet ye say, The way of the Lord is not equal.

To this final statement Jehovah replies,

> Therefore I will judge you . . . every one according to his ways . . . Repent, and turn yourselves from all your transgressions; so iniquity shall not be your ruin. . . . For I have no pleasure in the death of him that dieth . . . Wherefore turn yourselves, and live ye (Ezekiel 18: 30, 32).

It may seem that I am spending too much time on this angle of truth suggested by Daniel 1, but it is so important that I trust you will bear with me. Israel had stated a truth. We do suffer for the sins of our parents. But they had overlooked another truth. God will not condemn a man except for his *own attitude toward God's remedy.* Therefore, they will not be condemned except for their own personal decision and response to the light which God gives them. Before Calvary, men might have blamed God for their condition. Since God has made full and ample provision for salvation by the free gift of God, the responsibility now rests upon *you and me.* This takes care of the infants which die in infancy and those who are mentally unable to receive the truth of God. We need not worry one second about babes and children who die before the age of personal accountability; every one of them is saved since God has clearly indicated that we shall have to answer personally for what we have done with God's remedy, Jesus Christ.

An illustration may help. Imagine a young lady upon a bed of affliction. She is blind, paralyzed, helpless, racked by pain and suffering. The doctors tell her it is not because of anything she has done, but because of someone else's sin. Her grandfather in his youth had his fling, and contracted a disease, transmitted by the inexorable laws of nature to the third and the fourth generation. She is suffering because the virus of a terrible curse has been transmitted by birth to her from her grandfather whom she has never even seen. Now she may rebel against the seeming injustice of fate. She may become cynical and hard and blame God. But that will not change it. She is facing a sad fact, a fact hard to explain but a *dreadful fact*. We feel sorry for this girl. But now something happens. A physician, after a lifelong study has perfected an absolute cure for her disease. It is a cure which never fails. He sends word to the young lady, blind and despairing and helpless, and says, "I can cure you. I have an infallible remedy. I will come and give it to you, free and without charge. It cost me much, but costs you nothing. One dose of it and you will be completely and permanently cured. All I need is your consent to let me give it to you. Let me help you."

But the young woman is bitter and keeps repeating, "It just is not right, it is unfair; our fathers did eat the sour grapes and the children's teeth are set on edge. I will not take the remedy, although free, until I can understand why I should suffer for another's sin." All that will not help her at all. The offer of the doctor, however, has done one thing. It has placed the responsibility for her continued condition squarely upon her. Before the doctor came, she might hold her grandfather responsible, but now it is different. It is now her responsibility and hers alone. If she refuses the remedy, she has no one to blame but herself. What folly, what ignorant folly, for her to turn down such an offer.

Yet that is just the thing sinners do daily. If God had not sent the Great Physician to heal man's wounds of sin and conquer death, we can understand how men would try to blame Adam or God or someone else. But it is all different now. God sent His Son to die for the sinner and now offers salvation *full and free,* without money and without price to anyone and everyone who will believe God's promise, call upon the Great Physician and freely accept His salvation, purchased at such a price on Calvary. Do you not see, my unsaved friend, that it is now *all your own responsibility?* Since God gave His Son every excuse is gone. It is up to you. God has done His part; He can do no more.

The only sin which can damn a man now is *rejecting the offer of God.* In brief, it is simple *unbelief* in God's plan of salvation and His dear Son.

The Holy Spirit has come to convict men of *sin.* And that one sin which is defined is,

Of sin, because they believe not on me (John 16:9).

Oh, trust Him now and be saved.

We have taken all this time in the first part of the first chapter of Daniel because we need to know this basic fundamental truth before we can fully appreciate the rest of this wonderful book. In the next chapter we shall deal with the blessed reward of obedience as seen in the conduct of Daniel and his three companions.

CHAPTER THREE

Touch Not

But Daniel purposed in his heart that he would not defile himself with the portion of the king's meat, nor with the wine which he drank: therefore he requested of the prince of the eunuchs that he might not defile himself (Daniel 1:8).

Would to God that every Christian would, like Daniel, purpose in his heart to fully obey the Lord, no matter what the results, and determine never to be defiled by the offerings of this passing, fleeting world! Daniel stands among the heroes of the Bible above most all others as a child of God, whose whole life was pure and obedient and blessed. And if by the grace of God we can attribute these virtues to any one thing it was because he purposed in his heart to remain clean and separate even under the most trying and adverse conditions. In the chapters preceding this one on the first chapter of the prophecy of Daniel we have reminded you, that, according to the Lord Jesus Christ Himself, Daniel was a *prophet*. But Daniel is more than a prophetic book, it also contains some of the most pertinent and precious lessons of a practical nature for every believer.

In this present chapter we want to emphasize one great truth: the necessity of and the reward for living an obedient and separated life before the Lord. This I believe is the greatest and most dire need of the Church and the members of the body of Christ today. The call, ''Come out from among them, and be ye separate, saith the Lord,'' was never more needed than at this very moment. Daniel will have much to teach and encourage us in this chapter. Just because Daniel is a prophetic book, many have seen only the prophetic interpretation and missed its practical lessons of holiness. As a result we become hairsplitting theologians and experts of prophecy, but are as cold and dead spiritually as a cake of ice. We may become so intent upon the doctrine that we neglect the practical lessons of the all-important matter of personal spirituality and holiness and separation. God help us to avoid that pitfall, and before we take up the interesting prophecies of Daniel we would first of all learn the spiritual lesson of Daniel's life of devotion, holiness and purity, for until our lives are pure, God will not reveal His truth unto us. God will not open His truth and His Word to those whose lives are defiled and clouded by sin. So before we seek to know God's truth and will in His Word, we shall present the lesson of Christian separation and devotion, that you may the more clearly know God's will and understand His Word.

DANIEL AND HIS FRIENDS

From the first chapter of Daniel we gather that there were many other captives of Judah in the palace of the king of Babylon, who were chosen to become the attendants of the king. All of them were to be placed under special training and exercise and diet and then from these were to be chosen a few who were best fitted to occupy this important position in the king's palace. But only four of them were chosen and specially mentioned while all the others were forgotten and remain unmentioned in the record. And these four were *not* the ones who meekly submitted to the king's orders but were the ones who placed God's Word above the words of men, even the king, who refused to be conformed to the world and who steadfastly and unswervingly purposed to obey and serve God at any cost. And this determination to be loyal to the will of God was owned of God, recognized by men and rewarded in the end.

WOULD NOT BE DEFILED

In spite of the king's decree Daniel would not defile himself with the king's meat, but requested a purely vegetarian diet. Here is the record:

> Prove thy servants, I beseech thee, ten days; and let them give us pulse to eat, and water to drink. Then let our countenances be looked upon before thee, and the countenance of the children that eat of the portion of the king's meat: and as thou seest, deal with thy servants. . . And at the end of ten days their countenances appeared fairer and fatter in flesh than all the children which did eat the portion of the king's meat (Daniel 1:12, 13, 15).

Many are the precious lessons contained in these three precious verses. God does reward obedience. When we follow the Lord we do have something which reflects itself upon our countenances. These young men, because of being true to their convictions, had faces that were different from the faces of others. And peace of heart is ever reflected in joy of countenance and face. Furthermore, God honored the position of separation and testimony these men were willing to take. They refused to compromise with the world, they insisted upon obeying

God, and how wonderfully they were rewarded! Not only were their names immortalized in the record of Holy Writ for all eternity, but there were three other wonderful rewards. First, Daniel became the channel of God for a most wonderful revelation concerning the future. Second, he became the object of God's marvelous and miraculous preservation in the lions' den, just as his companions were delivered from and preserved in the fiery furnace. And then finally, they were rewarded by great exaltation, for Daniel was elevated to a high position and enjoyed a long and fruitful life. Revelation, preservation and exaltation, and God has the same promise for all of us who in this wicked world dwell as strangers and pilgrims. To those of His children who dare to be Daniels and not be carried away by the dictates and temptations of this world He promises also revelations of truth and preservation, and at the end of the road, exaltation and glorification.

GREATEST NEED OF CHURCH

Without fear of successful contradiction we dare to say that the greatest need of the Church today is a company of separated saints of God who will refuse steadfastly to be swayed by the world's program or the visible Church's apostasy. No greater blight has ever beset the Church of Jesus Christ than the blight of compromise and conformity to the world and its program. We are a redeemed people, a peculiar people and an holy nation. We are to shine as lights in the world and firmly refuse to bow before the gods of compromise and worldly standards. The line of difference and demarcation between the Church and the world has almost been wiped out, and those few of Christ's followers who dare to be different and refuse to go along with the crowd are so small in number that they are looked upon as odd and peculiar, and even fanatical and narrow-minded. It does cost something to be different and separate, but it is the only way which leads to the highest reward. The whole Bible pleads for a life and walk of separation among believers.

ISRAEL'S SIN OF COMPROMISE

It was the sin of compromise with the world that brought about the judgment of God upon the nation of Israel which resulted in Daniel being a captive in the land of Babylon. God had called the nation out of bondage in the land of Egypt and delivered them by blood and a mighty arm. He had protected them all the way for forty years by a strong hand. He had given them water from the rock and bread from heaven. Their clothes waxed not old nor did their shoes wear out. He gave them light from the glory by night and shade under the cloud by day. And then He brought them into a land flowing with milk and honey. He subdued their enemies before them and gave them an isolated place. He gave them a peculiar religion; a distinguishing special diet; a line of prophets, priests and kings; and even required of them a peculiar dress to keep them forever separate from the nations round about. In all this God wanted to teach them that they were His peculiar treasure and that they were to remain absolutely separate from the other nations. But Israel was disobedient. They began to intermingle with other nations, ate unclean food, intermarried with the Gentiles and lost their separated position. For this cause God sent them away into captivity and judged their land. The presence of Daniel and the other Hebrew youths in Babylon stands as mute testimony to the fact that God will have His people clean and that compromise with the world always results in the judgment of God.

Now of course you may say, "This was all under the law and in the Old Testament." But remember that these things were written for our instruction and admonition, and certainly we owe God more under the liberty of grace than under the whip of the law. The New Testament is very explicit in confirming the necessity of nonconformity to the world and separation for believers. Listen to Paul in Romans 12:1-2:

> I beseech you therefore, brethren, by the mercies of God, that ye present your bodies a living sacrifice, holy, acceptable unto God, which is your reasonable service. And be not conformed to this world: but be ye transformed by the renewing of your mind, that ye may prove what is that good, and acceptable, and perfect, will of God.

And again in II Corinthians 6:14-18:

> Be ye not unequally yoked together with unbelievers: for what fellowship hath righteousness with unrighteousness? and what communion hath light with darkness? And what concord hath Christ with Belial? or what part hath he that believeth with an infidel? And what agreement hath the temple of God with idols? for ye are the temple of the living God; as God hath said, I will dwell in them, and walk in them; and I will be their God, and they shall be my people. Wherefore come out from among them, and be ye separate, saith the Lord, and touch not the unclean thing; and I will receive you, and will be a Father unto you, and ye shall be my sons and daughters, saith the Lord Almighty.

This message is to believers. If you are not saved, of course this has no message for you, nor do we expect that you will take it seriously. But to you believers, let me repeat. The greatest need of the Church today is *separation*. We hear very little about Christian separation today. Not many voices are raised against the modern worldly practices of pleasure and dress and habits and conversation among professing Christians. It is too unpopular a subject and might entail disfavor and suffering. A certain preacher by the name of John the Baptist once lost his head because he dared to denounce sin. And today we too "stick our necks out" for the sword of decapitation when we boldly declare the will of God in regard to the matter of sin, especially sin among professing Christians.

How we Christians have failed! How we have compromised! Many a church dedicated by godly forebears and set aside for one thing only, the worship of God, has degenerated into an empty social center vying with the theater for entertainment and the restaurant for catering. Many of these churches have swimming pools, gymnasiums, pool tables and dance halls, while the voice of the Gospel is silenced and the message of salvation and grace is totally forgotten. The primary duty of the Church is a spiritual duty, preaching the Word, observing the ordinances, training the believers, teaching the saints and inviting sinners to receive Jesus Christ by faith. When the Church fails in these, it has lost its unique and separated position, and should change its name from "Church" to something else. In our eagerness to copy the world we have lost the one and only purpose we exist for as a Church.

True Individually

The Church is made up of individuals and so the worldliness of the Church is only a reflection of the worldliness of the individual members. No organization, no community, no group, no church rises any higher in spirituality, ethics or morals than the average of its members. And so all this departure of the Church from its primary God-given task of preaching the Gospel is a reflection of that same condition in the individual. What a change has come over us in a generation! What a change morally, spiritually and socially! Things which were condemned twenty years ago as gross immorality and sin today are countenanced and practiced by Christians as perfectly legitimate. It is not because the standard of morals has changed or sin is less sin than before, but because Christians dare not be different but must imitate and ape the world in its habits, fashions and conversation.

Paris decrees that the hair shall be cut until we cannot distinguish between the tender femininity of the women and the coarse and rugged masculinity of the men. And Christians, instead of holding their separated position, follow like meek lambs to the slaughter. The scandalous and positively immoral innovations of dress and attire, which I am sure are prime causes of the increasing evil of immorality and divorce and juvenile delinquency, are meekly accepted, and, worse than that, are copied by folk who confess to be Christians, with hardly a voice of protest even from those who are our spiritual leaders. Style decrees that finger nails shall be left to grow until hands look like bird claws, lips are painted with the color of the cyanosis of death. Now please remember, I am speaking about *believers*. I have no message for sinners, except, "Believe on the Lord Jesus Christ, and thou shalt be saved." Until you do that I have no message for you. I will not judge what you do. If you are unsaved there is nothing but judgment ahead for you and you know nothing of the peace and satisfaction God gives to those who are willing to trust Him and not depend upon the empty pleasures of this world to satisfy them. I cannot much blame you for drinking to the full of your sinful pleasures and gratifying your lusts in the brackish waters of this world for you have nothing but judgment ahead. So this message is not for you at all but for those of you who know the Lord.

The reason we Christians are not taken more seriously by the world, and why our testimony falls upon deaf ears most of the time, is because the world cannot see any difference between us and themselves. They see Christians frequenting the same places of worldly amusement, lining up at the same bar, using the same language, dressing in the same shameful way, painting their finger nails and toenails just lijke the world; they see Christians with half-pound earrings dangling, eyebrows plucked, lips painted, hair bobbed, just like the world. The only difference is that we have our names on the church rolls and go to church on Easter and Christmas and a few times between when we attend weddings or funerals. I am contending for a life of spirituality and separation among believers. That is the primary thing which is preventing revival and a renewal of the power of the Christian Church.

> Dare to be a Daniel,
> Dare to stand alone;
> Dare to have a purpose firm!
> Dare to make it known!

Does your neighbor know you are a Christian? Does the man who rides the bus know you are a Christian? The fellow who works with you? It did not take long to find out that Daniel and his three companions were followers of the Lord. The first test which came cleared away any doubts, for when it came to making a choice, they stood firm. Custom and precedent all decreed that they should eat of the king's meat, which in the story may well represent the good things and pleasures of the world. But they refused to be led by custom, accepted usage or precedent; they took as their only authority the Word of God. They would not be influenced by custom or style or popularity. They cared not what their friends might say or how they might be ostracized. They stood firm. The king's meat was unclean meat, and to partake of it would have defiled them, their testimony would have been lost and their rewards forfeited at the hands of God.

O Christian men and women, will you examine your hearts, your lives, your walk today, and in the light of God's Word and your wonderful salvation judge whether you in your conduct and conversation in social and business life, in your dress and in your habits are any different from the unsaved men and women about you? God grant you grace to be honest with God and with yourself, and "be ye separate" and get the blessing!

In our next chapter we shall attempt to bring one more lesson from this wonderful chapter on separation in the first chapter of Daniel. May God bless it all to all our hearts! I realize that these lessons will be sharply criticized and that to many they will not prove popular. I shall be called a "mossback," an "antique" and probably a "horse and buggy." Well, I am satisfied to be a horse and buggy and old-fashioned with Christ, rather than ride with the devil in a Cadillac.

CHAPTER FOUR

Dare to Be a Daniel

And the king spake unto Ashpenaz the master of his eunuchs, that he should bring certain of the children of Israel, and of the king's seed, and of the princes; children in whom was no blemish, but well favoured, skilful in all wisdom, and cunning in knowledge, and understanding science, and such as had ability in them to stand in the king's palace, and whom they might teach the learning and the tongue of the Chaldeans. And the king appointed them a daily provision of the king's meat, and of the wine which he drank: so nourishing them three years, that at the end thereof they might stand before the king. Now among these were of the children of Judah, Daniel, Hananiah, Mishael, and Azariah . . . But Daniel purposed in his heart that he would not defile himself with the portion of the king's meat, nor with the wine which he drank: therefore he requested of the prince of the eunuchs that he might not defile himself . . . Prove thy servants, I beseech thee, ten days; and let them give us pulse to eat, and water to drink (Daniel 1:3-6, 8, 12).

Daniel was a vegetarian in the palace of the king of Babylon. The request that he be given pulse to eat instead of the meat from the king's table was a request

for a vegetarian diet, for the word "pulse" refers to
herbs in the Scriptures. Now Daniel did not make this
request for simple reasons of diet or health as many
have supposed. There are people today who take this
action of Daniel as an argument against the eating of
meat, and insist upon a diet of herbs and fruits. They
even become very fanatical about matters of diet and
would condemn anyone who indulges in the eating of
animal tissues. But, as is always the case when we begin
to harp on one point, they become narrow and bigoted
and censorious. These people miss the point of Daniel
1 completely. Daniel had no objection to the eating
of meat. In fact God had made provision in the dietary
regulations of the nation of Israel for the eating of
clean foods, such as beef and lamb and mutton and certain kinds of fish and fowl. But Daniel's refusal to eat
the meat offered him in Babylon was because those
meats included certain kinds which were declared unclean by the Lord under the law. They had been strictly
prohibited as a sign of Israel's separation and peculiar
relationship to Jehovah. Among these prohibited meats
were pork, the flesh of carnivorous animals, certain
birds of prey and all fish without scales, a prohibition
which is still observed by orthodox Israelites today.
Now the primary reason for this prohibition was *not*
only dietary but spiritual and moral. They were not
denied these unclean foods because they were not good
to eat, for after Calvary and after the Cross and the
end of the dispensation of the law, this prohibition was
removed for the Church, and we today are not under the
dietary laws of the law. Peter had to learn this when he
refused to slay and eat of the animals which descended
in the sheet from heaven before going to the Gentiles

with the Gospel. In this sheet which Peter saw, we are told there were

> . . . all manner of fourfooted beasts of the earth, and wild beasts, and creeping things, and fowls of the air. And there came a voice to him, Rise, Peter; kill, and eat (Acts 10:12-13).

Peter had not yet learned the full lesson of grace and the end of the age of the law and so he refuses at first and says,

> Not so, Lord; for I have never eaten any thing that is common or unclean (Acts 10:14).

But a voice from heaven came again the second time and then the third time and the voice said,

> What God hath cleansed, that call not thou common (Acts 10:15).

Now of course we know the lesson Peter had to learn: that since Calvary the difference between Jew and Gentile as related to the Gospel had come to an end, the middle wall of partition had been broken down and now there is no difference, for all have sinned and all must be saved in the very same way, through faith in the Lord Jesus Christ. But the figure God used to press this lesson upon Peter was that of clean and unclean meats. To see only the resolve of Daniel not to eat meat as an argument against the eating of flesh is to miss the important spiritual lesson. Failure to distinguish between the law and grace only blinds men's eyes to real truth. This legalism and the denial of grace results only in confusion, bondage and uncertainty.

THE SPIRITUAL LESSON

Daniel then did not refuse the king's meat because he was a dietary fanatic, but an obedient child of God.

God had forbidden Israel the eating of unclean foods, freely indulged in by other nations, in order to facilitate their separated position. He wanted them to remain absolutely separate from the Gentile nations round about them; and to make it easier for them, He gave them an isolated land, a peculiar worship and ritual, one place of worship, peculiar regulations of dress, and a diet which would prevent them from fellowship with the unclean nations around them. The faithful Hebrew simply could not have social intercourse with these other nations, for that would mean that he would have to eat with them, and since they ate unclean food, he would have to defile himself and lose his separated position. The restrictions of diet were God's own provision to keep Israel in the place of blessing. Failure to observe this law brought God's judgment upon the nation. Isaiah clearly states this in Isaiah 65:3-4, where he says of the nation,

> A people that provoketh me to anger continually to my face; that sacrificeth in gardens, and burneth incense upon altars of brick . . . which eat swine's flesh, and broth of abominable things is in their vessels.

As a result God pronounces His judgment and says of this conduct of His chosen people,

> These are a smoke in my nose, a fire that burneth all the day . . . I will not keep silence, but will recompense, even recompense into their bosom (Isaiah 65:5-6).

NOT SO WITH DANIEL

This truth Daniel the young prince in Babylon knew. He knew that the king's meat was unclean and to eat it was to defile himself before God, and believing that we ought to obey God rather than men, he refused. It was

a serious thing to invoke the displeasure of Nebuchadnezzar, and disobey the greatest ruler in the world in
that day. Daniel refused to compromise with the world
no matter what the cost might be. We shall see later on
how God owned and honored Daniel's determination
and made it superlatively worth while to dare to invite
the displeasure of the world in obedience to God's Word.

OUR LESSON TODAY

So much for the primary interpretation of the passage
in Daniel 1; we now want to take up the practical
applications to our own heart. I realize that what follows will not only be unpopular with many of you, but
will also subject me to severe criticism. But I have a
conviction, a burning conviction, that God wants someone to speak frankly on the matter of Christian separation in these days, and I would not be disobedient to
this conviction, even though I realize keenly that it will
strike and cut, I fear, the majority of you believers
who ought to know better. Please remember what I am
about to say is born of a conviction that this is what we
need and what God wants. I am not apologizing, but
rather explaining my motive. If you disagree with me,
please do it in a Christian spirit. If you think I am
wrong, pray for me; if you feel deep, deep in your heart
that what I say is right, don't be disobedient and invite
the judgment of God.

A PECULIAR PEOPLE

Christians are called a "peculiar people" in the Bible.
The word "peculiar" comes from a Latin word,
peculium, which means a "private possession." It was
applied to things which were particularly one's own
personal property, and not for the public. A *veculium*

was something which was your very own private possession. And we are God's *peculium,* His own purchased
possession. We are not our own, we are bought with a
price, the inestimable price of the precious blood of the
Lord Jesus Christ. This is God's claim upon us, and we
are to realize that we are *His* and *His* alone, His
peculiar possession. The word "peculiar," therefore,
does not mean that we must be odd or funny or fanatical
in conduct or dress and be known by the outlandish garb
of a special sect, or by peculiar inflections of a pious
voice or silly eccentricities in diet. The rather, we
are peculiar in this, that we recognize God's claim upon
us, and therefore refuse, steadfastly refuse, to go along
with the sinful or questionable customs of the world,
and will have no part in anything whatsoever which is
displeasing to God and contrary to the plain teaching
of His infallible Word. John says, "Love not the world,
neither the things that are in the world." And Paul in
I Corinthians 7:31 tells us that while we are in the
world, we are to "use this world, as not abusing it: for
the fashion of this world passeth away." The Lord is
a reasonable God and willingness to be different and
be His "peculiar treasure" rather than court the favor
of this world, will be rewarded with blessings and joy
unspeakable and full of glory.

Plain Talk

And now five minutes of plain talk, while we again remind you that what we say is from a heart desirous of
pleasing God and helping you as Christians, for this is
for you if you are a Christian. The Bible is crystal
clear on the matter of separation in walk, conduct, conversation and dress of the believer. We believe it is
pleasing to God to adorn properly and comfortably

and beautifully these bodies of ours, the temples of the Holy Ghost, but some of us preachers must raise our voices against the extremes and immodesty of dress both in men and women today. There is no wrong in carefully and attractively adorning these bodies. Yet one of the saddest things, in recent years especially, is the eagerness with which Christians adopt the devilish extremes of modern attire. There is so much to say here that one knows not where to begin. Modern woman has bobbed her hair, painted her nails, calcimined her face, plucked her eyebrows and put on male attire until the last trace of femininity, daintiness and motherliness is gone. In regard to the hair I will let the Bible speak, lest you think it is merely a preacher's narrow idea. Listen:

> For if the woman be not covered, let her also be shorn: but if it be a shame for a woman to be shorn or shaven, let her be covered . . . Judge in yourselves: is it comely that a woman pray unto God uncovered? Doth not even nature itself teach you, that, if a man have long hair, it is a shame unto him? But if a woman have long hair, it is a glory to her: for her hair is given her for a covering (I Corinthians 11:6, 13-15).

O Christian woman, this is God's Word. Where is *your glory?*

The same is true of modes of dress adopted by the world and copied by Christians, and again I am addressing myself to those of you who still have enough love for the Christ who saved you to want to do His will and please Him, and who still believe the Bible is not outdated. While we may abhor the extremes of a generation ago with its bustles and rats and the dresses trailing in the filth of the streets, we denounce with greater emphasis the other extremes of today. The shameful abbreviation of dress with which both men and women appear in public is utterly unbecoming to Christians and a disgrace to the Name of Christ. Add to this the pagan practices of artificial eyelashes and clawlike finger nails, painting of toenails, plucking of hair, painting of face and lips with the colors of death, and it becomes a spectacle indeed. That the world practices these we can understand; why Christians do remains a contradiction to all we profess. What we have said so far is clearly taught in the Word. Listen to old narrow-minded Peter, speaking of *Christian women*:

> Whose adorning let it not be that outward adorning of plaiting the hair, and of wearing of gold, or of putting on of apparel; but let it be the hidden man of the heart, in that which is not corruptible, even the ornament of a meek and quiet spirit, which is in the sight of God of great price (I Peter 3:3-4).

And you, men, is your life a life of separation? Do you dress like a Christian or expose yourself in public till you have little more on you than a monkey? Among your friends does your conversation bespeak your profession, or do you go along with and laugh at, or even tell the debasing and vile jokes and stories that seem to be an indispensable part of the conversation wherever men congregate? Do you do business like a Christian? Do you shun from joining any organization where you cannot act and live like a Christian whether it be a club, a lodge or a union? Do you dare to invite ridicule and even material loss, or even the loss of your job because you will not support and go along with the "unfruitful works of darkness"? God is ready to honor a determined stand for Christ, and refusal to endorse anything which dishonors Him.

I am not an extremist or a fanatic, but am convinced that because of the Christian's fear of people's opinions and criticism, we have lost our power and testimony and blessing. But it paid a Daniel and it will pay us. As a result of all these let-downs and removal of the bars of moral restraint, and disregard of the Word of God, the world is heading for moral chaos today. Broken homes, divorce, childless marriages, juvenile crime and unchastity are sweeping like a flood tide over the nation, until even those who do not share the views I have expressed from the Word, do agree with us that unless there is a curbing of all these influences, America is morally and spiritually doomed.

This concludes the four chapters on Daniel 1. We have gone into some detail to bring out what seems to us the important lesson in this first chapter, and yet one which is usually overlooked, or passed rapidly by, to get at the second chapter with its more appealing and spicy diet of prophetic truth. Before we can appreciate Daniel the prophet, we must get the background of Daniel the saint in this first chapter. The revelations God made to Daniel in the chapters to follow, came only because Daniel dared to take a stand against the customs and fashions of the world, and in obedience to the Word of God, take an uncompromising and separated stand as one of God's peculiar people. Will you, too, stop now and check up on yourself and ask, "How much different am I, *a Christian,* than the world about me?" Then turn once again to Romans 12:1-2:

> I beseech you therefore, brethren, by the mercies of God, that ye present your bodies a living sacrifice, holy, acceptable unto God, which is your reasonable service. And be not conformed to this world: but be ye transformed by the renewing of your mind, that ye may prove what is that good, and acceptable, and perfect, will of God.

Dare to be a Daniel!

CHAPTER FIVE

The Times of the Gentiles

And in the second year of the reign of Nebuchadnezzar, Nebuchadnezzar dreamed dreams, wherewith his spirit was troubled, and his sleep brake from him. Then the king commanded to call the magicians, and the astrologers, and the sorcerers, and the Chaldeans, for to shew the king his dreams. So they came and stood before the king. And the king said unto them, I have dreamed a dream, and my spirit was troubled to know the dream. Then spake the Chaldeans to the king in Syriack, O king, live for ever: tell thy servants the dream, and we will shew the interpretation. The king answered and said to the Chaldeans, The thing is gone from me: if ye will not make known unto me the dream, with the interpretation thereof, ye shall be cut in pieces, and your houses shall be made a dunghill (Daniel 2:1-5).

And the decree went forth that the wise men should be slain; and they sought Daniel and his fellows to be slain. Then Daniel answered with counsel and wisdom to Arioch the captain of the king's guard . . . He answered and said to Arioch the king's captain, Why is the decree so hasty from the king? . . . Then Daniel went in, and desired of the king that he would give him time, and that he would shew the king the interpretation. Then Daniel went to his house, and made the thing known to . . . his companions: . . . that they would desire mercies of the God of heaven concerning this secret . . . Then was the secret revealed unto Daniel in a night vision. Then Daniel blessed the God of heaven (Daniel 2:13-19).

We have quoted at length these verses from Daniel 2 in order to refresh your memories concerning the setting of this wonderful chapter which contains one of the most prophetic pictures in the entire Bible. In this second chapter of Daniel we have a dream of a wicked king, wherein God revealed an outline of the history of the world in much detail and gives the course of time from Daniel until the glorious Second Coming of Christ. It has been called the *ABC* of Bible prophecy, and studied in conjunction with the last book of the Bible, Revelation, will give the clearest outline and understanding of Bible prophecy found anywhere. Daniel is the book of the Revelation of the Old Testament.

THE WORLD IS A STAGE

The world today is a vast stage with the curtain still down, while the actors are preparing for the last scene in the great drama of human history. The play is almost done; there remains but one more scene, the last days and the coming of the Lord to set up His kingdom. Behind the curtain we hear the commotion of the stage hands as they set up the machinery and set the stage for the last climactic scene. We hear the setting of the stage on every hand as man still seeks to bring a man-made world peace, and a federation which will guarantee the cessation of the plagues of war and destruction, pestilence, poverty and want, which have vexed humanity since sin began. Unrest throughout the world, preparations for war amid talking of peace, peace councils and agreements, while the clouds of judgment gather in this hectic atomic age, so soon to close.

Now the book of Daniel takes us upon this stage, behind the curtain before it rises. To the believing student of Scripture, God offers to reveal what is going to happen after the curtain rises. This privilege of knowing the events ahead, this favor of entering into the secrets of the future of these old nations and the world, is reserved for those who believe God's Word and receive His Son Jesus Christ by faith. To all others the curtain remains down, and Daniel has no message to them. To them the questions, "What lies ahead?" and "What about future peace, and the next war?" and "Will the nations be able to outlaw war?" and a million other questions remain in the realm of speculation, but to the believer all these things are known, for we can turn to Daniel and find the answer as certainly as Daniel received the interpretation of Nebuchadnezzar's dream.

TIMES OF THE GENTILES

This second chapter of Daniel deals with a period of time known in Scripture as the "times of the Gentiles," a period of time extending from the captivity of Judah some six centuries before Christ, and ending with the Second Coming of Christ at the beginning of the millennial kingdom age. This "times of the Gentiles" began with the reign of Nebuchadnezzar, and Daniel and his companions were among the captives when this time began. Because of Daniel's faithfulness to God, God now prepares to reveal through Daniel the course of this age from Judah's captivity to the setting up of the Messianic kingdom. This revelation was made at the very beginning of the Gentile age for a very definite reason. There were among the captives of Israel a number of faithful ones who had not been guilty of the sins of the nation, because of which they had gone into captivity. These faithful ones must have been much disturbed at the breaking up of the kingdom of Israel and Judah. God had made His promise to Abraham, Isaac and Jacob and David, and through all the prophets that they (Israel) were His covenant nation, that they would be the head among the nations of the world, that their Messiah would come in due time and set up the kingdom of Israel which should never, never end, and that the land of Palestine given to the nation by divine covenant to Abraham would be their safe and peaceful dwelling place forever and ever. Under David and Solomon it seemed that this glorious age had come, but a few hundred years afterward, the whole nation was taken captive and carried away to pagan lands to serve in bondage. They were out of the land, their independence was gone, they were ruled over by a heathen king.

The Question and the Answer

This must have been the question which arose in the hearts of the faithful who looked for the hope of Israel. Has God clean forgotten His promise and His covenant? Is this the end of the history of the glorious nation and the covenant people? Will all the promises of God concerning the kingdom go by the board? Was God mistaken, or did we misunderstand His Word, and instead of a literal kingdom, must we spiritualize His promises and look for something else? These and kindred thoughts must have arisen in the hearts of Daniel and all the faithful. To Daniel, therefore, God revealed the answer to all these questions. *No*, God has not forgotten His covenant, and although Israel will be scattered many centuries for their sins, in the end time God will restore

the nation, set up the kingdom and fulfill every promise
He has made concerning the blessing of His earthly
people in the land of Canaan forever and forever.
The period of time which will elapse between their
dispersion among the nations and their regathering in
the kingdom at the coming again of the Messiah, is the
burden of Daniel's prophecy, given at that particular
time to encourage and reassure the faithful ones, that
although for the present they are captives, in the end
they will be regathered and all that God had promised
to the fathers, and through the prophets, shall yet be
fulfilled. This period of time, we repeat, is called in
Scripture the "times of the Gentiles." God had committed the government of the world to the nation of Israel, administered through priests and prophets and godly kings. But the nation was disobedient, and God interrupted the kingdom and now commits it for a while to
the Gentile nations. This has been going on since the
days of Nebuchadnezzar, but is rapidly drawing to a
close, as the nations are engaged in a last desperate
death struggle to avert complete destruction of the world
in this atomic age. When it seems that all is hopelessly
lost, then the King will return and end the "times of
the Gentiles," and set up His glorious kingdom of peace
and righteousness.

The King's Dream

The revelation of this age was given to Daniel in
response to a dream of a wicked king. Nebuchadnezzar
had conquered the then known world and subjected all
nations under him. Then we are told in our chapter that
as he lay upon his bed he began to wonder about the
future, and what would be hereafter. He knew he would
not be here forever and probably knew his kingdom

would not stand always, for all the other world kingdoms
before him had fallen and given way to other conquerors.
He became so concerned that when he finally fell asleep
he dreamed a dream, which we know was God's picture
interpreted through Daniel of this present age and the
end time. At first the king called all the wise men of
Babylon and made a very unreasonable request. He
demanded of them to tell him not only the interpretation
of the dream but the dream itself. Whether he had
actually forgotten the dream, or whether this was a
test of the Chaldean fakirs, is beside the point. The
point is this, that God was about to reveal to Daniel
and through him to us what would happen during the
interval between Israel's dispersion and their final regathering.

This revelation was in the form of a dream. The king
saw a great image, consisting of a head of gold, chest
and arms of silver, a belly and thighs of brass and legs
and feet of iron. The ten toes of the image were a mixture of iron and clay. Then the king saw a great stone
cut out of a mountain without hands, a supernaturally
produced, miraculous stone, and the stone itself began
to grow and grow, until it filled the face of the whole
earth. In the next chapter we shall take up in detail the
meaning of each of these parts of the great image according to Daniel's interpretation, and the identity of
the great rock which destroyed the image, and filled the
whole earth. But here we want to give you the key. The
image represents the kingdoms and governments of this
world in its several historic stages. It represents man's
effort to make a federation, a world federation of nations, to secure peace and prosperity for all time. The
head of gold was the world empire of Babylon. The chest
of silver was the Persian empire which conquered and

superseded the Babylonian Empire. The belly and thighs
of brass was Greece which in turn conquered the Medo-
Persians, and finally the last was the Roman Empire
of iron, divided into the eastern and western empires
as seen in the two legs. The feet of ten toes is the final
form of Gentile world government, now this very day,
we believe, in the process of formation. There shall be
a federation of ten kingdoms, which will suddenly be
destroyed by the personal appearance of the Rock of
Ages, the Foundation Stone and the Smiting Stone,
even the Lord Jesus Christ Himself, and His kingdom
shall be established and cover the whole earth, and
shall never end. This is the brief summary of the dream
and interpretation of Daniel 2. We shall elaborate on it
in our next chapter.

The Second Coming of Christ, the Smiting Stone of
Daniel 2, will end the period of time, lasting over twenty-
five hundred years, known as the "times of the Gentiles." Jesus, in speaking of the destruction of Jerusalem, tells us this in predicting the final deportation
of the nation and the destruction of the capital of Palestine:

> And they shall fall by the edge of the sword, and shall
> be led away captive into all nations: and Jerusalem shall
> be trodden down of the Gentiles, until the times of the
> Gentiles be fulfilled (Luke 21:24).

This "times of the Gentiles" is not to be confused
with the "fulness of the Gentiles" spoken of by Paul
in Romans 11:25. While the "times of the Gentiles" and
the "fulness of the Gentiles" cover in a general way
the same historic period, they refer to quite opposite
peoples. The "times of the Gentiles" refers to the period
of time from Nebuchadnezzar to the Second Coming of
Christ, when the kingdom of Israel is in abeyance and

the nations are left to rule and govern the earth. The "fulness of the Gentiles" refers to the Church, the body of Christ. It covers this present age from Pentecost to the Rapture of the Church. The "fulness of the Gentiles" is the completion of the Church of Christ, the body of Christ.

The "times of the Gentiles" is rapidly drawing to a close and the "fulness of the Gentiles" is almost here. Then the Lord Jesus will come and take away His Church and begin the last form of man's rule on earth under the figure of the ten toes of the feet of the image and then the stone will fall from heaven in the Person of the Lord Jesus Christ. Man's rule will be at an end, his bungling job of trying to govern himself and set up a Utopian world kingdom without Christ will be over and then

> Christ shall have dominion over land and sea,
> And earth's remotest regions, shall His empire be.

From the very beginning of human history man has tried to set up a kingdom without God's King. It began in Genesis 10 and 11 under Nimrod who built the first Babylon. Then came Assyria, to be followed by Egypt, Babylon, Persia, Greece and Rome. There were six great attempts to establish a world kingdom. But the Bible says there will be eight in all before man's age comes to an end. This is clearly indicated in Revelation 17, where John is giving us a picture of the last form of human government:

> And there are seven kings [or kingdoms, for a king implies a kingdom]: five are fallen, and one is, and the other is not yet come; and when he cometh, he must continue a short space. And the beast that was, and is not, even he is the eighth, and is of the seven, and goeth into perdition. And the ten horns which thou sawest are ten kings, which

have received no kingdom as yet; but receive power as kings one hour with the beast (Revelation 17:10-12).

This passage speaks of seven kingdoms. We know from history that these have all existed except *two.* There were six, no more, no less. John said when he wrote nineteen hundred years ago that *five have fallen* and one is. Assyria, Egypt, Babylon, Persia and Greece (*five in all*) were no more and the sixth was the Roman Empire then in power. That, too, has since fallen. Now there remains only the last form of world confederacy and union, which will last only a little while and will be taken over by the eighth, the kingdom of the beast, the man of sin, the Antichrist who will reign for just a few years and federate ten great nations into the feet of Nebuchadnezzar's image only to fall before the brightness of the Lord's coming.

In Daniel's day the *two first* ones were already history, Assyria and Egypt, so he saw only the last six: the head, Babylon; the chest, Persia; the thighs, Greece; the legs, Rome; the feet and toes, the revived Roman Empire; and then in chapter 11, the last brief reign of the Antichrist.

Today we believe we can clearly trace the outline of the formation of the end-time confederacy, the Big Ten. We have heard of the Big Three and the Big Four and the Big Five. We wonder how soon we will be hearing of the Big Ten. We believe very, very soon. The end is at hand. The next event is the return of the Lord in the clouds to take us believers out before all the wrath of hell breaks loose upon the old world for a brief time under the reign of Satan's last man in an attempt to set up a kingdom without the King. God help us to be ready for the next greatest of all events, the coming of the Lord Jesus Christ.

CHAPTER SIX

Nebuchadnezzar's Image

Daniel answered in the presence of the king, and said, The secret which the king hath demanded cannot the wise men, the astrologers, the magicians, the soothsayers, shew unto the king; but there is a God in heaven that revealeth secrets, and maketh known to the king Nebuchadnezzar what shall be in the latter days. Thy dream, and the visions of thy head upon thy bed, are these; as for thee, O king, thy thoughts came into thy mind upon thy bed, what should come to pass hereafter: and he that revealeth secrets maketh known to thee what shall come to pass . . . Thou, O king, sawest, and behold a great image . . . This image's head was of fine gold, his breast and his arms of silver, his belly and his thighs of brass, his legs of iron, his feet part of iron and part of clay. Thou sawest till that a stone was cut out without hands, which smote the image upon his feet that were of iron and clay, and brake them to pieces. Then was the iron, the clay, the brass, the silver, and the gold, broken to pieces together . . . and the stone that smote the image became a great mountain, and filled the whole earth. This is the dream; and we will tell the interpretation thereof before the king (Daniel 2:27-29; 31-36).

In this brief record we have Daniel's answer to the demand of the king of Babylon to recall and interpret a dream which the king had dreamed but as promptly

forgotten. It was a most unreasonable demand and all
the wise men in Babylon were unable to meet it and
were, therefore, to be put to death. But Daniel, God's
servant, springs to the rescue, calls a prayer meeting
with his friends, and then goes to the king. In the
Scriptures we read that he tells the king exactly and in
detail the dream which he had seen. The king immediately recognizes the dream and then follows the
interpretation.

But before we take up the meaning of the dream of
this image, I would have you notice carefully three expressions which will give us the key to understanding
it better. These three are *latter days* (Daniel 2:28),
should come to pass hereafter (Daniel 2:29), and the
expression found in this same verse, *what shall come to
pass*. Here they are again, the three expressions:

1. Latter days
2. Should come to pass *hereafter*
3. *Shall come* to pass

DEALS WITH THE FUTURE

All three of these expressions emphasize the fact
which must not be lost sight of: this image is a picture
of *future things*. It is a prophecy and deals with
things which had not yet happened, but lay in the days
ahead, even to the *latter* days. We insist upon this
because skepticism and infidelity have attacked Daniel
again and again, and tried to prove that it is not a
prophetic book, and does not deal with future events.
But Daniel is very clear on the matter, and tells the
king that this image of gold, silver, brass, iron and
clay, is a picture of things to come.

THE INTERPRETATION

Bearing carefully in mind, therefore, the prophetic aspect of the dream, let us see Daniel's divinely-revealed interpretation. If we read it simply and literally, without prejudice or preconceived conclusions, it will be very clear and easy to believe and understand, for it is now over two and a half millenniums since Daniel spoke these words, and therefore we can turn to history itself to check the accuracy of Daniel's prediction. Here is the interpretation. We quote it in its entirety because of its clarity.

Thou, O king, art a king of kings: for the God of heaven hath given thee a kingdom, power, and strength, and glory. And wheresoever the children of men dwell, the beasts of the field and the fowls of the heaven hath he given into thine hand, and hath made thee ruler over them all. **Thou art this head of gold.** And after thee shall arise another kingdom inferior to thee, and another third kingdom of brass, which shall bear rule over all the earth. And the **fourth** kingdom shall be strong as iron: forasmuch as iron breaketh in pieces and subdueth all things: and as iron that breaketh all these, shall it break in pieces and bruise. And whereas thou sawest the feet and toes, part of potters' clay, and part of iron, the kingdom shall be divided; but there shall be in it of the strength of the iron, forasmuch as thou sawest the iron mixed with miry clay. And as the toes of the feet were part of iron, and part of clay, so the kingdom shall be partly strong, and partly broken. And whereas thou sawest iron mixed with miry clay, they shall mingle themselves with the seed of men: but they shall not cleave one to another, even as iron is not mixed with clay. And in the days of these kings shall the God of heaven set up a kingdom, which shall never be destroyed: and the kingdom shall not be left to other people, but it shall break in pieces and consume all these kingdoms, and it shall stand for ever. Forasmuch as thou sawest that the stone was cut out of the mountain

without hands, and that it brake in pieces the iron, the
brass, the clay, the silver, and the gold; the great God
hath made known to the king what shall come to pass
hereafter: and the dream is certain, and the interpretation thereof is sure (Daniel 2:37-45).

"ABC" AND "XYZ"

This passage is the ABC of prophecy, just as the
book of the Revelation may be called the XYZ of
prophecy. A clear understanding of this passage in
Daniel 2 is the very foundation and the framework
of the course of history as given by the Lord Himself.
Again please notice the expression in verse 45, "The
great God hath made known to the king *what shall
come to pass hereafter.*" The events were still future,
although some of them are authenticated history now.
Daniel tells the king that he is the first in a line of five
world kingdoms. "Thou art this head of gold." It is a
picture of the wealth and splendor of the Babylonian
Empire. It extended over the then known world and
was wealthy and beautiful beyond description, as all
history attests.

But Babylon was not to continue in that form; another power was to rise and conquer the kingdom. This
is represented by the chest and arms of silver. This we
know from history was Persia, the two arms representing the coalition of Persia and Media in one great
world empire, which subdued Babylon. Medo-Persia
was inferior to Babylon both in power and wealth, as
silver is inferior to gold. Medo-Persia was conquered
by Greece, under Alexander the Great, to continue for
a brief time and then we enter the iron stage when Rome
swept over the world in conquering power and ruled the
earth for centuries. But the Roman Empire became
divided into the eastern and the western empires, and

so we have the two legs of the image. This united Roman Empire was in power in the days of the Lord Jesus, still holding sway under the Caesars over the whole known world. All this is history, but we are not dependent upon history for our interpretation, for Daniel himself in his vision in chapter 7, identifies and names these successive empires, under the symbols of the four fearful beasts, the lion (Babylon), the bear (Persia), the leopard (Greece) and the nameless monstrosity (Rome). We shall deal with these when we study Daniel 7.

THE UNFULFILLED PARTS

So far then all is clear, for history has verified the accuracy of all Daniel's predictions. But the fact that all the fulfilled part was accurately and inerrantly fulfilled, makes it necessary for us to believe that the part yet unfulfilled (the feet and the ten toes) will also be still fulfilled in the future with the same infallibility. What do the ten toes of the feet of the image represent? They are a part of the same image as the head of gold, chest of silver, and the brass and the iron. It is a continuation of the rule of man upon the earth during the "times of the Gentiles." First we are told the *time* when these ten toes will be set up. The feet of the image represent the last form of Gentile world power. There are two feet, indicating there will be two great divisions or parts in this kingdom. There are ten toes which we shall see represent ten kings or ten nations, five on each foot. It all adds up to this. In the end time, just before the Lord Jesus Christ returns there will be a federation of nations, (a Big Ten) consisting of two groups of five nations each (two Big Fives). It will be the last great world federation of nations, loosely held together by

ties of common danger and fear of one another. The
toes are mixed iron and clay—the iron of totalitarianism,
and the clay of socialistic democracy. They can never
blend, just as the ideologies of totalitarianism today
and the ideologies of democracy today will never blend.
They may mix, but they will never really unite.

Forming Today

Rome in her power has ceased, but the spirit of
Babylon lives on and one more great attempt will be
made to unite all the world for power and for peace.
This last time it will not be by one great nation like the
head of gold or chest of silver, but by a federation of
great nations, ten in number. But it will be a weak federation, only held together like iron and clay without a
real union of common interest and ideals. Today we
seem to witness before our very eyes the formation
of this very thing. The nations, after millenniums of
war and bloodshed, and faced with atomic destruction,
are driven to face the fact that they must either federate
and unite, or perish. But there are two ideologies. The
ideology of clay and democracy, the iron of force and
aggression and totalitarianism. An attempt, no doubt
an honest attempt, is being made to bring them together
and one foot already reveals its five toes, the Big Five.
But as a preacher of the Gospel and a firm believer in
the truth of Scripture, I too know that there can never
be lasting peace and union until the Prince of Peace,
the Stone cut without hands out of the mountain, comes
again to set up His kingdom.

And so in the end time, and everything points to its
soon fulfillment, there will be a great world federation
of nations, seeking to make all the world one. Already
a universal language is being suggested, and a central

authority and a world capital and a United States of the World. How near the coming of the Lord must be, when we see all these things happening before our very eyes! In this connection let me refer you again to the parallel passage in Revelation.

And there are seven kings [or kingdoms]: five are fallen, and one is, and the other is not yet come; and when he cometh, he must continue a short space (Revelation 17:10).

This was written in John's day. Five kingdoms had already fallen and the sixth (Rome), was then in power. In Daniel's day only two had fallen and Nebuchadnezzar was the third. In Daniel, Babylon is first, for in Daniel we deal only with the future ones, and not the past. John says the last form of world power was still future, and would last only a little while. Out of this last ten-nation federation will arise the superman, the Antichrist, and for a brief period he will bring in a world government which at first promises to solve man's problems, but will fall and be destroyed at the coming of Christ. The last attempt of man to federate will begin to weaken until this superman, Satan in human form, will step in, take over the conference and the organization of the United States of the World, and promise the end of all man's struggles. But it will be a devilish ruse only, to wrest the power from the rightful King of all the earth, the Lord Jesus, and the Stone will fall and grind his kingdom to pieces. All this is vividly depicted in Revelation 17:11-12:

And the beast that was, and is not, even he is the eighth, and is of [or out of] the seven, and goeth into perdition. And the ten horns which thou sawest are ten kings [kingdoms], which have received no kingdom as yet; but receive power as kings one hour with the beast.

This is the last scene in the battle of the ages. It is the same as the picture in Daniel 2, where the ten toes represent this same ten-kingdom league of the latter days. Some Bible students believe that the ten toes will be a restoration of the old Roman Empire with all its power and glory. Others believe that since Rome is represented by iron, and the feet are both iron and clay, it will consist of a combination of the old Roman Empire and other states as well. That it will be mostly a restoration of the old Roman Empire is strongly suggested in Scripture, but the actual identity of the nations involved is immaterial. The important fact is this: the Bible tells us that there will be one more great attempt to make a world government on this earth. Ten nations will be prominent in this effort, divided into two parts with five nations on each side. But this attempt will utterly fail because they are not a unit, but have different personal and selfish interests at heart. Like iron and clay it will be an unstable mixture, entered into for expediency only, and not with a sincere desire to help all humanity.

It seems to me that the lines are being drawn clearly in the world today, following this exact pattern as given in Daniel and Revelation. And since this final federation occurs immediately prior to the return of Christ, we have every confidence when as ambassadors of Christ we cry out to the world, "The end is at hand." The next great event may well be the coming of the King of kings. But, before the final world ruler appears (the personal Antichrist to set up a brief reign of terror during the Tribulation Period), the Lord Jesus will return, take to Himself every true believer, and then after the brief reign of the last world dictator, will return as the *Stone, the Smiting Rock,* to put an end to man's bungling and failures, and set up His kingdom forever and ever. Here again is Daniel's own version of this imminent fact,

> And in the days of these kings shall the God of heaven set up a kingdom, which shall never be destroyed . . . but it shall break in pieces and consume all these kingdoms, and it shall stand forever.

Are *you* ready?

CHAPTER SEVEN

Three Hebrews in the Fiery Furnace

Nebuchadnezzar the king made an image of gold, whose
height was threescore cubits, and the breadth thereof six
cubits: he set it up in the plain of Dura, in the province
of Babylon . . . Then an herald cried aloud, To you it is
commanded, O people, nations, and languages, that at what
time ye hear the sound of the cornet, flute, harp, sackbut,
psaltery, dulcimer, and all kinds of musick, ye fall down
and worship the golden image that Nebuchadnezzar the
king hath set up: and whoso falleth not down and wor-
shippeth shall the same hour be cast into the midst of a
burning fiery furnace (Daniel 3:1, 4, 5, 6).

We come now to the third chapter of Daniel which
records for us that great image of Nebuchadnezzar, and
the refusal of three young Hebrews to fall down and
worship this strange god. As a result they are cast into
a seething fiery furnace, where they are miraculously
preserved by the angel of the Lord and wonderfully
delivered and exalted. To see in this interesting narrative
only a picture of how God will preserve all those who are
faithful to Him, is to miss part of the great message
here contained. To be sure, the wonderful and comforting
lesson of God's care for all who dare to stand firm for

Him is here and we do thank God for it. It is true that God does honor faithfulness in His children in all ages and will reward them. All this is true and we glory in this great fact. But there is far more here. Remember what Jesus said about Daniel; He tells us that Daniel was a prophet and that his prophecies deal with future events. So beyond the immediate lesson of God's care for His own, we look also for a prophetic lesson concerning the future.

THREE RULES

We remind you therefore again of the rules of interpretation which we gave you, and which we trust you have memorized by this time. Here they are again:

1. All Scripture has one primary interpretation.
2. All Scripture has several practical applications.
3. Most Scripture passages have also a prophetic revelation.

This story is a case in point which will illustrate this for us.

By primary interpretation the experience of the three Hebrew youths in the fiery furnace teaches God's care for His captive people Israel in the days of Nebuchadnezzar. By application the story teaches us that God always cares for His own and we need never be afraid to be faithful to our convictions and His Word. Then there is the prophetic revelation, which we believe is the most important one, because Daniel is first of all a prophetic book, according to the Lord Jesus Himself, and so we look for the prophetic lesson first of all. The three young Hebrews are a picture of the nation of Israel among the Gentiles. Cast into the furnace of affliction and persecution, they should perish by all human standards, but miraculously they are preserved, even in the fiery furnace of race hatred and persecution, because they are God's covenant people and will finally be marvelously delivered and exalted among the nations. This is the broad teaching. Now for the details so clearly given in this chapter.

THE GREAT IMAGE OF GOLD

In the first verse of Daniel 2 we have the king of Babylon erecting a great image and telling all the world to worship this image. All the world follows with the exception of a few, a little remnant who steadfastly refuse to do so. Now remember, that with the captivity of Israel and the ascendancy of the empire of Babylon the "times of the Gentiles" began, which was to run until the coming again of the Messiah the Christ at the end of the Tribulation. This age of the Gentiles begins and ends with a great image, a false god. Here we have Nebuchadnezzar's image in Daniel 3. In Revelation 13 we see another image, and yet the same image in principle, set up by the Antichrist of whom Nebuchadnezzar was merely a type. There in Revelation we have this image again, and all the world commanded to worship this image, again upon pain of death. And again just as in Daniel's day there will be a remnant of Hebrews who refuse, and are marked for death, but miraculously preserved by the Lord, their covenant God, and finally delivered and exalted to reign in the millennial age. The two pictures are parallel and identical in Daniel 3 and Revelation 13.

BABYLONIANISM IS A SYSTEM

But to thoroughly understand the prophetic meaning of the image in Daniel 3 and Revelation 13, we must go even farther back in Biblical history. For Babylon and Babylonianism began in the days immediately after the Flood of Noah. We have the record in Genesis 10 and 11. There you will recall a man by the name of Nimrod (meaning "the rebel"), who like Nebuchadnezzar was a type of the Antichrist, built the city of Babylon, and a great tower, and on the top of this tower he placed the image of his god "Belus" or Baal. This first Babylon or Babel was a picture of Babylon throughout all the ages to follow. For Babel or Babylon is a *system*, a political and religious system opposed to the true religion of Jehovah. It is Satan's counterfeit of God's kingdom and whether we see it in the form of the Egyptian Empire, or the Assyrian, or the Babylonian, or the Persian, or the Greek, or the Roman Empire, it is always the same for it is engineered by the same author, Satan. Babylonianism is an ideology; it is Satan's attempt to set up a kingdom in opposition to the kingdom of our Lord Jesus Christ. It began in ancient Babel under Nimrod. This man built a great city, one of the wonders of the world, and this city represented a political system. But he also built a tower, which was the seat of Babel's worship of the Babylonian god, and this tower represented a *religious system*. There was only one language and one government.

Nimrod, the founder of Babel, sought to establish a *world empire*, a world federation, politically and religiously. To keep men from being divided he devised *Babel*, by which he attempted to achieve one government, one religion, one language, one United Nations of the World. And so he called it Babel, which means, from the two fragments "Bab" and "El," the "gate to God." It was a false religion, a spurious plan of redemption by man's efforts and man's works. But

God came down, confused their tongue, and scattered and discomfited them, and called Babel not the way to God, but *"confusion."* Man's effort to bring about the ideal religion and government in the world is called by God "confusion" and will be finally destroyed when Jesus comes to cast down the image of which we read in Revelation 13.

Nimrod's ancient Babylon was destroyed, though its ruins remain to this day to indicate that the spirit of Babylon still lives on to be revived again and again but always to perish and arise again in another form, but always with the same program, *a world political federation, a world religious federation* and *a world language and government.* And in each case it was accompanied by the persecution of God's true people and the casting of them into the furnace of persecution and affliction, but always with this same result, that Babylon's program failed and God's people came through in the end.

Witness to all this stand the great world empires of the past. Egypt with its persecution of God's people is gone as the Pharaohs knew it. Assyria with its persecution of God's nation is gone and the people go on. So, too, with Nebuchadnezzar's Babylon. He sought to revive and consummate the dream of Nimrod, *one world of all nations.* He had successfully conquered the known world, subjected them all to his central government. He was seeking a universal language and for that cause he taught these captives in Babylon the language of the Chaldeans, as we are told in Daniel 1:4:

> Whom they might teach the learning and the **tongue of the Chaldeans.**

Then in addition, to make up the trinity of evil, he purposed to make *one universal religion.* He set up this golden image and sought to compel all nations, peoples and tongues to worship this one image, this one false god of Babylon. And just as in every other instance, there were those who were true to their God and refused to bow. They were subjected to the most cruel persecution, but God saw His people through. God's people continued but their persecutors were destroyed. And so Babylon fell as recorded in Daniel 5, and the next form of Babylonianism appears under Darius the Mede and we have the same story. Persia falls and Greece appears with the same program, a world federation of nations, a world religion and a universal language. How nearly Greece succeeded in gaining her objective may be gathered from the fact that so universal was the Greek language even in Jesus' day, centuries after Greece fell, that even our New Testament was written almost entirely in the Greek. But Greece fell and Rome came, and we know her history with its persecution of God's ancient people Israel. But Rome has gone and the covenant nation of Israel lives on in spite of Pharaoh's drowning program, Nebuchadnezzar's fiery furnace and lions' den, Haman's gallows, the Caesars' murders and deportation in the destruction of Jerusalem —in spite of Hitler's fury and Mussolini's hatred.

At the end of this age Satan will once more revive his Babylonian program and, under the direction of the two beasts of Revelation 13, will set up a world kingdom, will seek to force a world religion upon men in the setting up of the image in Revelation 13, and will once more attempt to destroy God's ancient Israel, only to come to the same end as did Nimrod, Pharaoh, Nebuchadnezzar and all the rest of the puppets in the line of Satan's succession. From all this you will see that the history of man is not a succession of isolated events. It is all part of one grand plan, a struggle between God and Satan, the seed of the woman and the seed of the serpent. History is a unit and while we see the events as isolated occurrences, underneath it all is one great line and program, the struggle of Satan against the Christ and God's people. With all this in mind read again the story of the image of Nebuchadnezzar in Daniel 3, and remember what this image represents. Study again then, the fate of the three young men in the fiery furnace and their marvelous deliverance and the destruction of those who had cast them into this place, as well as the end of the wicked king. Study all this in the light of Jesus' statement concerning Daniel as a prophet. In dealing with this image of Nebuchadnezzar, we must refer you to the mention Jesus makes of the *image* which will be set up in the last days by the last representative of the spirit of Babylon. It is found in Matthew 24. In this remarkable chapter Jesus is giving His so-called Olivet discourse, in answer to the question of the disciples concerning the end of the age. Jesus gives a long list of signs which would announce the end of the age. These signs, by the way, are now for the first time in all history in actual process of fulfillment. After giving these signs He gives us a description of the Tribulation, that period of great persecution between the Rapture of the Church and the public appearing of the Lord Jesus Christ. This Tribulation, remember, is the fulfillment of the prophecy of the fiery furnace in Daniel 3. In speaking of this terrible time Jesus says:

> When ye therefore shall see the abomination of desolation, spoken of by Daniel the prophet, stand in the holy place, (whoso readeth, let him understand:) then let them which be in Judaea flee into the mountains . . . For then shall

be great tribulation, such as was not since the beginning of the world to this time, no, nor ever shall be. And except those days should be shortened, there should no flesh be saved: but for the elect's sake those days shall be shortened (Matthew 24:15, 16, 21, 22).

THE ABOMINATION OF DESOLATION

Jesus says that in this Tribulation Period Daniel's prophecy concerning the abomination of desolation will be fulfilled. Jesus, of course, is referring to Daniel 9:27, 11:31 and 12:11, in all of which the image of the abomination of desolation shall be set up. We shall treat with that later, except to say now that according to Daniel and confirmed by Jesus' words, the Antichrist will promise peace to the world and Israel, but after three and a half years will break his promise and cause to be erected in the Temple at Jerusalem, then already rebuilt, a monstrous heathen image, and cause all who will not worship it to be killed. In Revelation we are given the details of all this. He does great wonders and deceives the people . . .

saying to them that dwell on the earth, that they should make an image to the beast, which had the wound by a sword, and did live . . . And he causeth all, both small and great, rich and poor, free and bond, to receive a mark in their right hand, or in their foreheads: and that no man might buy or sell, save he that had the mark, or the name of the beast, or the number of his name (Revelation 13:14, 16, 17).

But just as in the case of Egypt and Babylon, God remembers His covenant people and so Revelation relates the sealing of "the hundred and forty and four thousand" who were not destroyed in the Great Tribulation. These one hundred forty-four thousand are from the twelve tribes of Israel, twelve thousand from each tribe.

How clearly, therefore, in the light of Revelation and the words of Jesus in Matthew 24 do we see the prophetic picture presented to us by the image of Nebuchadnezzar and the three young men in the fiery furnace. Nebuchadnezzar is a type of the beast of Revelation 13. The image is the type and picture of the abomination of desolation. The fiery furnace is a picture of the Great Tribulation. The three young Hebrews are a type of the nation to which they themselves belonged. Their deliverance from the furnace tells us in prophetic preview God's future program of deliverance and exaltation. The fact that the men who threw them into the furnace were themselves burned, while the three young men escaped unharmed, is God's own prediction of what will happen to those who seek to destroy God's ancient people.

How near this time must be when God comes to judge this wicked world! Observe how the newspapers and the radio tell us of man's attempt to make once more a world government for his own safety, while God's people are being persecuted and scattered everywhere. Soon the Lord will speak once more, as He did before, but now for the final time. There will be only two camps, the camp of the redeemed and the camp of the lost. On which side are *you*? Soon the Lord will come to call out all believers, and to judge the world in terrible righteousness and judgment. Be ready for that day; "Believe on the Lord Jesus Christ, and thou shalt be saved."

CHAPTER EIGHT

The Faithful Remnant in the Tribulation

In the chapter preceding this we began the study of the third chapter of the book of Daniel, where we have the interesting and deeply instructive message and record of three young Hebrew princes, who with Daniel had been carried from their native country of Judaea to be slaves in the palace of the king of Babylon. After some time there, the king Nebuchadnezzar caused a great image to be made of gold, and then issued a decree to all the world that at a certain day and hour, when the herald made the proclamation, all men everywhere without exception, were to fall down and worship this image. In this chapter we shall see some more valuable lessons, as taught by the refusal of these three faithful servants of the Lord to bow the knee before the heathen gods of Babylon. But first let me remind you again, that, apart from the many practical lessons of the necessity of faithfulness to God, all this is also prophetic of events yet to come, for we must never lose sight of the fact that Daniel is first of all a prophetic book. This is corroborated by the Lord Jesus Himself who calls Daniel "the prophet" in Matthew 24.

Six Hundred Sixty-Six

This image of the king was a prediction and type of
another image which will be set up after the Church
has been raptured before the Tribulation. One of these
days the Lord Jesus, according to the sure promise of
God, will return in the clouds of heaven and shout from
the air, and at the sound of the trumpet and His mighty
voice all the saints of all past ages who have died will
be raised from their graves, and all the living believers
at that time will be instantaneously changed and will receive new bodies and together with the resurrected saints
will be caught out of this earth to meet the Lord in the
air. After the Church is gone there will arise a superman,
called in the Bible the Man of Sin, the Son of Perdition
and the Antichrist. He will bring in a brief peace, restore all the nation of Israel to the land of Palestine,
rebuild the Temple in Jerusalem and promise protection
and peace to God's scattered and persecuted nation of
Israel. But after about three and one-half years he will
suddenly turn coat, reveal his real, wicked identity, become the enemy of God's covenant people, set up an
image in Jerusalem and compel all the world to worship
this terrible image. But there will be a remnant of one
hundred forty-four thousand of the twelve tribes of
Israel, then residing in the land of Palestine, who will refuse to worship this image, and as a result become the object of the most terrible hate and persecution of the Antichrist. But God will seal them and miraculously deliver
them and exalt them above the nations in the day of the
return of the Lord. The number of this Man of Sin will
be the number of the beast and is given in Revelation
13 as the number six hundred sixty-six. Remember that
number. Anyone who does not carry this number and

have the mark of the beast, which I sincerely believe will be the number six hundred sixty-six, will be condemned to die. All of this record is given in detail in Revelation 13.

A PARALLEL IN DANIEL 3

In the light of this portion of the book of Revelation, the story in Daniel 3 becomes clear. Nebuchadnezzar is one of many types and shadows of this coming superman, the Antichrist. Babylon is a forerunner of the great world empire over which this Man of Sin will rule in the Tribulation Period. The image Nebuchadnezzar erected is a type of the image of Revelation 13 and is called in Scripture the "abomination of desolation." The three young Hebrews represent the remnant of the Tribulation, the one hundred forty-four thousand. Because they refuse to bow before Satan they are cast into a fiery furnace of the day of Jacob's trouble, but delivered by the Lord and highly exalted. Now turn again to Daniel and see how clear the whole picture becomes.

> Nebuchadnezzar the king made an image of gold, whose height was threescore cubits, and the breadth thereof six cubits (Daniel 3:1).

Notice the prominence of the number six in the dimensions of this image—*sixty* cubits high, *six* cubits wide. It immediately suggests the image of the last days and its measurements and its number six hundred sixty-six. Next notice the answer of these three youths to the demand of this wicked king. They refused and the gestapo of that day observed their apparent rebellion and reported to the king as follows:

> There are certain Jews whom thou hast set over the affairs of the province of Babylon, Shadrach, Meshach, and Abed-nego; these men, O king, have not regarded

thee: they serve not thy gods, nor worship the golden image which thou hast set up. Then Nebuchadnezzar in his rage and fury commanded to bring Shadrach, Meshach, and Abed-nego . . . Nebuchadnezzar spake and said unto them, Is it true . . . do not ye serve my gods, nor worship the golden image which I have set up? (Daniel 3:12-14).

And here is the answer of these brave young men, an answer that speaks eloquently of a conviction that was dearer than life and a lesson we need so much to learn in these days of conformity and compromise with the world. Hear them as they answer the highest authority on the earth of that day.

Shadrach, Meshach, and Abed-nego, answered and said to the king, O Nebuchadnezzar, we are not careful to answer thee in this matter. If it be so, our God whom we serve is able to deliver us from the burning fiery furnace, and he will deliver us out of thine hand, O king. But if not, be it known unto thee, O king, that we will not serve thy gods, nor worship the golden image which thou hast set up (Daniel 3:16-18).

We would love to linger here and speak at length on the lesson on separation, for it is needed so much today, but we have dealt with this subject in some detail when we studied the first chapter of Daniel, so will have to pass over many of the practical lessons here. One, however, needs a word or two and that is the Christian's relationship to the government of the land and the powers that be. If anything is clear in the Bible it is this, that the believer is to be a good, faithful, loyal and patriotic citizen of the land which affords him a home and protection. Jesus said, "Render therefore unto Caesar the things which are Caesar's; and unto God the things that are God's." We are to support and pray for our government and our rulers. We are to pay our taxes and dues, obey the laws and be examples of good, decent, honest, law-abiding citizenship. Anyone who knows his Bible knows this to be the will of God.

But there is also another truth. These three young men were, so far as the record goes, faithful and obedient up to a certain point. But when the laws of the land conflicted with their service of God and their obedience to God's will, they did not hesitate for a single moment to put the will of God above the commands of the government. It was so in the eating of unclean foods in Daniel 1 and here again in Daniel 3. Peter and the apostles affirmed the same fact again in Acts when they said to the authorities who would restrain them from preaching the Gospel, ''We ought to obey God rather than men.'' It meant persecution and hatred, but also became the occasion for marvelous blessings of deliverance.

THE FIERY FURNACE

As a result, therefore, of the steadfastness of the three youths, Nebuchadnezzar becomes infuriated and commands them to be cast into a furnace of fire. Every little detail of the record is significant.

> Then was Nebuchadnezzar full of fury, and the form of his visage was changed against Shadrach, Meshach, and Abednego: therefore he spake, and commanded that they should heat the furnace one seven times more than it was wont to be heated. And he commanded the most mighty men that were in his army to bind Shadrach, Meshach, and Abed-nego, and to cast them into the burning fiery furnace. Then these men were bound in their coats, their hosen, and their hats, and their other garments, and were cast into the midst of the burning fiery furnace. Therefore because the king's commandment was urgent, and the furnace exceeding hot, the flames of the fire slew those men that took up Shadrach,

Meshach and Abed-nego. And these three men, Shadrach,
Meshach, and Abed-nego, fell down bound into the midst
of the burning fiery furnace (Daniel 3:19-23).

To the casual reader all these details and the repetition
of these men's names may seem unimportant, but to the
believer in the verbal inspiration of all Scripture, every
detail becomes highly important. A lifetime of preaching
would be insufficient to gather all the blessed and
precious truths contained in this graphic picture. Remember first of all the prophetic implication, as depict-
ing what will happen in the latter days when Israel
shall pass through the furnace of affliction in the Tribulation and be as miraculously preserved as these young
men were. But beyond the prophetic lesson there is also
a most comforting lesson for every believer here. To
all who will stand firm for their faith in God and the
Lord Jesus Christ, there is also the promise of persecution. It has ever been thus. No saint in any age of
history has ever been popular with the world. If you
and I are going to stand for what we believe to be the
truth of God, and refuse to be swayed from it no matter
what the cost, we too shall find that the world is no friend
to grace. And in the measure that we dare to stand true
for God and be on fire for Christ, in that measure we
shall suffer persecution. The Christian is a stranger
here. We are citizens of a heavenly country and only pass
through this world as strangers and pilgrims representing our Lord and King the Lord Jesus Christ. The more
godly our lives, the less fellowship we can have with
the world and the more we feel that we do not fit here.
The older I become the more I begin to feel this fact
of my being a pilgrim and a stranger here. The things
of the world not only do not attract me, but are positively

repulsive to me. The things the world loves we hate, and they hate the things we love. And the more we realize the fact that we have little in common with this world and its program, the more we will be considered odd and have to suffer the ridicule and hatred of the world. The closer we walk with God the more we can understand the song, written by one who knew his home was not here:

> I am a stranger here, within a foreign land,
> My home is far away, upon a golden strand;
> Ambassador to be of realms beyond the sea,
> I'm here on business for my King.
>
> This is the message that I bring,
> A message angels fain would sing;
> "Oh, be ye reconciled," thus saith my Lord and King,
> "Oh, be ye reconciled to God."

God have mercy on the Christian who is popular with the world. Jesus said, "In the world *ye shall* have tribulation: but be of good cheer; I have overcome the world." If you doubt this fact, then remember what James says, "The friendship of the world is enmity with God." If you want to test the truth of this statement, then take the definite stand for your God that Shadrach, Meshach and Abed-nego did and you will soon find out. Go out tomorrow as a believer and refuse to listen to the lewd jokes of your companions, speak up for Christ when His Name is taken in vain, and spring to the defense of your Christ when men and women curse and swear. Refuse tomorrow to enter with your fellow workers in their worldly, sinful indulgences. When they tempt you with sin, speak up and say, "I belong to Christ. I can't go with you. I belong to Christ; I do not drink. I belong to Christ and I don't gamble. I belong to Christ and I will not go along with you in this shady

deal." See how quickly your friends will drop you and
avoid you, when you go all the way for Christ. The
trouble with most Christians is that they get along together too well with the world, just because they will
not stand true to their profession, but compromise and
hide their light under a bushel.

But to those who will dare to stand true there is a
great blessing. See the picture of the three young men.
To be sure, they were cast into the fiery furnace, but
what a glorious experience it proved to be! Notice the
record again:

> Then Nebuchadnezzar . . . rose up in haste, and spake
> . . . Did not we cast three men bound into the midst of the
> fire? . . . Lo, I see four men loose, walking in the midst of the
> fire . . . Then Nebuchadnezzar came near to the mouth of the
> burning fiery furnace . . . and said . . . come forth, and
> come hither. Then Shadrach, Meshach, and Abed-nego, came
> forth of the midst of the fire . . . upon whose bodies the
> fire had no power, nor was an hair of their head singed,
> neither were their coats changed, nor the smell of fire
> had passed on them (Daniel 3:24-27).

After all their trial they came out safe and the answer
is given in verse 25, where Nebuchadnezzar saw a
fourth man in the fire and he recognized him as the Son
of God, Jesus Christ Himself, appearing in a theophany,
who in human form, as He often did in the Old Testament,
had come down to deliver these three men from the wrath
of the enemy. So, too, in the Tribulation Period, when
Israel is cast into the furnace of affliction, the nation
will be delivered by the personal coming of their Messiah,
the Son of God, the Lord Jesus Christ.

PRACTICAL LESSON

This is true of all God's people who will be found faithful and refuse to bow before the gods of this age. The Lord has not promised to keep us *out* of the fire of persecution and tribulation, but He has promised to be *with us in trouble* and to see us through. His own promise is, "I will be with [them] in trouble." "In the world ye shall have tribulation: but be of good cheer; I have overcome the world." Are you passing through deep waters, my friend? Are you hated and opposed and persecuted for your faithfulness to Christ and your stand for Him? Do the members of your own family ridicule you and friends forsake you because of your belief and your refusal to go with them into the world? Then take heart; the Lord is with you and will see you through. Notice that the only things which were burned in the fire were the *ropes that tied them.* We are told in verse 21 they were bound in all their clothes. In verses 21, 23 and 25 we are told they were cast *bound* into the furnace and that they fell down *bound,* but when the king looked again they were *walking* about in the furnace. Cast in *bound,* hand and foot, and then *walking free.* The only thing the fire touched was the bonds that held them. How wonderful! And to you who also are passing through the fire because of your faith in Christ, remember the fire cannot hurt you, but only serve to free you and exalt you in due time.

When through fiery trials thy pathway shall lie,
My grace, all-sufficient, shall be thy supply;
The flames shall not hurt thee; I only design
Thy dross to consume, and thy gold to refine.

Then the king promoted Shadrach, Meshach, and Abednego, in the province of Babylon (Daniel 3:30).

CHAPTER NINE

The Burning Bush

> Lo, I see four men loose, walking in the midst of the fire, and they have no hurt; and the form of the fourth is like the Son of God (Daniel 3:25).

These are the remarkable words of Nebuchadnezzar, king of Babylon, in the interesting narrative of three young Hebrew princes, slaves in Babylon, who refused to bow before the image which the pagan king Nebuchadnezzar had set up in the plain of Dura. Because of their faithfulness to Jehovah they firmly rebelled against the king's edict, and as a punishment for their defiance of the king they were cast into a fiery furnace. The men who cast them in were seared to death, but the young men were miraculously preserved by their God. When the king next came to see the fiery furnace he found the three young men unharmed and walking in the midst of the fire, only the cords which held them having been burned off. But there was an additional personage in the fire, too, whom the king immediately recognized as the Son of God. Where the king got his knowledge of the Son of God we do not know; probably the very appearance of this glorious fourth person was such that it could have been no other. Nebuchadnezzar is greatly disturbed and immediately commands that the youths be released and be exalted to a great and high place in the capitol of Babylon.

TYPICAL OF ISRAEL

We have repeatedly reminded you of the prophetic nature of the book of Daniel and we know now, from the rest of the Scriptures and God's revealed plan, that these three youths are a type of Israel among the nations during the "times of the Gentiles," that period of time from the captivity of Judah until the re-establishment of Israel in the land of Palestine, and the setting up of the Messianic kingdom of Israel. One can never know God's prophetic program until the lesson taught in this incident is clearly understood. Israel today as a people is scattered among the nations and suffering in the fiery furnace of persecution and affliction. But God will not forsake the nation, because of an unconditional promise and covenant of grace made with their fathers, Abraham, Isaac and Jacob. This truth is taught throughout the entire Bible. After God's program for the nations has been accomplished, and Israel has passed through the last great burning of the day of Jacob's trouble in the Great Tribulation, their Messiah, the same One who walked with the young men in the fiery furnace, will once more appear, slay their enemies and deliver His people and exalt them in the kingdom. We trust you will not feel that we are placing too much emphasis and spending too much time on this subject, for it is so important and so little understood by the average Christian that we feel fully justified in elaborating on this truth still further.

The Burning Bush and Moses

We have another incident in the history of Israel which is a parallel lesson. In this passage we have a burning bush instead of a fiery furnace, but the lesson is the same as in Daniel 3. Here is the record as given in Exodus 3: 1-3:

> Now Moses kept the flock of Jethro his father in law, the priest of Midian: and he led the flock to the backside of the desert, and came to the mountain of God, even to Horeb. And the angel of the Lord appeared unto him in a flame of fire out of the midst of a bush: and he looked, and, behold, the bush burned with fire, and the bush was not consumed. And Moses said, I will now turn aside, and see this great sight, why the bush is not burnt.

Here we have the Lord once again in a flame of fire in the midst of a bush but the bush remains unharmed. Just as in the case of the three youths in Daniel 3, we have here the prophetic picture of God's preservation of His people, His covenant nation, while in bondage among their enemies. The setting of the entire incident is exceedingly interesting. Moses had escaped death through the love and perseverance of his parents who had hid him for three months, whereas the king had commanded all the male babies of the Israelites to be cast into the Nile. After three months his mother deposited him by the river's brink, where he was providentially picked up by Pharaoh's daughter and promptly adopted as her son. By divine direction the mother of Moses herself was engaged as nurse so that she had the training of her own child Moses, during the formative years of his life. During these few years that Moses was taught by his own mother, and before he was taken permanently to the king's palace, he was thoroughly instructed as to his future work in delivering Israel from bondage, for after forty years Moses went out from the palace of the king with the intent and purpose of revealing himself to his fellow Israelites as their deliverer. Seeing one of his kinsmen suffering at the hands of an Egyptian slave driver, he promptly defended his brother and slew the Egyptian, in the firm faith that Israel would take this act as a cue for them to rally to his standard and acknowledge him as their deliverer, so that he might lead them out of Egypt into Canaan. All this is corroborated by the Scriptures. In Acts 7:23-25 we read of Moses:

> And when he was full forty years old, it came into his heart to visit his brethren the children of Israel. And seeing one of them suffer wrong, he defended him, and avenged him that was oppressed, and smote the Egyptian: for he supposed his brethren would have understood how that God by his hand would deliver them: but they understood not.

From these verses you will notice that Moses *knew* that he was God's chosen deliverer of Israel and supposed that even his brethren knew all about it. This is further proven by Hebrews 11:24-25:

> By faith Moses, when he was come to years, refused to be called the son of Pharaoh's daughter; choosing rather to suffer affliction with the people of God, than to enjoy the pleasures of sin for a season.

Moses knew God's plan for Israel and he knew his part in that plan. But when he was rebuked by his own brethren the next day and they rejected his offer to help them, he became angry and disgusted, picked up and ran away to Midian, and there became a sheepherder in the wilderness of Sinai. For forty years he remained there in obscurity, far, far away from the place of duty

and service. A man trained for forty years to be a king
and picked to be the next Pharaoh of Egypt, a man
educated in all the wisdom and knowledge of his day,
was spending his time tending a little flock of sheep
on the backside of the desert! He thought that God was
all through with the nation of Israel. When he remembered their disobedience, their ingratitude and their
unworthiness, he just could not understand how God
could have anything to do with that sinful nation, and
supposed that God had given them up and there was no
future for them. And so he was content to be a shepherd.
How many thousands of Christians there are today who
are just as ignorant of God's grace as Moses was! They
too believe that God is all through with the nation of
Israel, that they will never be restored to the land of
Palestine again. They make the Church Israel, spiritualize all the prophecies referring to Israel as applying
to the Church and see no future program for the nation.
These people need to hear the message of the fiery
furnace and the three young men, and they need to
learn the lesson of the burning bush, which Moses had
to learn.

God's Eternal Covenant

Moses had forgotten that God had made a covenant
of grace with this nation, to Abraham. This covenant
was a covenant of *grace*, that is, it was an unconditional
promise of God, wholly independent of the merits or
worth or faithfulness of the nation. No matter how un-
worthily the nation may conduct itself, God will not
break His covenant. "Listen, Moses," God seems to
say, "you may have given up your people and turned
your back on them but *I have not,* for I have promised,
and I will keep My word. I am going to do all I have

promised." This is the whole setting of the burning bush, the picture of the indestructible nation of Israel in the fires of persecution. In Exodus 2:24-25, the two verses just preceding the story of the burning bush, we read,

> And God heard their [Israel's] groaning, and God remembered his covenant with Abraham, with Isaac, and with Jacob. And God looked upon the children of Israel, and God had respect unto them.

Exodus 2 records the failure of Moses but the *faithfulness* of Jehovah. He (God) remembers His covenant. It does not say that He remembered the virtues of the people or their goodness, but that He remembered His covenant. Their deliverance did not depend on their *goodness or merits* but only on God's faithfulness.

This was the first lesson Moses must learn, and a lesson many of God's dear people must still learn, that salvation is of grace and does not depend upon our faithfulness but *God's* faithfulness. This was the lesson of the burning bush. Moses turns aside to see the great sight of the indestructible bush and then we read:

> And when the Lord saw that he turned aside to see, God called unto him out of the midst of the bush, and said, Moses, Moses. And he said, Here am I. And he said, Draw not nigh hither: put off thy shoes from off thy feet, for the place whereon thou standest is holy ground. Moreover he said, I am the God of thy father, the God of Abraham, the God of Isaac, and the God of Jacob. And Moses hid his face; for he was afraid to look upon God (Exodus 3:4-6).

What a lesson! God had not forgotten. He is still the covenant-keeping God of the fathers and will keep His word in spite of all the unfaithfulness of His own children. Look at the bush, Moses; it is burning, burning, but is not consumed. And the reason it was not consumed was simply this: *God was in the bush.* This is plainly stated:

> And the angel of the Lord appeared unto him in a flame of fire out of the midst of a bush (Exodus 3:2).

The "angel of the Lord" is the Lord Jesus Christ. It is one of the many names for the Son of God in the Scriptures. He is the same One as the fourth man whom Nebuchadnezzar saw walking with the three young men in the fiery furnace, and whom he identified as the *Son of God.* Here is the same One in the burning bush, but He is here called the "angel of the Lord."

The Picture Clear as Crystal

I am sure that by this time the picture is clear from the record of the fiery furnace and the burning bush. Israel is the burning bush in the wilderness—burning, burning, burning, in the persecutions of the ages. Burning under the taskmasters' whip in Egypt, oppressed by Nebuchadnezzar, by Greece and Rome, by a Haman, a Hitler, a Mussolini, and countless others, but never, never consumed. All because God has a program for the nation that no man, no nation or nations, can stop. There will be one last great burning, when, after the Church is caught away, the nation shall enter the Great Tribulation, called significantly "the time of Jacob's trouble" (Jeremiah 30:7), but again God will remember His covenant and deliver them, and the burning bush will become the fruitful tree of Jehovah, planted in the land and filling the face of the earth with her fruit.

It is sad, indeed, that today there are so many Christians like Moses who believe that God has terminated His dealings with Israel and that they will not be re-

gathered in the land, never to be plucked up again, but
to dwell there with David their king under the personal
presence and protection of their Messiah, the ''angel
of the Lord'' of the burning bush, and the ''Son of God''
in the fiery furnace. To those of you who do not believe
that the literal nation of Israel, because of God's covenant, will finally, sometime in the future, be literally
restored to the land of Palestine forever, let me refer
you to Amos 9:13-15, and then you decide.

> Behold, the days come, saith the Lord, that . . . I will
> bring again the captivity of my people of Israel, and they
> shall build the waste cities, and inhabit them; and they
> shall plant vineyards, and drink the wine thereof; they shall
> also make gardens, and eat the fruit of them. And I will
> plant them upon their land, and they shall no more be pulled
> up out of their land which I have given them, saith the
> Lord thy God.

God says that He will plant them again in their own
land. Now you may say that they did return to the land
in the return from the captivity under Ezra, Nehemiah
and Zerubbabel. Very true, but God says in Amos 9:15
that someday they will return *never to be driven out
again.* That has never yet happened. Either this is not
true and God was mistaken, or else there is a time
coming when they shall return never to leave again.
Think it over. Read it again and God help you to see
the light.

Then the burning bush shall become the fruitful tree
of the Lord according to God's own Word.

> He shall cause them that come of Jacob to take root:
> Israel shall blossom and bud, and fill the face of the world
> with fruit (Isaiah 27:6).

This, in the barest outline, is the prophetic message
of the fiery furnace of Daniel 3 and the burning bush

of Exodus 3. It is the truth God's people need to know
in order rightly to divide the Word of truth. To take
the promises God made to the nation of Israel in regard to Palestine and their future glory and restoration,
and to spiritualize them to apply to the Church, is one
of the greatest evils which has ever beset the Church.
It blinds our eyes to grace, and closes our vision to the
program of God for these closing days of this age. May
God make us to read His Word, simply believe it, and
then live it.

CHAPTER TEN

Why Do the Heathen Rage?

The theme of Old Testament prophecy is the coming of the "King of kings, and Lord of lords." These prophecies deal with two comings, generally spoken of as the first and the second comings of the Lord Jesus. However, the Bible has a great deal more to say of the second coming than of the first. The first coming is meaningless without the second. The second is the consummation and vindication of the first. In this chapter we shall study just one passage which deals with the events connected with this glorious event, *the coming of the King.* It is found in the Second Psalm:

> Why do the heathen rage, and the people imagine a vain thing? The kings of the earth set themselves, and the rulers take counsel together, against the Lord, and against his anointed, saying, let us break their bands asunder, and cast away their cords from us. He that sitteth in the heavens shall laugh: the Lord shall have them in derision. Then shall he speak unto them in his wrath, and vex them in his sore displeasure. Yet have I set my king upon my holy hill of

Zion. I will declare the decree: the Lord hath said unto me,
thou art my Son; this day have I begotten thee. Ask of me,
and I shall give thee the heathen for thine inheritance, and
the uttermost parts of the earth for thy possession. Thou
shalt break them with a rod of iron; thou shalt dash them
in pieces like a potter's vessel. Be wise now therefore, O ye
kings: be instructed, ye judges of the earth. Serve the Lord
with fear, and rejoice with trembling. Kiss the Son, lest he
be angry, and ye perish from the way, when his wrath is
kindled but a little. Blessed are all they that put their trust
in him.

This Second Psalm is one of the Messianic Psalms.
We recognize the fact that all Psalms are Messianic
in their meaning, as is all the Word of God. By this,
of course, we mean that they all point to the Messiah,
the Lord Jesus Christ. But certain Psalms are particularly called Messianic because they are definitely
quoted in the New Testament by the Lord Jesus Himself
or the writers of the New Testament, as referring to
the Lord Jesus. This one, the Second Psalm, is quoted
by the New Testament writers in several books, as
pointing to the second coming of the Lord Jesus Christ.

The Lord Jesus, the same One who was born in Bethlehem's stable, is coming again the second time to reap
the harvest of Calvary; to take home His Church, to
judge the world and to set up His theocratic kingdom
on the earth. This Psalm deals exclusively with the
latter events and gives us one of the many pictures of
the course of this age. It is of the utmost importance
that the Christian should know what God has to say
about the future and the events which we may expect
to happen. No one can be His best for God unless he

knows what God is doing. Now the Lord has very plainly stated, over and over again in His Word, just what the course and the end of this age will be. There is certainly no excuse for any believer being ignorant of His plan. The present wars and turmoil in the nations, with famines, earthquakes, storms, signs in the heavens, false prophets and christs, the spreading wave of anti-Semitism, the apostasy of the Church and the threatened break-up of civilization have all been foretold as being signs of the close of this dispensation, and as heralding the return of the Lord. The next event in the program of God is the return of the Lord Jesus Christ from heaven with a shout, with the voice of the archangel and the trump of God. When that occurs, and it is near, all the dead in Christ shall arise from their graves; all living believers will be changed and shall be caught up-to meet the Lord in the air. After that will follow seven years of the greatest travail, war and death the world has ever known. At the close of this period of Tribulation the nations will gather in the Valley of Jehoshaphat, north of Jerusalem, in Palestine, for an attack upon the city of Jerusalem. They will be interrupted by the sudden appearing of the same Lord Jesus Christ from heaven with His saints. He will utterly destroy these armies and set up the perfect government upon the earth. Then will follow a period of one thousand years when Christ shall be King over all the earth. There will be no war, no poverty, no conflict. Animals will lose their ferocity and the lion shall eat straw like the ox. Even the serpents will be harmless, docile and gentle. Men shall beat their implements of war into useful instruments of industry and agriculture. The knowledge of the Lord shall cover the earth as the waters cover the sea.

In this Second Psalm notice the program as it is revealed. The Psalm divides itself into seven natural parts, as follows:

1. The Silent Lord on the Throne   vss. 1-3
2. The Laughing Lord of the Nations   vs. 4
3. The Speaking Lord from Heaven   vs. 5
4. The Judging Lord   vss. 6-9
5. The Reigning Lord of the Earth   vss. 6-9
6. The Warning Lord of Patience   vss. 10-11
7. The Saving Lord of Love   vs. 12

THE SILENT LORD

How often we hear in these days, from the lips of the unbelievers as well as from the hearts of those who are confused by the program of God, the question, "If there is a God in heaven why does He not do something?" Have you not heard men say that? They point at the awful, devilish and hell-begotten atrocities of the world dictators with their blitzkriegs of terror and desolation; the bombing of civilian communities, hospitals and children's homes; the laying waste of whole cities and countries; the spilling of the blood of countless thousands of innocent victims who had neither part nor voice in bringing all this about. The only answer to this question is given in the Scriptures. This is the time of God's silence. He is permitting men to go on in their wicked way in order that He may prove in the end that the heart of man is as corrupt and desperately wicked as ever. With all the centuries of our flaunted civilization, its education and reform, the heart of man has never been improved. The unregenerate heart of man is no different, whether educated or illiterate. The more refined and educated the heart of man the more dangerous he becomes, without the love of God within his bosom. Witness the nations today. What progress has been made in every field of endeavor! Yet man, instead of using the increased knowledge and invention to make a better world, is using them to destroy others and himself.

All this is according to God's program. Nowhere in the whole Bible is there a verse to support the contention that this age is going to get better and better until at last by the mutual understanding of men and nations, by conference and education, by reform and legislation, by the preaching of a social gospel we shall finally come to our senses and banish war and bring in an age of peace and contentment. *No! No! No!* That is not God's Word. Instead it teaches us that wicked men shall wax worse and worse, deceiving and being deceived. Instead it tells us that in the last days perilous times shall come and there shall be wars and rumors of wars, violence, hatred and destruction. That golden age will never come until the Prince of Peace comes. David describes the days in which you and I are living in these words:

> Why do the heathen rage, and the people imagine a vain thing? The kings of the earth set themselves, and the rulers take counsel together, against the Lord, and against his anointed, saying, let us break their bands asunder, and cast away their cords from us (Psalm 2:1-3).

God is silent through it all. He lets men, in their mad delusion, rave about working out their own salvation. God is still on the throne, however, even though He does not intervene. The cause of the whole matter that vexes the world today is this: the world is at enmity against God. If we could dig to the bottom of the Communist, Fascist and Nazi philosophies, we should find that it is rebellion against God and that they are all being egged on by Satan himself in an effort to banish the Church of Jesus Christ from the earth. Although God is silent, He is not indifferent, as we see in the second part of Psalm 2.

THE LAUGHING LORD

Not often is it said that God laughs. But as He looks down upon the world today God laughs. It is not a laugh of indifference but a laugh of derision. As the great God has watched the armies of Europe in their mad, deluded struggles to master the world, He has laughed at their puny efforts. He who in the beginningless eternity planned the universe, reached down His omnipotent hand into nothing, threw it out into nowhere and from His almighty fingers there sparkled forth the jeweled stars and planets. He hung each one in the chandeliers of heaven, garnished them all with stardust, framed them in an iridescent horizon and sent them dancing, swinging to the music of the spheres. Yes! This Almighty One laughs at man's feeble efforts to make a heaven out of earth by his own efforts. He who "measured the waters in the hollow of his hand, and meted out heaven with the span, and comprehended the dust of the earth in a measure, and weighed the mountains in scales, and the hills in a balance" . . . *He laughs.*

He before whom "the nations are as a drop of a bucket, and are counted as the small dust of the balance . . . [who] taketh up the isles as a very little thing" . . . *He laughs.*

But He will not always laugh nor ever be silent. This the inspired writer tells us next in the third part of Psalm 2.

THE SPEAKING LORD

Today the nations are raging and God indeed is laughing at their rage. The next thing will be the voice of the Lord. It is the *coming* of the Lord *for His Church* before He comes to judge the earth. How near that event must be! David says here that He will speak to those who are raging now, "in his wrath." David saw only the Lord's dealing with the nations. The New Testament tells us that when He comes to speak to the nations, He will speak first to His Church. Listen to I Thessalonians 4:16:

> For the Lord himself shall descend from heaven with a shout, with the voice of the archangel, and with the trump of God: and the dead in Christ shall rise first: then we which are alive and remain shall be caught up together with them in the clouds, to meet the Lord in the air: and so shall we ever be with the Lord.

One of these days Jesus Christ will come again. God will speak instead of laugh, and the answer to the question "Why does not God do something?" will be abundantly answered. After the Lord takes out His believing Church, consisting of everyone who is trusting in the finished work of Christ, He will begin to deal with the wickedness which today is turning the world into a veritable inferno of hell. Every Christian, however, will be caught out before the Lord pours His vials of wrath upon the nations.

What a blessed hope! What a meeting that will be when all the saints meet at the feet of Jesus! My heart longs for that day, that day which is the only hope of the believer in this dark age. To meet all our loved ones who are asleep in Christ! To see Mother, Father, Sister, Brother, Husband, Wife, in that city of peace! I can see my own dear mother as her emaciated, wrinkled form lay on that bed. When she saw the gates swing open, she smiled and pressed my hand as I sat by her death-bed, and whispered, "I'll soon see Jesus now." Just a little while after, she slipped into His arms. I can see Father, as he lay there not so long after Mother went. He repeated one of his favorite Dutch Psalms, and said, "Oh, the glory of meeting Him." I see, too, my older brother as he lay in that casket with a smile on his lifeless face and I know, thank God, I shall meet him again; and I see my baby sister who was given by the Lord to grace my parent's humble home for only a little while. The Lord gently plucked that unopened bud and placed it in His own bosom to unfold and to spread its fragrance in a place near His own heart where all babies go when they die. As I stand beside those four graves in a little cemetery in western Michigan, though I lift weeping eyes, I can still shout the victory cry:

> O death, where is thy sting? O grave, where is thy victory? (I Corinthians 15:55).

Soon the Lord will shout from heaven and those bodies will arise to be joined with their conscious spirits now reposing in the bosom of the Lord. Hallelujah!

> Behold, I shew you a mystery; We shall not all sleep. but we shall all be changed, in a moment, in the twinkling of an eye, at the last trump: for the trumpet shall sound, and the dead shall be raised incorruptible, and we shall be changed (I Corinthians 15:51-52).

Before we consider the remainder of the Second Psalm, let me ask you, "Are you ready for the coming of the Lord?" Jesus said, "When ye shall see these things come to pass, *know* that it is nigh, even *at the doors.*" One of these days the heavens will split and the Lord shall *shout* from the air and every saved one will go to meet his loved ones and Him. All the rest will be left behind to face the wrath of God. You have loved ones up there now waiting for you. But you will never meet them again unless you accept their Lord and their Saviour. Do you remember the day when that little flaxen-haired, blue-eyed darling went home and the little one lisped, "Jesus is coming for me"? Do you not long to see that little sweetheart again? Then come to Christ today so that when He shouts from the air you too will rise to meet with that great company.

Believe on the Lord Jesus Christ, and thou shalt be saved (Acts 16:31).

In the following chapter we shall cover the last four parts of Psalm 2 and see Jesus crowned and reigning over all the earth—the *judging Lord*, the *reigning Lord*, then the *warning Lord* and finally the *saving Lord*.

CHAPTER ELEVEN

The Coming Reign of Christ

Jesus Christ is King!

In all the Old Testament prophecies He is presented as the King who will come and set up His kingdom of righteousness and peace upon the earth. When He came the first time, He came as King. His coming was announced by an angel. His birth was heralded by a heavenly host. As King, His ministry was proclaimed by John the Baptist. The charge on which He was crucified was that He had made Himself a King. He hung on the Cross as a King with a crown of thorns upon His brow. He arose a King when He routed the powers of darkness, broke the bands of death, and came forth the mighty conqueror of death, sin and hell. Yes, Jesus Christ is King.

We have seen the program of God in the setting up of the millennial kingdom, as portrayed in the Second Psalm. This Psalm is only one of hundreds of passages throughout the Word where the Lord gives us the details of the program for this age, which will result in the ushering in of an era of peace and prosperity under the beneficent sway of Jesus Christ the King of kings and Lord of lords.

The second Psalm, as we have mentioned previously, divides itself quite naturally into seven distinct steps in the fulfillment of God's plan for the earth, and the nations. These steps are:

1. The Silent Lord on the Throne
2. The Laughing Lord of the Nations
3. The Speaking Lord from Heaven
4. The Judging Lord
5. The Reigning Lord of the Earth
6. The Warning Lord of Patience
7. The Saving Lord of Love

At present God is silent. While we know that He is on the Throne, He is not actively intervening in the world today so far as interrupting the madness of the nations is concerned. He is apparently unconcerned that man is seeking his own destruction and the annihilation of civilization. But God is not in any sense a disinterested bystander. He is only permitting the nations to fulfill His plan and purpose until that exact moment when the time comes for Him to intervene. While man is seeking to accomplish his own destiny and salvation by the instruments of war and destruction, God is said to "laugh." After the laughter, will come His voice. God will speak in a twofold way.

First, He will come in the clouds of heaven with a *"shout."* It is the same voice of the Lord which created the worlds; the same voice that spoke from heaven on Mt. Sinai; the same voice that said to the waves, "Peace be still"; the same voice that said to a dead man in a tomb in Palestine, "Lazarus, come forth"; the same voice as that which rent the rocks and caused the earth to reel as He cried on that day of days, "It is finished." That same voice will shout and "the dead in Christ shall rise first: then we which are alive and remain shall be caught up together with them in the clouds, to meet the Lord in the air.''

That shout will have a message, too, for all the nations of the earth. It will be the shout of war. It will usher in that ''day of the Lord,'' the description of which occupies such a large place in the Scriptures. David describes it in this Second Psalm as follows:

> Then shall he speak unto them in his wrath and vex them in his sore displeasure.

This day of His ''wrath'' is known by many names in the Scriptures. Besides the name, ''day of the Lord,'' it is called the ''great tribulation,'' the ''day of vengeance of our God,'' the ''days of recompence,'' the ''time of Jacob's trouble,'' the ''day of clouds and of thick darkness'' and many others. This day will begin at the catching away of the Church at the Rapture and will end with the return of the Lord Jesus Christ from heaven to set up His Universal Kingdom of peace on the earth—a period of seven years.

THE JUDGING LORD

A day of great sorrow! The importance of this day may be seen from the fact that so much of prophecy deals with this brief period of time. We shall give only a few of the many references of this great and terrible day of the Lord.

In Isaiah 2:19, we read concerning this day as follows:

> And they [men] shall go into the holes of the rocks, and into the caves of the earth, for fear of the Lord, and for the glory of his majesty, when he ariseth to shake terribly the earth.

In Isaiah 13:9-11, 13, 15-16, we read:

> Behold, the day of the Lord cometh, cruel both with wrath and fierce anger, to lay the land desolate: and he shall destroy the sinners thereof out of it. For the stars of heaven and the constellations thereof shall not give their light: the sun shall be darkened in his going forth, and the moon shall not cause her light to shine. And I will punish the world for their evil, and the wicked for their iniquity; and I will cause the arrogancy of the proud to cease, and will lay low the haughtiness of the terrible . . . Therefore I will shake the heavens, and the earth shall remove out of her place, in the wrath of the Lord of hosts, and in the day of his fierce anger . . . Every one that is found shall be thrust through; and every one that is joined unto them shall fall by the sword. Their children also shall be dashed to pieces before their eyes; their houses shall be spoiled, and their wives ravished.

Let me refer you to one more passage from the many, many others, to show you what God has to say about this awful coming day. Turn to Isaiah 34:1-6:

> Come near, ye nations, to hear; and hearken, ye people: let the earth hear, and all that is therein; the world, and all things that come forth of it. For the indignation of the Lord is upon all nations, and his fury upon all their armies: he hath utterly destroyed them, he hath delivered them to the slaughter. Their slain also shall be cast out, and their stink shall come up out of their carcases, and the mountains shall be melted with their blood. And all the host of heaven shall be dissolved, and the heavens shall be rolled together as a scroll: and all their host shall fall down, as the leaf falleth off from the vine, and as a falling fig from the fig tree. For my sword shall be bathed in heaven: behold, it shall come down upon Idumea, and upon the people of my curse, to judgment. The sword of the Lord is filled with blood.

We might go on almost indefinitely with quotations from the Book to show how much the Lord has to say on this subject of the judgment upon the earth in the time of the end. For a detailed description of this time, read the last book of the Bible, the Revelation. You will find that its message has to do almost exclusively with the *day of the Lord.* In the first chapter of Revelation, we have a picture of the Lord Jesus who was rejected the first time but who will reject His enemies when He returns the second time.

In chapters 2 and 3 of Revelation we have a preview of the history of the Church on the earth from the Cross to the second coming of the Lord. This history is pre-written in the seven letters to the seven churches in Asia—the seven stages of the history of the Church from Ephesus to Laodicea. Then in Revelation 4:1-2, the Church is taken out, as John sees the door opened in heaven and hears the *Voice* saying, "Come up hither." From this point on, the Church is never again mentioned because the rest of the book of Revelation deals with God's judgments upon the earth. The Church is taken out first, Revelation 4, and then that great and terrible day of the Lord comes. In Revelation 4 and 5, we have a brief description of what John saw when he was caught up into heaven and this is the prophecy of what will occur when the Church is caught away. Then in Revelation 6 to 19, we have a vivid description of what will happen on this earth after the Rapture. There will be wars, pestilence, disease and death. Four horsemen appear in rapid succession in Revelation 6. First, the white horse of *false* peace, then the red horse of war and bloodshed, followed by the black horse of pestilence and finally the pale horse of death. The rest of the chapters give us in detail that terrible time when the *superman,* the *antichrist,* will reign; when an army of two hundred millions will ascend from the pit to spread death on the earth, and hailstones weighing one hundred twenty pounds shall fall from heaven.

After the final battle of Armageddon, which will be interrupted by the personal appearing of Jesus Christ, the Bible states that the blood of the slain will reach even to the bridles of the horses. According to Ezekiel, it will take seven months to bury these bodies of the slain. To those of you who are interested in knowing how much the Bible has to say about this great "day of the Lord," I refer you to the following Scriptures: Isaiah 63:1-6; 66:15-24; Jeremiah 25:29; Ezekiel 30:3; Joel 2 and 3; Malachi 4.

Immediately at the end of this period the Lord returns to destroy the armies of the dictators. You will find the reference in Revelation in the nineteenth chapter beginning at verse 11. After conquering His enemies, He sets up His millennial kingdom; read Revelation 20 and 21. After the judgment of the Great White Throne, we have the new heavens, the new earth and eternity.

Now the outline of Revelation corresponds exactly with this Second Psalm. Here, too, we have first the raging nations, then the Voice of the Lord, the destruction of the satanic oppressors and finally the setting up of the kingdom.

Now we come to the fifth division of Psalm 2, the reigning Lord on the earth.

The Reigning Lord

Yet have I set my king upon my holy hill of Zion (Psalm 2:6).

Zion, of course, is Jerusalem and the holy hill is the hill on which the city is built. God says that in spite of the raging of the godless nations, who have substituted godlessness for godliness and folklore and mythology for the Bible, He will set up His own King to reign on the earth. Then next we hear the *King* speak and He says:

> I will declare the decree: the Lord hath said unto me, Thou art my Son; this day have I begotten thee. Ask of me, and I shall give thee the heathen for thine inheritance, and the uttermost parts of the earth for thy possession. Thou shalt break them with a rod of iron; thou shalt dash them in pieces like a potter's vessel (Psalm 2:7-9).

Yes,

> Jesus shall reign where'er the sun
> Doth his successive journeys run;
> His kingdom reach from shore to shore,
> Till moons shall wax and wane no more.

These are terrible days in which we live and yet they are wonderful days, for while wickedness and violence are increasing on every hand, the Bible tells us that "all these things *must* come to pass." All that we see around about us is in fulfillment of the sure word of prophecy. Not a single thing is happening except according to the program of God. In succeeding chapters we hope to show how that every single detail of the present world conditions was foretold by the prophets and by our Lord Jesus Christ. While the unbeliever knows not what to think of conditions in the world today, the regenerated student of the Word sees in all these things the fulfillment of His Word and the evidences of the faithfulness of God.

The next event in the program of God is the coming of the Lord Jesus Christ from heaven. I have the firm conviction that we are rapidly approaching the end of an age—an age that will close by the sudden translation of the blood-bought Church of the Lord Jesus Christ. God have mercy on the Christian who does not study the Word and is ignorant of the signs of the times. The Lord has said so clearly, "When these things begin to come to pass, then look up . . . for your redemption draweth nigh."

It may be at morn, when the day is awaking,
When sunlight through darkness and shadow is breaking,
That Jesus will come in the fullness of glory,
To receive from the world His own.

It may be at midday, it may be at twilight,
It may be, perchance, that the blackness of midnight
Will burst into light in the blaze of His glory,
When Jesus receives His own.

Oh, joy, oh, delight! should we go without dying,
No sickness, no sadness, no dreading, no crying,
Caught up through the clouds with our Lord into glory,
When Jesus receives His own.

O Lord Jesus, how long, how long
Ere we shout the glad song?
Christ returneth, Hallelujah!
Hallelujah, Amen! Hallelujah, Amen!

THE WARNING LORD

A solemn warning! The Second Psalm ends with a solemn warning and a gracious invitation—a solemn warning to the nations and a gracious invitation to everyone to put their trust in the Lord. Oh, that the nations would learn that all progress and civilization without Christ is but futile and doomed to failure! Oh, that the leaders of the nations would learn that there can be no perfect government and no equitable social order until He comes to take the kingdom "whose right it is," and

He "shall reign and prosper"! The prayer of every
child of God should be the last prayer of the Bible,
"Even so, come, Lord Jesus."

THE SAVING LORD

The gracious invitation! The Psalm ends with these
blessed words, "Blessed are all they that put their trust
in him." The word "blessed" means "happy." Only
those who have put their trust in the Lord Jesus can be
really happy—happy because they are in harmony with
God's program, happy because they know that soon
their Lord will come and all this turmoil of the nations
will cease and the earth at last will be at rest.

Soon the shout will resound from heaven and He who
came once before "despised and rejected of men," shall
come as the "Lion of the tribe of Juda." Then,

> Christ shall have dominion over land and sea,
> Earth's remotest regions shall His empire be.

My friend, are you ready for that day? Each day
brings us nearer that glad event for the children of God
and that sad event for those who reject Him.

> Kiss the Son, lest he be angry, and ye perish from the
> way, when his wrath is kindled but a little. Blessed are all
> they that put their trust in him (Psalm 2:12).

Accept Him today and be saved.

CHAPTER TWELVE

Bad News and Good News

Earthquake rocks Caribbean. Hundreds are killed. Thousands are made homeless by giant quake. Great tidal wave rushes miles inland leaving untold dead and numberless homeless in its wake. Riots kill two thousand and wound many more thousand. Hotel bombed by the terrorists. One hundred killed. Hundreds wounded. Thousands idled by newest strike. All production at a standstill. American plane shot down over friendly territory. American flyers bombed. America issues a strong protest. Russia masses troops on the frontier. American warships patrol the Mediterranean. Man kills wife and three daughters and turns gun on himself. Flames destroy hotel. Forty dead. Tornado rips through town. Hospitals jammed. Red Cross rushing supplies. All doctors available being rushed to the scene. Delegates at Conference in deadlock. Tension rises. Angry remarks being made. Peacetime army at an all-time high. Atomic warfare, according to leading scientists, will destroy all of our present civilization.

These are the headlines gathered at random from one day's newspaper reports as I am preparing this chapter;

and all of the news, practically all of it is bad news. To-day as we read our newspapers and listen to our reporters over the air, we hear very, very little of good news. Most of it is exceedingly bad. Newspapers are "bad news" papers. By this we do not mean that the newspapers are bad, but rather that if the newspaper prints the bad news, it becomes a good newspaper, for if the newspaper is a good newspaper, it is a "bad news" paper; or let me repeat, a good newspaper reports the news as it really is, and most of it in these days in which we are living is, we must admit, very bad news. So the good newspaper prints bad news!

How happy, therefore, we are that we can have printed and tell over the air news that is not bad—that we can herald to all men everywhere the good news! For "good news" is the meaning of the word "Gospel." The word *evangelium* means "good news." The good news is that God has provided a way out, that when man has reached his utter extremity and has no way to turn, God's plan and God's purpose still are the best. This subject of good news was suggested to us as we studied this book of Daniel where we have three Hebrew youths who because of their faithfulness and devotion to the cause of their God and their Jehovah, were nevertheless cast into a fiery furnace with the purpose of destroying them utterly. But strangely enough, God sent His own Son, in the person of the fourth individual in the fiery furnace, to keep them without harm and to deliver them and to exalt them to a high and holy position. This is, indeed, good news, for the God who delivered the friends of Daniel in the fiery furnace, and Daniel in the lions' den, is the same God today. And all those who will heed the good news and trust the promises of God and be faithful unto Him may, like Daniel's friends, be assured

that out of it all will come something that will be in-
finitely profitable and edifying—something that will
bring its reward in the end. We have been studying
Daniel, and, of course, we have been occupied mostly
with the prophetic aspect of this wonderful book. However, now and then, we want to insert at least one lesson
of a more practical nature in order that we may receive
all of the benefit and all of the blessing which God has
for us in this wonderful prophetic volume. And so we
find that there is good news for all who are willing to
heed God's command.

Good News for the Nations

As we study this prophecy of Daniel we find that while
it records for us the failure of the nations in seeking
to establish a man-made government upon the earth, it
also brings the good news of ultimate delivery. After
man's day is past, God is going to usher in a day wherein the nations of the world are going to be blessed. They
will live in peace and tranquillity, one with another,
when war shall cease, when there will be no armies and
no more navies, when there will be no more instruments
of destruction, but every man shall sit under his own
vine and under his own fig tree, and none shall make him
afraid. That is the good news that God has today. As we
look round about us and we see everything dark and becoming darker day by day, we thank God that we can cry
out to the nations that this day is coming, according to
the promise of the Almighty God Himself. All of these
events, discouraging as they are to those who do not
know the program of God, are nevertheless very clearly
and minutely outlined in the Scriptures and we are
specifically admonished that when we see these things
coming to pass—the things that are happening in the

world today and which we read from the headlines—then we are to look up, not to look down, but heads up, for our "redemption draweth nigh." Isaiah the prophet says concerning that glorious day:

> And many people shall go and say, Come ye, and let us go up to the mountain of the Lord, to the house of the God of Jacob; and he will teach us of his ways, and we will walk in his paths: for out of Zion shall go forth the law, and the word of the Lord from Jerusalem. And he shall judge among the nations, and shall rebuke many people: and they shall beat their swords into plowshares, and their spears into pruninghooks: nation shall not lift up sword against nation, neither shall they learn war any more (Isaiah 2:3-4).

These are the words of God; they cannot fail. Everything round about us today is pointing to the very soon coming of the One who will make all of these things possible.

WE ALSO HAVE GOOD NEWS FROM THE WORD OF GOD FOR THE NATION OF ISRAEL

The hope of Israel, of course, has been, throughout all the ages, a national return to their homeland, the land of Palestine, out of which they have been scattered for so many centuries. Today there is unusual activity, more than at almost any other period in history, concerning the restoration of the land to the people, God's ancient covenant nation. In recent years we have seen the rapid rise of Zionism, a movement which has for its design and purpose the return of the nation of Israel, the covenant nation, to the covenant land promised to them by Almighty God through Abraham, Isaac and Jacob. Because we hear so much about Zionism in these days and because it is so little understood by great masses of people, it might be profitable at this time to give a few facts in regard to this world-wide movement with which, I am sure, all true Christians are heartily in accord. Zionism is a movement which has for its purpose the setting aside and the restoration of the land of Palestine as a homeland for the scattered nation of Israel in the world today. Now Zionism is divided into two groups, the Nationalist group and the Judaean group. The Nationalist group claims that it is the traditional, historic and legal right of the nation of Israel to have absolute possession of the land of Palestine, where they may set up a national independent society for the establishment of an independent nation, a revival of the glory of ancient Israel under the Davidic kingdom.

Then there is the Judaean group who, while they do not call for the setting aside of the entire land of Palestine as an exclusive Jewish state, nevertheless want it to be open so that it may be made the fountainhead, the center, the capital as it were, for Jewish culture and religion for the world, such as Rome today is the fountainhead of Catholicism, and Mecca the fountainhead of Mohammedanism; and other examples might be given. Now, while Zionism today is meeting with a great deal of opposition, and from the human standpoint it seems almost impossible of realization, we Christians who believe the record of the Word of God and the program of God in regard to the nations as well as Israel, find in this movement many, many hopeful signs. The Bible is replete with prophetic references that in the end time, after this dispensation begins to run to its close, God is going to regather His ancient covenant people one by one, and will restore them again unto the land which He had promised unto their fathers. There are literally hundreds of these Scripture passages, but we quote only a few, and then trust that they will act as an in-

centive for you to study the prophets of the Bible more
thoroughly for the voluminous evidence of the absolute
return of the nation to the land again. We believe that
the Nationalist dream of Zionism is going to be completely realized when their Messiah comes to deliver
them, and the Davidic kingdom is again re-established
in the land of Canaan. Let me call your attention to the
following prophetic passages:

> And now therefore thus saith the Lord, the God of
> Israel, concerning this city, whereof ye say, It shall be
> delivered into the hand of the king of Babylon by the sword,
> and by the famine, and by the pestilence; behold, I will
> gather them [that is, the nation of Israel] out of all
> countries, whither I have driven them in mine anger,
> and in my fury, and in great wrath; and I will bring them
> again unto this place, and I will cause them to dwell
> safely: and they shall be my people, and I will be their
> God . . . Yea, I will rejoice over them to do them good,
> and I will plant them in this land assuredly with my whole
> heart and with my whole soul . . . Men shall buy fields
> for money, and subscribe evidences, and seal them, and take
> witnesses in the land of Benjamin, and in the places about
> Jerusalem, and in the cities of Judah, and in the cities
> of the mountains, and in the cities of the valley, and in the
> cities of the south: for I will cause their captivity to
> return, saith the Lord (Jeremiah 32:36-38, 41, 44).

> Thus saith the Lord; If my covenant be not with day
> and night, and if I have not appointed the ordinances
> of heaven and earth; then will I cast away the seed of
> Jacob, and David my servant, so that I will not take any
> of his seed to be rulers over the seed of Abraham, Isaac,
> and Jacob: for I will cause their captivity to return, and
> have mercy on them (Jeremiah 33:25-26).

> Therefore, behold, the days come, saith the Lord, that
> they shall no more say, The Lord liveth, which brought
> up the children of Israel out of the land of Egypt; but,
> The Lord liveth, which brought up and which led the

seed of the house of Israel out of the north country, and from all countries whither I had driven them; and they shall dwell in their own land (Jeremiah 23:7-8).

As far back as the book of Deuteronomy, God already revealed through Moses what would be the history of his people:

Thy God will turn thy captivity, and have compassion upon thee, and will return and gather thee from all the nations, whither the Lord thy God hath scattered thee. If any of thine be driven out unto the outmost parts of heaven, from thence will the Lord thy God gather thee, and from thence will he fetch thee (Deuteronomy 30:3-4).

This is the theme of all prophecy. As we turn to the book of Isaiah—Isaiah is just full of these wonderful prophecies and promises to Israel—we read this:

And it shall come to pass in that day, that the Lord shall set his hand again the second time to recover the remnant of his people, which shall be left, from Assyria, and from Egypt, and from Pathros, and from Cush, and from Elam, and from Shinar, and from Hamath, and from the islands of the sea (Isaiah 11:11).

Here is another promise from the same book:

Fear not: for I am with thee: I will bring thy seed from the east, and gather thee from the west; I will say to the north, Give up; and to the south, Keep not back: bring my sons from far, and my daughters from the ends of the earth; even every one that is called by my name: for I have created him for my glory, I have formed him: yea, I have made him (Isaiah 43:5-7).

These words were spoken in connection with the history of Israel. In Jeremiah we read this:

And I will be found of you, saith the Lord: and I will turn away your captivity, and I will gather you from all the nations, and from all the places whither I have driven you, saith the Lord; and I will bring you again into the

place whence I caused you to be carried away captive
(Jeremiah 29:14).

Just one more reference:

I will surely assemble, O Jacob, all of thee; I will
surely gather the remnant of Israel; I will put them together as the sheep of Bozrah, as the flock in the midst of
their fold: they shall make great noise by reason of the
multitude of men (Micah 2:12).

Now we might go on almost indefinitely in this strain,
because prophecy is filled with similar promises. What
wonderful, wonderful good news we have for the nation
of Israel today! This regathering of the nation and return to the place of blessing will not come by the plans
and program of men, but will be accomplished by the
Lord Himself, and that gives us confidence to believe
that when it comes it is going to be done in absolutely
the right way.

Good News for the Church

But not only have we good news for the nations of the
world, and good news for the nation of Israel, but we
have good news for the Church of the Lord Jesus Christ.
The true Church of the Lord Jesus Christ, composed of
people from every tribe and tongue and nation and color
and denomination, is being gathered even now, called
out by the Holy Spirit. All those who believe and trust
the finished work of the Lord Jesus Christ, no matter
who they may be, become members of the body of the
Lord Jesus Christ which is His Church. And we are
told that this Church shall remain here until just before
the breaking of the final judgment upon this wicked
world, called the Tribulation Period. The Lord Jesus
Christ has told us that we were to look for all these bad

and ominous signs which are disturbing the world today, for they would be the indication of the nearness of His return. He said concerning it, "When these things begin to come to pass, then look up . . . for your redemption draweth nigh." So the good news to the Church today is this, that we are living, we believe, in the very end time of this age, and very soon now we shall hear the shout from heaven, "Come up hither," according to the promise of God given in the Scriptures in so many different places. In First Thessalonians we read:

> For the Lord himself shall descend from heaven with a shout, with the voice of the archangel, and with the trump of God: and the dead in Christ shall rise first: then we which are alive and remain shall be caught up together with them in the clouds, to meet the Lord in the air: and so shall we ever be with the Lord. Wherefore comfort one another with these words (I Thessalonians 4:16-18).

That is good news. In First Corinthians we read this:

> We shall not all sleep, but we shall all be changed, in a moment, in the twinkling of an eye, at the last trump: for the trumpet shall sound, and the dead shall be raised incorruptible, and we shall be changed (I Corinthians 15: 51-52).

Good news in a world filled with bad news!

THEN FINALLY, THERE IS GOOD NEWS FOR YOU

There is good news for you who are reading these words this very moment. If you are a Christian, of course, there is good news, for we know that we are rapidly approaching the world's glad day of the return of the Lord Jesus Christ. But I have good news also for you who are still without Christ, who can look forward and see nothing else but death, nothing else but eternity. You have no hope, you have no assurance, you have no peace. There is good news for you, and the good news is this, that way back nineteen hundred years ago God sent His Son into the world because He realized that man could not save himself, but was hopeless, utterly depraved and helpless, and therefore needed a Saviour. And so He sent, in the fullness of time, His Precious Son who took upon Himself the responsibility of a lost world that was plunging into an eternal hell, and bore our sins in His body on the Tree. He assumed our responsibility and went to Calvary and there He died for all those who had fallen in Adam. Now the good news is this, that Christ died according to the Scriptures, that He was buried, that He arose again, and that today there is salvation, freedom from want and fear and oppression, freedom from death and freedom from the specter of eternity, to all those who will put their trust in Him. It is so simple. That is what makes it good news. Just right where you are, bow your head, believe the record that God gave of His Son, receive the Lord Jesus Christ, repent of your sin, turn away from self and all your own goodness, and put your trust in the promise of God who said "that whosoever shall call on the name of the Lord shall be saved." God grant you grace to do it now.

CHAPTER THIRTEEN

The Tree Vision of Nebuchadnezzar

Nebuchadnezzar the king, unto all people, nations, and languages, that dwell in all the earth; Peace be multiplied unto you. I thought it good to shew the signs and wonders that the high God hath wrought toward me. How great are his signs! and how mighty are his wonders! his kingdom is an everlasting kingdom, and his dominion is from generation to generation (Daniel 4:1-3).

These are not the words of a Hebrew saint, nor of one of the usual writers of the Scriptures. The fourth chapter of the prophecy of Daniel contains the testimony of a pagan, heathen, Gentile king, Nebuchadnezzar, relating for us his conversion and how he came to the knowledge of the true God and Jehovah. As you know, the Bible is a Hebrew book, written in the main, both the Old and the New Testaments, by Hebrews whom God chose and inspired by His Spirit to set down the record of His will, His plan, His purpose, His program for the ages. The fourth chapter of Daniel, however, is a very outstanding exception to this rule, for as we have stated, it contains the personal testimony of the conversion of this heathen king.

If we are to understand the Bible correctly, we must

remember that it deals very largely with the history of
one single nation, the nation of Israel, the nation which
is at the center of God's program and plan for the dis-
pensations and the rest of the world nations. It deals
particularly with one particular land, the land of this
nation, the land of Canaan, which God gave by covenant
to Abraham, Isaac and Jacob, and through them to the
twelve tribes of Israel. That promise holds good today
and is just as sure and unbreakable as in the day when
God first gave it to His servant Abraham as recorded in
the thirteenth, fourteenth and fifteenth chapters of Genesis. If, therefore, we are to understand the Bible and
all of its revelation, we must remember that the key to
the Scriptures is the plan of God concerning the nation
of Israel in setting up a kingdom here upon the earth,
and that during the interval of the nation's rejection
and the setting aside of the kingdom, God is calling out
for Himself a Bride, the Church of the Lord Jesus. After
the Rapture of the Church, God will again begin to deal
with His ancient people, and fulfill all the covenant
promises which He has made to the prophets of old as
contained in the record of the Bible. It is, therefore,
significant and worthy of special note that in this fourth
chapter of Daniel, we have the record not of a Hebrew
writer but of a Gentile king concerning the dealing of
God in revelation.

Purpose of the Prophecy of Daniel

To the casual observer, the book of Daniel looks very
much like twelve disconnected and unrelated chapters
telling the experiences of this man, Daniel, while he was
a slave in the palace of the king, Nebuchadnezzar. However, when we remember that the Holy Spirit who wrote
all the other sixty-five books of the Bible is the one

Author, and that there is a unity and a progression and a oneness of purpose in every one of these books and all of them are related together, we begin to see in the prophecy of Daniel not merely a historic record of certain events which took place thousands of years ago, but a revelation of God, and we see that all these chapters are connected one to the other and reveal to us what God's purpose and plan is for these days which lay ahead in Daniel's day. These twelve chapters in Daniel, therefore, are not isolated experiences, but they are related accounts of God's progressive revelation of the things which He wants His children to know. The main purpose of Daniel was to give us a vision of the "times of the Gentiles" up until the second coming of the Lord Jesus Christ. So what we find in Daniel is a record of the course of the ages from Daniel's day through the present dispensation of the grace of God, through the Tribulation Period, and up to the millennial period which shall be ushered in by the second coming of the Lord Jesus Christ, the Messiah.

Four Pictures of Babylon

In order to make it more easy for you to understand the purpose and the teaching of the prophecy of Daniel, let me remind you that we have in this interesting book, four distinct and separate and yet related pictures of the course of this age.

The first is found in the second chapter. You will recall it—the image of Nebuchadnezzar with its head of gold, with its chest and arms of silver, with its belly and thighs of brass, with its legs of iron and with its feet and toes of iron and of clay. We have already pointed out that this was a prophetic picture of the course of history from Babylon even unto the last form of Gentile world power and dominion which will be destroyed when the Lord Jesus Christ comes again. We have pointed out that the head of gold represented Babylon; the chest represented the kingdom of Persia; the belly and the thighs of brass represented the conquering hosts of Greece; and finally the Roman Empire, which in turn conquered the kingdom of Greece, was divided into two parts represented by the two legs and then for a time discontinued. We believe that we are standing on the very threshold of that time when the ten toes will make their appearance in the two-headed federation of nations of the end time just before the coming of the Lord.

This was the great image which the king Nebuchadnezzar saw and was a picture of the course of Gentile dominion during the time of the rejection of the King. The most significant part of this vision was that after having viewed the great image of gold and silver and brass and iron and clay, he saw a great stone coming down from heaven. It smote the image in its feet and ground it to powder, and then the stone itself became a great rock which eventually filled the entire earth. Now the picture was simply this—during the time of our Lord's rejection the Gentile world powers will seek to bring about a millennium, a period of peace and world federation and world government which will have no need for God or for God's Christ, but at the end of man's efforts, after he has failed, the Lord Jesus Christ, the Rock of Ages, shall return and smite these governments and grind them to powder. Then He Himself will become the King of kings and the Lord of lords and His kingdom shall be over all until it fills the entire earth. This is the testimony of prophecy that at the end of man's reign, after man has exhausted every means at his disposal to bring about a world peace and security, the Lord Jesus Christ will come and He alone will bring peace and happiness and prosperity to this poor old dying world which is today in the very last throes of its desperate attempt to save itself without the Lord Jesus Christ. That is the first picture which we have of the course of the age.

Then the second one of these pictures is the tree vision of Nebuchadnezzar which we have in this fourth chapter. In this tree vision Nebuchadnezzar had another dream in which he saw a great tree with branches giving shelter to the beasts of the field, and where birds could find nesting places. Then a voice from heaven commanded to hew down the tree, and it fell, and after seven years the stump again budded forth and became another tree. This is just another picture of the same thing that we have in the second chapter of the way the Gentile world power will increase and grow until it is cut down. We have an additional thing here in the fourth chapter, however, for we find that the tree that was cut down will ultimately be restored. This teaches us that in the millennial age even the Gentile nations will own and acknowledge the Lord Jesus Christ and be saved.

We have a third picture of the course of this age. It is found in the next chapter which we shall take up in due time—a picture of Belshazzar's impious feast, when he took the vessels of the Lord from the Temple of Jehovah and made merry with "his princes, his wives, and his concubines," only to be stopped in the middle of the feast by a hand that came from heaven and wrote his doom upon the walls of the dining hall. Then we have one other picture and that is found in Daniel 7, where Daniel sees the four beasts, the lion, the leopard, the bear, and then the indescribable monstrosity which runs parallel to the image that we found in chapter 2. But now we want you to consider the vision of the tree in the fourth chapter of Daniel. It is one of the longest chapters in Daniel, and we shall not take the space to quote it in its entirety but shall give you the more important features. Nebuchadnezzar, the one who had seen the vision of the great image in the second chapter, is still king in Babylon and Daniel is still serving him there in the capacity of adviser. Then one night the king had another dream. He saw a great tree growing, which had attained such gigantic dimensions that it overshadowed the entire earth. Under its branches the beasts of the field found shelter. In its branches the birds of the heaven found a place for their nesting and for their protection. And then a very strange thing happened. Let me quote the record as we have it in the fourth chapter of Daniel:

> I saw in the visions of my head upon my bed, and, behold, a watcher and an holy one came down from heaven; he cried aloud, and said thus, Hew down the tree, and cut off his branches, shake off his leaves, and scatter his fruit: let the beasts get away from under it, and the fowls from his branches: nevertheless leave the stump of his roots in the earth, even with a band of iron and brass, in the tender grass of the field; and let it be wet with the dew of heaven, and let his portion be with the beasts in the grass of the earth (Daniel 4:13-15).

This is the account of the king himself in regard to the dream which he had dreamed. And then Daniel is called in after all the wise men and the soothsayers, the magicians and the astrologers of Babylon had failed to give any kind of an explanation. When the Lord shows Daniel the meaning of this particular dream, he is astounded and amazed and for a time is absolutely silent, seeking wisdom from on high that will enable him to break the news of the judgment contained in this dream to the king, Nebuchadnezzar. After his period of silence we have the record of Daniel's interpretation as follows:

> It is thou, O king, that art grown and become strong: for thy greatness is grown, and reacheth unto heaven, and thy dominion to the end of the earth . . . This is the interpretation, O king, and this is the decree of the most High, which is come upon my lord the king: that they shall drive thee from men, and thy dwelling shall be with the beasts of the field, and they shall make thee to eat grass as oxen, and they shall wet thee with the dew of heaven, and seven times shall pass over thee, till thou know that the most High ruleth in the kingdom of men, and giveth it to whomsoever he will (Daniel 4:22, 24, 25).

Now in studying this interpretation of the king's dream, we must bear in mind that Daniel is, indeed, a prophecy, and while all of these accounts contain many, many valuable moral and ethical lessons which can be very profitable to us and which we should not overlook, nevertheless the purpose of Daniel is to prophesy concerning the things which are to come. This, we remind you, was definitely stated by the Lord Jesus Christ in the Gospel according to Matthew where He specifically reminds us that Daniel was a prophet. In the light of the prophetic nature of Daniel, Nebuchadnezzar, the king of Babylon, is representative of world government, not only in his particular time and age in which he lived, but is representative of man's effort at governing himself in every age of man's dominion until the kingdom of the Lord Jesus Christ shall be set up.

Just as Nebuchadnezzar succeeded in conquering the entire world and uniting all the people under one great Babylonian system of government, so too the Bible tells

us that toward the end of this age there will emerge a
world government, a world federation of nations under
one federal headship which shall guarantee unto man
a man-made prosperity, a time when war shall cease,
when there will be no poverty, no strife, no disagreement,
but the Utopia of man's dreams, the millennium of man's
making shall find its fulfillment. When that time comes,
then as in Nebuchadnezzar's case, the pride of man will
reach its very apex. Man will imagine that he himself
has brought about all this wonderful achievement and
accomplishment through education, science, human wisdom, without acknowledging the Lord Jesus Christ. The
Bible is filled with descriptions of this end-time world
federation when man shall have reached the very pinnacle of human success only to find that it is a paper
house of dreams, that it cannot stand, that until Christ
reigns there can be no lasting peace, there can be no
success by the efforts of man alone.

Man, like Nebuchadnezzar, will be walking upon the
housetop of his own accomplishments and viewing all
that he has made, saying, "Is not this great Babylon,
that I have built?" But just the very moment when man
dreams that he has accomplished his desired purpose will
be the signal for the coming again of the rightful Owner
and the rightful Governor, even the Lord Jesus Christ.
He will shout from the air and take His Church into
heaven with Himself, and then will follow a period of
seven years of tribulation which we may well call the
folly, the insane madness of the nations of the earth.
Nebuchadnezzar became mad for seven long years during
which he was with the beasts of the field, living like an
animal, and the kingdom of Babylon was without his
leadership. This is typical and prophetic of that seven-
year period of time between the Rapture of the Church

and His second coming again, during which God is going to remove all restraints, permit the Antichrist to have free reign, and man will succeed in almost annihilating himself were it not for the sudden intervention of the Lord Himself. And so the voice that came from heaven and commanded that the tree representing Nebuchadnezzar, the king, be hewed down and cut to the ground, is a picture of the coming of the Lord who will cause the nations to become stark mad in their insane delusion of self-achievement and self-grandeur, and then will follow the seven years of greatest confusion the world has ever known.

THE END IS NEAR

We believe that the time of the cutting down of this great tree of world power is very, very near at hand. We are today experiencing as never before an effort on the part of man—sincere efforts, well-meaning efforts —to bring about some kind of negotiation, some kind of an understanding, some kind of a union and federation of the nations of the world that will forever guarantee the security of the inhabitants of this earth, and will increase the prosperity and bring to an end the wars that have devastated this world since time began. And we say this, not critically but sadly, that in all of these deliberations we hear little or nothing of God. There is no acknowledgment of the God of heaven, whatsoever. And so we believe that in the end time, after man has reached the very pinnacle of his own effort and achievement, the Lord Jesus Christ is going to come back again to destroy the wicked nations of the world, and set up His glorious and wonderful millennial kingdom of peace under the leadership of the only King of heaven and of earth, even the King of glory, the Lord Jesus Christ.

You have probably noticed in the reading of the passages from Daniel 4, that the purpose of all this was that Nebuchadnezzar might learn to know that God is still the King of heaven, that God is still on the Throne. And the purpose of God judging the nations and judging the world, which we believe to be in the very near future, will be that man may learn to know that without God everything must fail, and that God is still the King of heaven and of earth. In the next chapter we shall learn about the conversion of the Gentiles at the coming of the Lord Jesus Christ as indicated by the conversion of Nebuchadnezzar the king, after his seven years of madness.

CHAPTER FOURTEEN

The Conversion of the World

> Now I Nebuchadnezzar praise and extol and honour the
> King of heaven, all whose works are truth, and his ways
> judgment: and those that walk in pride he is able to abase
> (Daniel 4:37).

These are the concluding words of the testimony of
the king of Babylon, Nebuchadnezzar, after his conversion. You will recall he had seen a great tree growing
until its shadow covered the entire earth, giving shelter
to the beasts of the field, and the birds of the heaven.
Then he had seen a watcher, a holy one, coming down
from heaven, and giving the order and the instruction
to cut down the tree, with the provision that the stump
and the roots be allowed to remain in the ground. The
king was greatly disturbed and after all his magicians
and astrologers and soothsayers were unable to give
him the interpretation, Daniel was called in and told
the king that this tree represented the king himself,
and as the king represented the kingdom, it also represented the kingdom of Babylon; and that because of his
pride God would take him out of his seat of dominion,
would cause him to be mad, insane, for a period of seven

years during which he would make his habitation with
the beasts of the field.

God's Word Never Fails

After a lapse of about twelve months all these words of
Daniel came to pass, and Nebuchadnezzar was suddenly
stricken with great madness and driven by his own subjects from his kingdom and made his habitation for seven
long years among the beasts of the field; only to be
restored when he lifted up his eyes unto the God of
heaven.

Now this fourth chapter of Daniel contains the record,
the words of the king Nebuchadnezzar himself, as to the
details of his conversion. We are happy to have this
record of conversion of this wicked king, not only because of its moral and ethical instruction but also because of its prophetic significance. We have often pointed out that Babylon represents the kingdoms of this
world, the kingdoms of men without the Lord Jesus
Christ, the King of kings. As such, Nebuchadnezzar represented the course of the history of the nations until
at the end time, after man's day has run its course, they
shall be lifted up with pride at their own achievements,
imagining, foolishly imagining, that they have finally
brought about the Utopian condition of world security,
world peace and world prosperity; then God is going to
come and strike down the world powers and set up His
own King, the Lord Jesus Christ, upon the throne and He
shall reign forever and forever.

In the previous chapter you will remember we tried
to trace the history of man's rule upon the earth up until
the coming of the Lord Jesus Christ. The thing to remember is that Nebuchadnezzar was stricken with this
madness for a period of exactly *seven years,* which we

believe to be prophetic of the seven years of tribulation, between the Rapture of the Church and the second coming of the Lord Jesus. This seven-year period is called the "great tribulation," "the time of Jacob's trouble," "the day of indignation." It will be characterized by the nations who will seek to set up a kingdom in opposition to everything that is godly and Christian under the leadership of the Man of Sin, the personal Antichrist, who will seek to dethrone the Lord Jesus Christ and set up his reign of terror in opposition to the reign of peace promised to all the prophets and to those who believe His Word. One of these days the Lord Jesus Christ will return to this earth again, but first He will come and shout from the air and take out the Church, His Body, together with all the Old Testament saints and when they have been safely removed from the earth, He will usher in a period of tribulation, persecution, suffering and death, a period of pestilence, famine, earthquakes and all sorts of judgment which shall threaten to annihilate man from the face of the earth except for the fact that God will shorten these days for the sake of His elect people, Israel. Then at the end of seven years of this terrible tribulation the Lord will come. This is represented by the watcher, the holy one, who comes down from heaven in Nebuchadnezzar's dream and causes the ax to be laid to the tree. It is the same as the stone cut without hands out of the mountain in Daniel, chapter 2, which smites the image of Nebuchadnezzar; the same thing as the tree vision in chapter 4. The stone itself becomes so large that it fills the entire earth. All of these accounts tell us that man's day will come to an end, that man's effort to set up an ideal world peace and world government without acknowledging the Lord Jesus Christ must come to a bitter and a dismal end.

Then the Lord Jesus coming with His Church will set up the long-promised kingdom of the Messiah, promised by the prophets and the seers of old to His faithful people.

WORLD CONVERSION AT THE COMING OF CHRIST

There is one little detail given in this fourth chapter of Daniel which is very often overlooked. You will recall that when this holy one, this watcher from heaven, commanded that the tree was to be cut down, a very definite instruction was given. The stump of the tree and its roots were to be left in the ground and at the end of the seven years this stump was to sprout again, representing first of all, of course, the fact that Nebuchadnezzar would be restored when he acknowledged the King of heaven, and was converted. All this came to pass historically. But prophetically this stump means that after the seven years of the madness of the nations in the Tribulation, the Gentile nations, too, will be converted and while Israel will be restored in the land, these Gentile nations will occupy the countries of the world, acknowledge the Lord Jesus Christ as Saviour, and every knee shall bow to Him and every tongue confess that Jesus Christ is Lord to the glory of God the Father.

The fact that Nebuchadnezzar was not converted until *after* the seven years of madness and the stump of the tree did not sprout again until *after* it had been cut down for a period of time is of such great importance that we must insist upon your careful study of this important truth, because upon it depends the proper attitude toward the program of God in this dispensation. There are those who tell us that during this present dispensation, before the setting up of the kingdom, before the coming of the Lord Jesus Christ, the world is going to be converted by the influence of the social gospel; by the preaching of the church, by education, reformation, legislation and scientific development man will finally learn his lesson, will accept the Gospel, all will be converted and the world will be ushered into an age of peace and joy and happiness and prosperity and freedom from war and want and poverty, and *then,* at the end of that period of time, the Lord will come again to judge the quick and the dead and to usher in eternity. Then there is another school which teaches quite the opposite; it claims that this world will not become better and better but rather, according to the testimony of the Word of God, worse and worse until it seems that man will ultimately destroy himself. However, before this happens the Lord Jesus will return, take out His Church, then allow the seven years of the Tribulation, represented by the seven years of madness of Nebuchadnezzar, at the end of which He will return *with* His Church, destroy His enemy, the nations shall be converted, Israel shall be restored to the land, and then the millennial rest and peace of one thousand years will be ushered in.

OF VITAL IMPORTANCE

There are, generally speaking, two schools of thought in regard to the return of the Lord Jesus Christ. These are called the postmillennial and the premillennial schools. There is a third of more recent origin called the amillennial, to which we will give no attention at all because it is so far fetched and so utterly impractical that we have no space for it. However, because of the widespread acceptance of the postmillennial—it is held by a very large segment of Christendom today—we must give a little time to that particular subject.

Two Schools of Thought

Against the postmillennial theory of the return of the Lord Jesus Christ, there are two very serious objections. Before we take up these two objections, let me give you the meaning of the word, "postmillennial." It comes from three Latin words, *post* and *mille* and *annum*. *Post* means "after"; *mille* means "thousand"; and *annum* means "years." So we have the meaning, "after the thousand years." The postmillennialists, then, teach that the Lord Jesus will not return until after the one thousand years of millennial peace and prosperity. As we stated before, there are two serious objections to this particular view.

The first is that it is not Scriptural. There is not one shred of evidence in the entire Bible to support the theory that the world will become better and better, morally, ethically or in any other way, until man has reached perfection and all men shall acknowledge the Lord Jesus Christ, and then after that the Lord is to come. To the contrary, as we shall show when we study the premillennial view, the Scriptures abound with statements showing us that this age will degenerate consistently until at last it seems all hope for mankind is gone and then the Lord Himself is going to step in and take a hand in the affairs of men. The second objection which we raise to the postmillennial view is that it is not borne out by the facts of history. After six thousand years of man's rule and all his attempts to produce a government that shall be the ideal universal government for all men, he finds himself today in greater straits than ever before. He has tried everything conceivable; the highest and the best educated men of all ages have sought an answer to the problem of war and of national disagreement only to find themselves today at greater odds than at any other time of human history.

Until the human heart is changed, until human nature is different, until men accept the Lord Jesus Christ as their personal Saviour and the only hope for this world, there can be no progress. After six thousand years of human effort we have experienced within a generation two of the greatest, the costliest of all the wars of history. Man has succeeded in developing instruments of destruction and death such as were not dreamed of only a generation ago. Today, in this atomic age, we are told that we are just beginning in the development of modern warfare. Not only is it true in the matter of international relationship, but in the moral realm, in the domestic realm, in the religious realm, the same thing is true. There are more crimes being committed; there is more wickedness, drunkenness and immorality. The divorce rate is higher than ever in the history of the world, while the birth rate is decreasing among the more civilized. There is more violence and corruption on every hand than the world has ever seen before. Every fact of history refutes the idea that the world will become better morally, economically, socially, in its relationship between men and nations and religion.

The Premillennial Teaching

Now place against this postmillennial theory the teaching of the Word of God and we shall find that it teaches not a postmillennial but a premillennial return of the Lord Jesus Christ. The word "premillennial" simply means "before the thousand years," and the premillennial school teaches that this world will, according to the foreknowledge and program of God, continue in its wickedness, in its own self-destruction, until finally the

Lord will come in and rescue the Church and the world and His people from complete annihilation. Then through His coming and His personal presence He will set up the kingdom long promised to the seers of old. According to this teaching we believe that things will continue to become worse and worse and worse. Despite all the talk of progress and development, all of the dreams of mankind in regard to the freedom and the securities of the nations and the peoples, all these things will ultimately fail until the Lord Jesus Christ is acknowledged.

Remember that we are studying the fourth chapter of Daniel where Nebuchadnezzar was kept in his madness until he acknowledged the God of heaven and recognized Him as the King over all and then his kingdom was restored. And so we believe that it is according to the testimony of the Scriptures that this age will continue its downward course while the Lord calls out a people for His Name to constitute the Bride which shall be taken out before the Tribulation Period. In answer to the question of the disciples in the twenty-fourth chapter of the Gospel of Matthew, Jesus gives a long list of signs which shall be indicative of the end of this age, and they certainly are not signs of improvement and development but they are signs of degeneration. He mentions among others the false christs that shall come and the wars and the rumors of wars and the famines and pestilences and earthquakes·in divers places, and then the antiracial attitude of many nations and the infidelity of friends and false prophets. Certainly this is not a picture of the world becoming better and better toward the end but rather becoming worse and worse. In I Timothy 4:1-2, we read:

> Now the Spirit speaketh expressly, that in the latter times some shall depart from the faith, giving heed to seduc-

ing spirits, and doctrines of devils; speaking lies in hypocrisy; having their conscience seared with a hot iron.

This certainly is not a picture of a world that is becoming better and better, but rather of one that is constantly degenerating. In II Timothy 3:1-5, we read:

> This know also, that in the last days perilous times shall come. For men shall be lovers of their own selves, covetous, boasters, proud, blasphemers, disobedient to parents, unthankful, unholy, without natural affection, trucebreakers, false accusers, incontinent, fierce, despisers of those that are good, traitors, heady, highminded, lovers of pleasures more than lovers of God; having a form of godliness, but denying the power thereof.

We might go on and on quoting passage after passage to indicate that God has truly revealed through His prophets that this world will become worse and worse under man's rule and will not become better and better until at last the Lord Jesus Christ Himself shall step in and take the reins of government.

God's Program for This Age

What the Lord, therefore, is doing during this dispensation is not the wholesale conversion of the world. Instead He is, through the preaching of the Gospel, gathering out a select number called the body of the Lord Jesus Christ—those who believe on the Lord Jesus Christ and are saved and numbered among the members of the body of the Lord Jesus. When the Lord Jesus comes to take this body out, the dead in Christ shall rise first and the living believers shall be caught up with them into the clouds to meet the Lord in the air. Then after the seven years of the Tribulation we shall have the setting up of the millennial kingdom and the conversion of the world, and all the Gentiles shall learn to know the Lord Jesus Christ when the knowledge of the Lord shall cover the earth as the waters cover the sea. Probably no clearer passage of Scripture on this subject can be found than in the book of Acts, where the apostles had come together in order to talk about the message of grace going to the Gentile peoples of that age. Here it is given very, very clearly.

> Simeon hath declared how God at the first did visit the Gentiles, to take out of them a people for his name. And to this agree the words of the prophets; as it is written, after this I will return, and will build again the tabernacle of David, which is fallen down; and I will build again the ruins thereof, and I will set it up: that the residue of men might seek after the Lord, and all the Gentiles, upon whom my name is called, saith the Lord, who doeth all these things (Acts 15:14-17).

In this brief passage you will find God's program. First, during this dispensation, He visits the Gentiles. Now notice carefully that it is to take *out* of them a people for His Name. It is not the conversion of the world; it is the taking *out from among the nations,* here one and there one, a few here and a few there, of people for His Name. And then notice carefully that it is after this—after He has visited the Gentiles to take out of them a people for His Name—that He will return and build again the tabernacle of David and set up the kingdom. After these events have taken place we shall have the conversion of the world.

This then is the simple program of God. During this dispensation there is the calling out of the Church, His Bride; at the end of this dispensation there will be the return of the Lord and the setting up of the long-promised kingdom of David "that the residue of men might seek after the Lord, and all the Gentiles, upon whom my name is called, saith the Lord."

CHAPTER FIFTEEN

The Rise and Fall of Babylon

Belshazzar the king made a great feast to a thousand of his lords, and drank wine before the thousand. Belshazzar, whiles he tasted the wine, commanded to bring the golden and silver vessels which his father Nebuchadnezzar had taken out of the temple which was in Jerusalem; that the king, and his princes, his wives, and his concubines, might drink therein . . . In the same hour came forth fingers of a man's hand, and wrote over against the candlestick upon the plaister of the wall of the king's palace: and the king saw the part of the hand that wrote . . . The king cried aloud to bring in the astrologers, the Chaldeans, and the soothsayers. And the king spake, and said to the wise men of Babylon, Whosoever shall read this writing, and shew me the interpretation thereof, shall be clothed with scarlet, and have a chain of gold about his neck, and shall be the third ruler in the kingdom. Then came in all the king's wise men: but they could not read the writing, nor make known to the king the interpretation thereof . . . Then was Daniel brought in before the king. And the king spake and said unto Daniel, Art thou that Daniel, which art of the children of the captivity of Judah, whom the king my father brought out of Jewry? . . . And I have heard of thee, that thou canst make interpretations, and dissolve doubts: now if thou canst read the writing, and make known to me the interpretation thereof, thou

shalt be clothed with scarlet, and have a chain of gold
about thy neck, and shalt be the third ruler in the kingdom.
Then Daniel answered and said before the king, Let thy
gifts be to thyself, and give thy rewards to another; yet
I will read the writing unto the king, and make known to
him the interpretation (Daniel 5:1, 2, 5, 7, 8, 13, 16, 17).

This fifth chapter of Daniel records the downfall of
the great kingdom of Nebuchadnezzar, the kingdom of
Babylon. This record has been abundantly confirmed by
secular history as well. We have already seen that in
Daniel we have four pictures of the course of Gentile
world dominion. One we saw in the second chapter in
the great image of the dream of Nebuchadnezzar; the
second one that we saw was the dream of Nebuchadnezzar concerning the great tree that covered the
earth but was cut down; then we have in this chapter
Belshazzar's impious feast and the sudden judgment
of God upon the nation of Babylon as the Medes and the
Persians took over. We have one more that we shall
take up later on—the vision of the four beasts in Daniel
7, 8 and 9. Now all of these four pictures give us a
wonderful, harmonious, prophetic vision of the course
of time from the time of Judah's captivity until the
time of Israel's restoration in the millennial kingdom,
from the time of Nebuchadnezzar and the height of
Babylonian power until the downfall of the nations' godless attempt to set up an ideal world kingdom without
the Lord Jesus Christ, the King of kings. All of the
world's history was foreknown by the Almighty and follows a definite pattern which God Himself foreknew and
has laid down in utmost detail in the books of the Bible,
not only in Daniel, but in all prophetic revelation.

We have continually been reminding you of the fact
that Babylon represents more than a physical kingdom.

Babylonianism is a system, an anti-Christian, anti-God system of man's endeavor to dethrone Almighty God and to bring about in this world an ideal Utopian kingdom and federation which shall not need the direction and the revelation of God in any sense whatsoever. While Babylonianism assumes various forms—under Nimrod way back in the eleventh chapter of Genesis, and then under the Egyptian form, the Babylonian, the Persian, the Grecian and the Roman form—the spirit of Babylonianism is always the same and never changes, and at the end time, just before the return of the Lord Jesus Christ, a man will arise of whom Nimrod and Nebuchadnezzar and Alexander the Great and many others were only types. This man will be a superman, half demon and half human, the Antichrist, the Man of Sin, who will succeed for a very brief time in bringing about that which Nimrod and all of his successors failed to bring about —a world union, a world commonwealth that shall promise all the ideals that man has been striving for throughout the millenniums of his past history. However, just when this Man of Sin seems to have reached the very acme and the pinnacle of his success, the Lord Jesus Christ will come in judgment and destroy man's anti-Christian system and set up upon this earth His own kingdom of prosperity and peace and righteousness, and reign forever and forever.

Now, we have a number of pictures throughout the Scriptures which give this wonderful revelation. We have already reminded you that the tree vision of Nebuchadnezzar and the image of Nebuchadnezzar are all pictures, but probably the most graphic and the most descriptive of them all is this story of Belshazzar and his great drunken feast in the palace of Babylon, and the sudden judgment of God as the Medes and the

Persians captured the city on the very night of this great debauch. This chapter should be read in connection with chapters 16, 17 and 18 of the book of the Revelation where we have the description of the final fall and doom of Babylonianism and the restored Babylonian system during the Tribulation Period of which this chapter in Daniel is a type and a shadow and a prophecy.

BABYLONIANISM FOLLOWS THE SAME PATTERN

In studying the various types of Babylonianism through the Scriptures, beginning with Nimrod's kingdom in the tenth and eleventh chapters of Genesis, we find that it always follows the same identical pattern. We may sum up the pattern of anti-Christian Babylonianism under three words: first, *federation;* second, *desecration;* and finally, *frustration.* The first attempt is to set up a world-wide kingdom under one particular head or nation who will dominate all the governments of the world. When this has been partly achieved, we find that it results in desecration, a denial of God, a denial of His Word, a denial of all things that are sacred. Then as the judgment of God falls upon them, we have the third stage, the frustration of all man's plans and the fulfillment of the plan of Almighty God.

This is most graphically illustrated in this fifth chapter of Daniel in the history of Belshazzar. Under his father, Nebuchadnezzar, and also under him, Babylon had attained the very pinnacle of its power; it had conquered all the known kings of the world and had succeeded in bringing them under the domination and under the government of the Babylonian Empire. But as a result of this, being lifted up with pride, they began to desecrate the holy things of the Lord. It is well in studying the fifth chapter of Daniel to remember one very outstanding truth, and that truth is that the judgment of God fell upon Belshazzar and upon the kingdom of Babylon as a direct result of one act on the part of the wicked king, and that one act was that he reached out and touched the holy things of God. We are told in verse 2, again in verse 3 and still again in verse 23, that the occasion for the judgment of God was that Belshazzar commanded to bring the golden and silver vessels which his father, Nebuchadnezzar, had taken out of the Temple which was in Jerusalem, that the king and his princes and his wives, and so forth, might drink therein. The crowning desecration that brought forth the displeasure of God and the judgment that fell upon Babylon was when he stretched forth his hand and touched the things which God has declared holy, which God has consecrated. He desecrated these things, and the cup of iniquity was full, and as a result judgment fell upon the wicked king and his kingdom. While this fifth chapter of Daniel with its record of Belshazzar's wicked feast, the writing on the wall and the interpretation of Daniel contains many, many moral and valuable instructions for our everyday living, we must remember that Daniel is primarily a prophetic book; and I want to repeat, because of its tremendous importance, that we **must remember** that the occasion for the judgment of God upon this Babylonian king was that he stretched forth his hand and touched the holy things of the Lord, the vessels of gold and of silver out of the Temple in Jerusalem, in Judea, in the land of Palestine, the Holy Land. These things which had been given by God, consecrated by God for a very definite purpose, this wicked Gentile king desecrated, and, as a result, God comes with His dire judgment upon him.

An Interesting Story

The fifth chapter of Daniel makes very interesting reading. It has been a favorite in all ages past. Belshazzar, the king, made a tremendous feast. It was a drunken debauch, a drunken party, to which he had invited a thousand of the nobles, the princes and lords of the kingdom of Babylon. Significantly, Daniel is not present. Undoubtedly he had been invited, for we are told that Belshazzar's father, Nebuchadnezzar, had elevated Daniel to the second place in the kingdom. He was among the nobility and ruled over a greater part of the kingdom of Babylon. Undoubtedly, therefore, he had been invited, but Daniel, maintaining his position of absolute separation from the world while he was in the world, refused to be present at the impious feast of Belshazzar. During the feast the fingers of a man's hand appear out of apparently nowhere, and begin writing upon the wall of the great banquet hall in which the feast was being carried on. Now the writing was in an unknown language, and the king was unable to interpret the writing upon the wall. As a result he calls in all the magicians and the soothsayers and the astrologers which had failed before, had failed his father Nebuchadnezzar and had failed him, and they were unable to give him any light whatsoever. Then the widowed queen, the wife of Belshazzar's father, Nebuchadnezzar, comes into the banqueting hall. I am glad to note here that evidently she, too, was not present at this party, at this debauchery and this desecration of the holy things of God. But, when she hears about the incident, she comes in and tells the king about Daniel and the service he had rendered to her husband, Belshazzar's father, in days gone by, and assures him that Daniel would be able to give the king the interpretation.

So Daniel is brought in and is made a great offer of riches and wealth and position which he turns down. He says that these gifts may be given to someone else, but he will tell the king the interpretation of this writing upon the wall. Putting it as simply as we possibly can this is the interpretation. The words *"mene, mene, tekel, upharsin,"* as found in verse 25, meant this: *"mene;* God hath numbered thy kingdom, and finished it." Because Belshazzar has reached out his hand and touched things that God has consecrated, declared holy, the end of his kingdom has come. *"Tekel;* Thou art weighed in the balances, and art found wanting." In addition to the destruction of the kingdom, there is a personal judgment which is falling upon the king himself. While you notice the word *mene* has to do with the kingdom, the word *tekel* has to do with the king personally. *Thou* are weighed and art found wanting. *"Peres* [another form of the word *upharsin,* found in verse 25]; Thy kingdom is divided, and given to the Medes and the Persians."

Then we have the brief record at the close of the chapter that that very same night the king was slain and the kingdom taken away from him. Now history tells us, (secular history), that Babylon was built across the River Euphrates. It had a great wall which made it almost impossible for a conqueror to make any impression upon it, a great moat ran around the wall, and inside they felt absolutely secure. The River Euphrates with its moat around the city made it seem that no enemy could possibly take the kingdom. But the Medes and the Persians under their leader had diverted the course of the River Euphrates into the moat, possibly around the city, and had caused the river bed itself to become absolutely dry. Having dried up the river, the army was able to march underneath the wall and take them by surprise while the king and all his leaders and captains were insensible in their drunken debauch.

BABYLONIANISM REVIVED

This is the end of the Biblical record of the kingdom of Babylon as it existed under Nebuchadnezzar and under his son Belshazzar. But the spirit of Babylon, we have reminded you, continues to live on, and never dies, until the Lord Jesus Christ Himself comes to annihilate it forever and forever. We find the spirit and the program of Babylonianism carried on just as zealously as before, under the Medes and the Persians, later on under the Grecian form of Gentile world dominion and then under the Roman Empire. At the end of this age it will reach its height and its pinnacle under the Man of Sin, the Antichrist. At the close of this dispensation, and we believe it will be very soon, the Lord Jesus Christ is going to take out from this world all of His elect members of the body of the Lord Jesus Christ. After they are gone, there will arise on the scene a man who will be the antitype of king Belshazzar and who will once more seek to bring together all the nations of the world in a Babylonian, antireligious, anti-Christian system of political power. He will seek to federate all the nations of the world, and it will seem that he will succeed for a time, but his mistake, too, will be that he will stretch forth his hand to touch the holy things of God. He will seek to conquer the Holy Land which God gave to Abraham, Isaac and Jacob as an everlasting possession. He will stretch forth his hand to touch God's holy covenant people, the nation of Israel, and as in the case of Bel-

shazzar, it will be the occasion for the sending forth
of the judgment of Almighty God. After the Church has
been taken out, the Antichrist, after having brought
together the nations of the world in a temporary peace
and prosperity, will stretch forth his hand to touch the
Promised Land, that he may conquer that which God
gave by covenant promise to only one nation, the nation
of Israel, and he will begin to persecute God's ancient
covenant people. This will be the signal for the coming
of the Lord Jesus Christ and the destruction of Babylonianism.

As we mentioned before we have the record of all this
given very graphically, a fulfillment of the fifth chapter
of Daniel, in the sixteenth, seventeenth and eighteenth
chapters of the book of the Revelation of Jesus Christ,
where we have in great detail the history of Babylonianism in its final form, under its final head, the Antichrist,
and its complete and ultimate destruction when the Lord
Jesus Christ comes. Now this record in Revelation is
the antitype, the fulfillment of that which was taught
by the smiting of the image of Nebuchadnezzar by a
great stone from heaven in Daniel 2, by the cutting
down of the tree in the tree vision of Daniel 4, and
by the fall of Babylon so graphically given in Daniel
5, the chapter which we are studying at this particular
time.

There are in the world at this very moment, a great
number of movements which seem to indicate beyond a
shadow of doubt that the time of the reviving of Babylonianism in the world is very, very near at hand. All
eyes are centered upon a little land today, situated at
the eastern end of the Mediterranean Sea, which is
best known to us as the Holy Land, the Promised Land,
the land of Palestine, the ancient land of Israel and the

land of Canaan. Not a day goes by that it is not in the
headlines, because there centers one of the most crucial
problems of all history, and of all the problems that
confront the nations today as they seek a solution for
the world's ills, there is no greater problem than the
Palestine problem. Now man has failed to take into con-
sideration God's prophetic program. If men would only
turn to the Word of God and find what God has to say
in regard to this land, and the people to whom this land
belongs, and to whom it has belonged since the days of
Abraham, Isaac and Jacob, we would have peace and
prosperity; but man would rather seek his own solution,
and so the awful turmoil in the world continues, until,
like Nebuchadnezzar, men will recognize the God of
heaven and be willing to follow His program with regard
to the holy things of God, His holy nation, His Holy
Land, and His sacred program.

In the next chapters we are going to take up in some
detail what we believe to be the Bible teaching concerning
the land of Palestine and its place among the kingdoms
of the world today. We believe that God has given in His
Word the solution for man's problems, and if men and
the leaders of the nations would only turn to the Word
of God instead of seeking by their own wisdom and logic
and understanding and ingenuity to bring themselves
out of the maze and the mess of misunderstanding which
is gripping the world today, all these problems could
be solved. However, we know that in the program of God
it will not come until the Lord Jesus Christ Himself
returns again to this earth. In the succeeding chapters
we shall deal with this problem of Palestine according
to the Word of God.

We trust that you will ask yourself the question now,
however, as we come to the close of this chapter, "Am

I ready for these end-time events?'' Let me remind you that before the final revival of Babylonianism and the doom of the ungodly kingdoms of this world, the Lord Jesus Christ is coming back again to take His Church unto Himself, to take us into heaven with Himself at the Judgment Seat of Christ, and those who shall be left behind will have to pass through the awful judgment of the Tribulation Period so graphically described in the book of the Revelation. May I ask you, ''Are you ready to meet the one and only King of kings, the Lord of lords, the Lord Jesus Christ?'' Belshazzar was feasting amidst the judgment that was impending. Then God's warning finger came, and then the judgment fell. You, too, my friend, if you are unsaved, are feasting amidst the ominous rumblings of coming judgment, and this is God's warning to you to flee from the wrath to come before it is too late. God help you to look to Christ now and be saved.

CHAPTER SIXTEEN

The Handwriting on the Wall

Belshazzar the king made a great feast to a thousand of his lords, and drank wine before the thousand. Belshazzar, whiles he tasted the wine, commanded to bring the golden and silver vessels which his father Nebuchadnezzar had taken out of the temple which was in Jerusalem; that the king, and his princes, his wives, and his concubines, might drink therein. Then they brought the golden vessels that were taken out of the temple of the house of God which was at Jerusalem; and the king, and his princes, his wives, and his concubines, drank in them. They drank wine, and praised the gods of gold, and of silver, of brass, of iron, of wood, and of stone (Daniel 5:1-4).

In the previous chapter we pointed out that the occasion for the judgment of God upon Belshazzar, king of Babylon, was the fact that he stretched forth his hand to touch the things which God has consecrated and declared holy, even the vessels which king Nebuchadnezzar had taken from the holy Temple in the holy city of Jerusalem in the Holy Land, and had taken God's covenant people captive and scattered them throughout the kingdoms of the world. This act always brings forth the judgment of Almighty God. Way back in making His covenant with Abraham, He had said "Thou shalt be a blessing: and I will bless them that bless thee, and curse him that curseth thee." And it is the record of history, indelibly written, that any nation which has ever persecuted God's ancient people, Israel, and has captured the Holy Land which belongs to this covenant people, has always suffered the wrath and the judgment of Almighty God, and so it will be even unto the end.

Now before taking up the Biblical account of God's purpose for the land of Palestine, and for His ancient people, Israel, I want it thoroughly understood that what I have to say is not in criticism of what any of the nations of the world are doing today. It is not my business to criticize or to find fault, but rather in a positive and constructive way to set before you the program as it is outlined in the Word of God and the solution of the problem of the Middle East today as it is given beyond a shadow of doubt in the words of prophecy. God has not left us in darkness, and if the leaders of the nations today would turn to the Word of God and the words of the prophets they would have in a moment the solution to the problem which has been vexing the nations throughout all these centuries and millenniums as regards this little parcel of land which we call the Holy Land. It is a small section of land comprising a territory only one-fourth as large as the entire state of Ohio, no larger than New Hampshire or Vermont, and yet it has been the very hub of controversy and of bloody strife and revolution throughout all the ages.

Once a year all of Christendom celebrates the birth of a Man who was born in a stable and laid in a manger in this little land at the eastern end of the Mediterranean. It was there where the Prince of Peace, the Lord Jesus Christ, came, where He taught, where He suffered, where

He was crucified and died, where He was buried and where He arose again. It is the place from which He ascended into heaven, and to which, according to prophecy, He will return again when He comes to take the kingdoms of the world and to make them His very own. But not only once a year is this land in the headlines, but every day in the year we read in our papers and hear reports over the radio of the difficulties and the problems of the Holy Land, the land of Palestine. We are led to ask, *why?* Why should there be all this commotion about a small piece of land which we could tuck away three times over in Lake Michigan alone, and yet which is more important, apparently, to the peace of the nations than any other land in the world today? We want you to consider very carefully, therefore, some of the things that we shall point out as revealed in the Word of God.

The program of God centers about one people and one land so far as the governments of this world are concerned. That one people is Israel, and that one land is the land of Palestine, the land of Canaan. Israel is the nation composed of the natural descendants of Abraham through Isaac and through Jacob and his twelve sons. The land is that territory according to the original grant given to Abraham, from the River Nile to the River Euphrates, and bounded on the west by the Mediterranean Sea. In history Israel possessed only a very small part of this land, the part known as Palestine, but in prophecy the Lord has promised the entire country to them for an everlasting possession.

These two, the people of Israel and the land of Israel, were included in the covenant which God made with Abraham when He called him out of Ur of the Chaldees. It was a covenant of grace that God made with Abraham. Now remember, a covenant of grace is a covenant which

God makes with Himself in the interest of another. A covenant of grace is always an unconditional covenant, and depends for its complete fulfillment upon the faithfulness of God alone and is in no way dependent upon the faithfulness or behavior of man *for whom* the covenant has been made. There are no "ifs" in the covenant of grace. The moment a single condition is added which man must fulfill, it ceases to be of grace and becomes immediately a covenant of works. This covenant of grace occupies a large part of the record of the life of Abraham. God repeated it seven times to Abraham alone. Then He repeated it again to Isaac, and then to Jacob, and then to Moses. Later He repeated it to David and to Solomon, and again and again to the children of Israel through the prophets. We shall study just a few of these references to this covenant. The first is in Genesis 12:1-2:

> Now the Lord had said unto Abram, Get thee out of thy country, and from thy kindred, and from thy father's house, unto a land that I will shew thee: and I will make of thee a great nation, and I will bless thee, and make thy name great; and thou shalt be a blessing.

Notice two things about this covenant of grace which God made with Abraham. First, God does it all. There are no conditions on the part of Abraham, except to believe God in that which He promises to do. God says, "I *will* shew thee [the land]." He says, "I *will* make of thee a great nation." He says, "I *will* bless thee." God does it, you will notice, all because it is a covenant of grace, and independent of anything which Abram is to do.

Secondly, notice that the covenant has to do with a land. God says, "[Go] unto a land that I will shew thee." And then notice, too, that it has to do with a seed, for He says, "I will make of thee a great nation." The two objects of the covenant of God's grace made to Abraham are a *people* and the *land* which this people is to possess. No matter where you pick up the line of the covenant, it is always with reference to the land and the people of this land. Israel and the land are forever inseparable, and are inseparably associated from the very first. Please bear these two words in mind, Israel and the land of Palestine. They are inseparable. Notice in this connection the following quotation from Genesis:

> And the Lord said unto Abram, after that Lot was separated from him, Lift up now thine eyes, and look from the place where thou art northward, and southward, and eastward, and westward: for all the land which thou seest, to thee will I give it, and to thy seed forever, And I will make thy seed as the dust of the earth . . . Arise, walk through the land in the length of it and in the breadth of it; for I will give it unto thee (Genesis 13:14-17).

Then in Genesis 15:18 we read:

> In the same day the Lord made a covenant with Abram, saying, unto thy seed have I given this land, from the river of Egypt unto the great river, the river Euphrates.

In this passage we have God giving to Abraham the boundaries of the land which his seed was to possess. It includes far more than is usually considered when we speak of the land of Palestine, yet God promised all this land to Abraham and his seed, and therefore the promise must still lie in the future. The prophecies of the Old and New Testaments both assert that this glorious time when Israel shall return to the land and possess all of it is very near at hand. Now read Genesis 17:4, 7, 8.

> As for me, behold, my covenant is with thee, and thou shalt be a father of many nations . . . And I will establish my covenant between me and thee and thy seed after thee

in their generations for an everlasting covenant, to be a God unto thee, and to thy seed after thee. And I will give unto thee, and to thy seed after thee, the land wherein thou art a stranger, all the land of Canaan, for an everlasting possession; and I will be their God.

In this reaffirmation of the covenant, we have God giving the term during which the covenant shall last, and please notice that it was to be an everlasting covenant. Space prevents us from giving the many other passages where the covenant is restated and confirmed to Isaac, to Jacob, to Moses, to David and through the prophets, but in each case the same two elements are repeated and we repeat them.

First—it is all of grace. God does not promise this to Abraham on condition that his seed shall be found faithful. There are no ''ifs'' in this covenant anywhere. God knew what an unfaithful nation Israel would be during the days of the prophets and the kings and how they would rebel and turn from God, and how they would reject God's own Son when He came into the world. However, all this could not in the least affect the covenant of grace which God made, for when He ''made promise to Abraham, because he [God] could swear by no greater, he sware by himself.''

Secondly—the covenant deals with just two things: the seed of Abraham, Israel, and the land of Palestine. Now four hundred years after God made this covenant with Abraham, He made another covenant with the seed of Abraham. It was made at Mt. Sinai and was the covenant of the law and therefore a covenant of works. Now a covenant of works depends upon the faithfulness of man for its blessing while the covenant of God's grace depends on the faithfulness of God. For this very reason a covenant of works always fails, while a covenant of

grace can never fail. The moment the blessing depends
on man's behavior or faithfulness it immediately breaks
down. Now God made a covenant of works, you remember, with Adam in the Garden of Eden and Adam
failed. God made a covenant of works with Israel on Mt.
Sinai and we know Israel failed.

But God made a covenant of grace with Noah after
the Flood in which He promised that "while the earth
remaineth, seedtime and harvest, and cold and heat,
and summer and winter, and day and night shall not
cease." That covenant has never failed. Now when the
Israelites had come out of Egypt and were on their way
to the land that God had promised through Abraham,
He made a covenant of works with them at Sinai and
said, "if ye will obey, and if ye will keep My commandments, and if ye will serve Me, then I will bless you and
prosper you, but if you will not do all these things, then
I will curse you and drive you forth from the land until
the time for your restoration." Read Leviticus 26, Deuteronomy 29 and 30 and many other similar passages.

In these passages God predicts and promises what He
will do to Israel if they fail to keep the covenant of
works. Listen to His words:

> And if ye will not for all this hearken unto me, but
> walk contrary unto me; then I will walk contrary unto you
> also in fury; and I, even I, will chastise you seven times
> for your sins. . . And I will bring [now notice] the land into
> desolation: and your enemies which dwell therein shall be
> astonished at it. [And now notice the prediction.] And I will
> scatter you among the heathen, and will draw out a sword
> after you: and your land shall be desolate, and your cities
> waste. . . And upon them that are left alive of you I will
> send a faintness into their hearts in the lands of their
> enemies; and the sound of a shaken leaf shall chase them;
> and they shall flee, as fleeing from a sword; and they shall
> fall when none pursueth (Leviticus 26:27, 28, 32, 33, 36).

Surely these words need no comment in the light of Israel's history and her dispersion and in the light of the present developments throughout the world, the racial unrest and the wave of racial animosity which is sweeping over the earth today. And so today the nation is out of the land because she failed, not because their God has failed.

GRACE STILL STANDS

But all the failures of the nation and all the years of her dispersion cannot break the covenant of grace which God made with Abraham. After He has purified and chastened the nation, He will fulfill every single promise of the Abrahamic covenant and bring Israel back and plant them forever in their land and they shall never again be pulled up out of the land. Read the words of the Lord concerning this people in Amos 9:14-15:

> And I will bring again the captivity of my people of Israel, and they shall build the waste cities, and inhabit them; and they shall plant vineyards, and drink the wine thereof; they shall also make gardens, and eat the fruit of them. And I will plant them upon their land, and they shall no more be pulled up out of their land which I have given them, saith the Lord thy God.

And now read Leviticus 26:44-45:

> And yet for all that, when they be in the land of their enemies, I will not cast them away, neither will I abhor them, to destroy them utterly, and to break my covenant with them: for I am the Lord their God. But I will for their sakes remember the covenant of their ancestors, whom I brought forth out of the land of Egypt.

This was before the law was given; even though Israel breaks the covenant of works and must be punished and chastened because of it, it in no way affects God's covenant of grace. Here is where the great mass of Christians stumble. They imagine that because Israel has failed, God has forsaken them as a nation and God is all through with Israel and they will never go back to the land again, and the Church has become spiritual Israel instead. All this error results from a misunderstanding of grace. A covenant of grace cannot be broken because it depends upon the faithfulness of God and not upon man's faithfulness. The enjoyment of that covenant of grace depends on man's faithfulness, to be sure, but it can never affect God's part in fulfilling it all. To teach, therefore, that Israel will not go back to the Holy Land as a nation and possess it forever as God's earthly covenant people and to teach that the Church now has taken Israel's place, is to reveal ignorance of the basic meaning of grace, for God's grace never fails.

THE NEW TESTAMENT TRUTH

In Galatians, the Apostle Paul uses an illustration to prove that man is not saved by works but by grace, and the illustration he uses, strangely enough, is the covenant of grace made with Abraham. Here is the record:

> And this I say, that the covenant, that was confirmed before of God in Christ [the covenant with Abraham], the law [the covenant of works], which was four hundred and thirty years after, cannot disannul, that it should make the promise of none effect. For if the inheritance be of the law [that is, of works], it is no more of promise: but God gave it to Abraham by promise (Galatians 3:17-18).

Now do not hurry over that passage. Notice what Paul says. He says that the law covenant which Israel failed to keep cannot set aside or disannul the covenant of promise which God made previously, so even though Israel fails under the law, God's promise to Abraham concerning their everlasting possession of the Holy Land still stands.

THE LAND BELONGS TO ISRAEL

It is as true today as it was in Abraham's day that the land of Palestine belongs to Israel and no one else. God still considers the land as belonging to Abraham's seed. In Leviticus 25:23 we read:

> The land shall not be sold for ever: for the land is mine; for ye are strangers and sojourners with me.

God says that the land is His and that the Israelites are sojourners with Him. It is the land of God, the land God promised; it is the land where the Son of God became a Man; it is the land where He walked for thirty-three years; it is the land where He suffered and was crucified and died; it is the land where He was buried and where He arose; it is the land from which He ascended into heaven; and it is the land to which He is coming back again. He is coming back, and when He comes He will not land in America, or in Britain, but "his feet shall stand in that day upon the mount of Olives, which is before Jerusalem on the east." This is the Holy Land, preserved for a holy people.

God has an earthly people and He has a land. Both of these He promises to vindicate and defend to the end. He promised Abraham to "bless them that bless thee, and curse him that curseth thee," and history has proved that God keeps His word. Every nation which has ever persecuted Israel has gone down under God's judgment. God has dealt with every one of them: Pharaoh of Egypt, Nebuchadnezzar, Alexander, the Roman Empire and even the more modern nations of these latter days. They all have come under the judgment of God, because they, like Belshazzar, have stretched out their hand to touch Israel, called in the Bible the "apple of his eye."

TRUE OF THE LAND ALSO

What was true of the people is just as true of the land which God included in His covenant with Abraham. No nation has any right to the Holy Land of Palestine but the nation to whom God Himself has given it, and history has proved that every nation which has conquered Palestine and taken it away from Israel, all or in part, has invited the judgment of the Almighty. No nation, I repeat, which has conquered the land or the people of Israel has ever escaped the judgment of God. History stands a mute monument to the proof of this assertion. Even the Crusades failed because the Christians, while they wanted to deliver the land from the sons of Ishmael, were not intent upon giving it back to its rightful owners, the sons of Isaac. Had the Crusaders gone forth with the firm intention of delivering the land and giving it exclusively to the rightful owners, no armies or combination of armies could have stopped them, for God would have been on their side.

The solution of this world's ills lies in this one formula: bring God's covenant people into God's Holy Land. Thank God, this is going to be accomplished when the Lord Jesus Christ comes again. Oh, that the nations of this world and its leaders might learn to seek what God has to say in His Holy Word concerning the problems that are vexing the nations today. God help us to study His Word in these last closing days so that when the Lord shall come we shall be ready for His appearing and not be ashamed at His coming. Are you ready? May God help you, and may God bless you.

CHAPTER SEVENTEEN

The Jews and Palestine

No single country of all countries of the world has been so much in the public eye, so much in the news, the past months and years as the land of Palestine. This is the land which God promised to Abraham and to his seed as an everlasting possession, and even though it has been in the hands of the nations of the world for many, many centuries, God's covenant still defines it as the land which God promised to a particular, peculiar nation, the nation of Israel, the descendants of the twelve tribes of Jacob.

It is significant that Palestine should be called the Holy Land, for the word "holy" has several meanings in the Scriptures. It does not, as some suppose, always mean holiness in character or conduct or walk. It is also applied to inanimate objects, the tabernacle, the vessels of the tabernacle and a large number of other things. We ourselves are called a holy people in our position, and because we are holy, separated unto God, He expects of us holiness in conduct. The word "holy" when applied to a land or to inanimate objects means "set aside for a definite purpose." Now the land of Palestine is the

Holy Land because in His eternal purpose and program, God has set it aside for the one purpose of occupation by His peculiar people, the descendants of Jacob, and because it is God's Holy Land, anyone who tampers with it and seeks to separate its people from their possession comes under the judgment of God. This is the record of history.

We have a striking example of it in this chapter in Daniel which we are now studying. Belshazzar, the king, stretched forth his hand and touched the holy things of God, the vessels that had been taken from the holy Temple of Jerusalem in the land of Judah. As a result, God brought swift and speedy judgment upon the nation and Babylon fell and came to a dismal end. Today the same thing is still true in principle, and the Holy Land, that little parcel of land situated at the eastern end of the Mediterranean Sea, is still the key to the world's problems. When the nation of that land to whom God has promised it by covenant is given full and free possession of this land, then only will the nations be at rest and the peace for which men strive shall finally be realized.

In recent years, there has been much indication of the fact that this is about to be consummated, and we believe that we are at the very threshold of that glorious time when Israel shall be fully restored to the land again and the millennial rest will be ushered in by the coming of the Messiah. Many Bible students were quite certain some twenty or twenty-five years ago that we had just about reached that period in history when Israel would be restored to the land and it would be the signal for the return of the Lord Jesus Christ. It is a well-known fact established by history that when the tide of war was turning against the Allies in World War I, it was a humble, modest Jewish chemist, Dr. Chaim Weitzman, now world famous and very much in the news again, who came forward in the zero hour of the apparent defeat of the Allies with a formula for the most powerful explosive ever discovered up to that time, T.N.T., and donated that discovery to his beloved country, Britain, and that turned the tide of victory for the Allies. Lloyd George's *Memoirs* gives a graphic account of this whole procedure.

Then it was that Lord Balfour announced that in the event of victory over the enemy, the land of Palestine would be set aside and given to Israel as her national homeland. Well, you remember the war ended, and the Balfour declaration gave Britain the mandate over the entire land of Palestine, the Holy Land. Here we believe was the golden opportunity. She had it in her power and her right to clear the land of its unlawful possessors and make it exclusively the homeland for God's scattered people. However, for reasons of expediency or otherwise, this dream, this promise, was never fully realized. We want it understood that we are not criticizing in any way the action of the nation in doing this, but only giving you the historic facts. So instead of Palestine being set aside as a homeland for the nation of Israel, the Arabs, the direct descendants of Ishmael, were permitted to remain in the tent with the seed of Isaac, and the history of Abraham's tent was repeated. If only the nations had been able to see their way clear to keep their promise to set aside the Holy Land as a national refuge and return it again to their rightful possessors to whom God has promised it, God might have raised many, many more of the seed of Jacob like Dr. Weitzman to bring blessing and help to the nations of the world. If you are on God's side, you will always have a majority, for God

is always able if you only obey His will. Surely it is
purely a matter of faith, and sadly tragic, that at that
crucial hour this well-intentioned promise of restoring
the land again to Israel was not kept. And so the awful
crisis continues and the unrest in the land is gaining by
leaps and by bounds.

ISAAC AND ISHMAEL

You will recall that Abraham's eldest son was Ishmael,
and his covenant son, Isaac. Ishmael, the first-born, was
born of the Egyptian woman in the tent of Abraham,
and Isaac was the second, born thirteen years later. It
was to Isaac that God had promised that He would give
—and to his seed forever—the land of the promised
covenant, even the land of Palestine. Now as long as
Ishmael was alone in the tent of Abraham, there was no
trouble of any kind, but when thirteen years later Isaac
was born, the trouble began. The advice of Sarah was,
"Send Ishmael away out of the tent," and Abraham
refused. Then Sarah said to him: "Cast out this bondwoman and her son: for the son of this bondwoman shall
not be heir with my son, even with Isaac." God appeared
unto Abraham and said: "In all that Sarah hath said
unto thee, hearken unto her voice," and Abraham obeyed,
and peace was restored. Isaac and Ishmael cannot dwell
in the same tent at the same time. Now, of course, you
know that Isaac was the father of Israel, and Ishmael
was the father of the Ishmaelites. The present-day Arabs
are the direct descendants of Ishmael. They were in the
land first, of course, because Ishmael was born in the
tent before Isaac was there, but God has promised it,
not to Ishmael, the son of the bondwoman, but to Isaac,
the son of the covenant. Now historically, again we find
that the Ishmaelites who are the descendants of Ishmael

were in the land first when all of this controversy arose some twenty or twenty-five years ago, but when the land was set aside for the coming of Israel, Ishmael must go. Well, you remember the story. The land had been promised as a homeland for the descendants of Isaac, and there the trouble has been ever since, and will continue until God's program so clearly laid down shall be obeyed. The Palestine problem will continue until in obedience to God the sons of the bondwoman are put out to make way for the sons of promise.

DIVIDING THE LAND

Then came probably the greatest mistake and the greatest error of all. Before we take up this tragic error, may I again say that we are not seeking in any way to be critical but only setting forth the teachings of the Word of God in the hope that they may come to the attention of those who are in a position to do something so that God's plan, which can never be ignored, may be carried out. In seeking to quiet the unrest in the Holy Land, and to put a stop to the continual fighting of Jews and Arabs, the proposal was put forward to divide the land into a number of divisions or states. And so just recently the proposal was again revived to divide the land and split it into three or four separate parts. The northern part was to be set aside for the Arabs; the small part in the south, in Judaea, was to be for the descendants of Isaac, the Israelites; then the other parts would be under the nations' control as a central federal government that should have jurisdiction over both parts. Oh, if the nations had only known what this proposal really means. It marks the beginning of one of the saddest periods of human history, and is an omen of the approaching end. The Word of God is very, very clear

that to divide the land, the Holy Land, is to commit a
crime that God will not permit to go unjudged. We remember what a protest went up from the Zionists all
over the world and the strong denunciation from the
people of Israel when this was first proposed. And the
proposal has not in any way solved the problem but the
difficulties, on the contrary, have only continued to increase and will increase until we give heed to the ''Thus
saith the Lord.''

THE DOUBLE SIN

In Joel 3, the Lord tells us the reasons why He is
going to judge the nations in the latter days, especially
in the Tribulation Period, and He gives two very definite reasons for the coming of God's judgment upon
the nations. Read carefully Joel 3:2:

> I will also gather all nations, and will bring them down
> into the valley of Jehoshaphat, and will plead with them
> there for my people and for my heritage [now note very,
> very carefully] Israel, whom they have scattered among
> the nations, and parted [or divided] my land.

Now note the two reasons why God says He is going
to judge the nations in the end time. First, they have
scattered ''my people'' among the nations. Secondly,
they have parted or divided ''my land.'' And don't miss
this. God says it is *My* land and He is referring to the
land of Palestine which we know usually as the Holy
Land. The first sin many of the nations have committed
by persecuting God's people, and we have seen them go
down one after another, for God's Word cannot be
broken. The second great error—and we are praying
that God will open the eyes of the leaders of the nations
and cause them to repent and enjoy the blessing of the
Lord—the second of these sins is the proposal to divide,

to partition, the land of Palestine. Or turn, if you will, to Daniel 11. Here we read this description of the act of the Antichrist:

> Thus shall he [that is, the Antichrist] do in the most strong holds with a strange god, whom he shall acknowledge and increase with glory: and he shall cause them to rule over many, and shall divide the land for gain (Daniel 11:39).

And then follows the description of God's judgment upon the Man of Sin and his ruin because of this particular sin. All this, please note, follows immediately upon the statement that he shall divide the land for gain.

THE LAST STRAW

According to the clear teaching of the Word of God, the next event in the program of God is the catching away of the Church of the Lord Jesus. Then the Man of Sin, the Antichrist, the antitype of Nimrod and Nebuchadnezzar and the Caesars will appear upon the scene. He will first of all promise the nation of Israel that he will restore them to their land, and when he has by deception gained their confidence, he is going to turn upon them in the midst of the Tribulation Period, and will repeat the sin of dividing the land of Palestine. And when he stretches out his hand to touch that which is holy, that which God called "my land," it will be the last straw, it will be the occasion for the coming of the judgment of Almighty God upon the Man of Sin and upon all his armies and upon all his program, and they shall be miserably destroyed at the return of the Lord Jesus Christ in power and in great glory. It is well to remember this because it is taught in type as well as direct statement throughout the Scriptures. Just remember that Belshazzar who is a type of this coming

Man of Sin made this great mistake of stretching forth
his hand to touch the things which God had called holy.

Now we have taken a great deal of time and gone into
considerable detail in order to set before you what we
believe to be according to the Word of God the basic
problem of the world today, and the only hope for the
longed for and sought for peace for which man is striving. Israel is still God's chosen nation. That does not
mean that they as individuals can be saved without the
Lord Jesus Christ, but as a nation they are still God's
chosen nation. Palestine, the Holy Land, is still God's
chosen land, and there can be no peace in this world
until the nation and the land according to God's purpose
are again wholly united. Every peace effort, all of the
wisdom of diplomats and endless bloodshed will never
bring about a government which will assure lasting
tranquillity and prosperity. Only as the nation is back
in the land and the Messiah is their King, will the time
come when "they shall beat their swords into plowshares,
and their spears into pruninghooks . . . [and] neither
shall they learn war any more." The key to lasting peace
is the land of Israel and the Israel of the land. The Lord
has commanded us to "pray for the peace of Jerusalem:
they shall prosper that love thee." When Jerusalem is
at peace the world will be at peace. Let us pray that
the leaders of the nations may soon see that God is on
the side of those who recognize His program. We believe
that any nation which vows to exterminate Israel and
seeks to conquer Palestine will ultimately be defeated
and destroyed. Soon the day will be here when the oppressors shall cease, and

> Jesus shall reign where'er the sun
> Doth his successive journeys run;

His kingdom reach from shore to shore,
Till moons shall wax and wane no more.

We have tried to set before you the program of God. May we again say that we have not in any way tried to enter into any political argument or set ourselves up as judges of what the nations are doing or to be critical in any destructive sense, but only to set before you what we believe from the very depths of our heart to be the inspired program of Almighty God with the firm conviction that until the nations of the world learn God's program and are willing to follow His formula for peace, there can be no lasting peace. Let us pray for our leaders; let us pray for our nation; let us pray for the nations of this world; let us pray that the time will soon come when every knee shall bow to the Lord Jesus Christ and "every tongue . . . confess that Jesus Christ is Lord, to the glory of God the Father." Then shall peace like a river cover the earth. Then shall Israel be at rest in her own land. Then shall the nations know war no more. Every man shall dwell safely under his own vine and under his own fig tree, and the long hoped for, long prayed for, millennial age of peace will come when the nations shall be at rest and Christ shall have dominion over land and sea. God hasten the day. In closing may we ask, "Are you ready for that time?" Very soon we believe from all indications round about us, the Lord Jesus Christ will return and you will have to stand before Him personally to give an account of what you have done with Him. On whose side are you today? God help you. God bless you.

Pray for the peace of Jerusalem   they shall prosper
that love thee.

CHAPTER EIGHTEEN

Daniel in the Lions' Den

Now when Daniel knew that the writing was signed, he went into his house; and his windows being open in his chamber toward Jerusalem, he kneeled upon his knees three times a day, and prayed, and gave thanks before his God, as he did aforetime (Daniel 6:10).

No commentary on the book of Daniel would be complete without at least one or two chapters on the prayer life of this remarkable man of God. As in the case of all the other great heroes of the Old and the New Testaments, the life of Daniel was characterized by a deep devotion, a gratitude toward God and an utter sense of dependence upon Him. This is expressed in the records of his prayer life as we have them related in this book. There are at least three instances in the book of Daniel where we find him praying and calling upon the Lord —three little looks into the private life of this man whom God used in such a wonderful way. We have already found Daniel praying in the second chapter, when after Nebuchadnezzar had demanded that his dream which he could not recall should be interpreted, Daniel calls a meeting with his three friends who later were placed in the fiery furnace, and they called upon the Lord for a solution to their problem. And here again in the sixth chapter of Daniel, the record of Daniel in the lions' den, we find him in his house before the open window facing Jerusalem, the city of promise and the city of his fathers, calling upon God and thanking Him there. And then once more, we have Daniel praying in the ninth chapter, one of the classic chapters in the entire Bible on the subject of prayer, where we have a record of one of Daniel's prayers in full, a pattern, as we shall see, for our own prayer life. We shall deal with it in greater detail when we come to chapter 9. While only a little is said about Daniel's prayer life in this sixth chapter, most of it is taken up with the setting and background of what brought on this particular circumstance. We find in this one verse, the tenth verse of Daniel 6, a great deal of information concerning the private life of this remarkable man of God.

THE SETTING OF DANIEL'S PRAYER LIFE

There is probably not a chapter in the entire book of Daniel which is more familiar than the sixth chapter which records for us the casting of Daniel into the den of lions, and his supernatural preservation by the angel of the Lord. But most of us have overlooked this little hint in the tenth verse which speaks to us of the secret of Daniel's preservation: his devotion, his faith, his complete reliance upon the power of God to deliver him in the time of trouble. Now the setting of this particular chapter is necessary to understand all of the detail. The kingdom of Babylon had fallen; Darius, the king of the Medes, had taken over the kingdom, and in order that it might be a stable kingdom he had organized it in a very thorough way. We read of this organization in the first two verses of this sixth chapter:

> It pleased Darius to set over the kingdom an hundred and twenty princes, which should be over the whole kingdom; and over these three presidents; of whom Daniel was first: that the princes might give accounts unto them, and the king should have no damage.

We are rather surprised that Daniel, who had been taken as a slave in the captivity of Judah, should have been given this high place of honor and distinction in the kingdom of the Medes, in the kingdom of Darius. Yet we find Daniel as the chief president ruling over the dominion under the king. As such he soon became the object of the jealousy of the others who sought his exalted position, and they began to lay traps for him. They sought some occasion whereby they might accuse him before the king, but they found none whatsoever, and they realized that unless they could set some kind of a trap which would make the test of Daniel's faithfulness to his God the real thing, they would never be able to unseat him from his high position. In order, therefore, to get rid of Daniel, they went to the king, Darius himself, and requested, appealing to his pride, of course, that the king issue a decree that for a period of thirty days no one in the entire kingdom of Darius would be allowed to utter a prayer or ask a petition of any god or man, save only of the king himself, and failure to obey this decree of the king would be punishable with the awful experience of being cast into a den of lions, there to be destroyed. We have the record in verses 7 to 9 of this chapter where we read:

> All the presidents of the kingdom, the governors, and the princes, the counsellors, and the captains, have consulted together to establish a royal statute, and to make a firm

decree, that whosoever shall ask a petition of any God or man for thirty days, save of thee, O king, he shall be cast into the den of lions. Now, O king, establish the decree and sign the writing, that it be not changed, according to the law of the Medes and Persians, which altereth not. Wherefore king Darius signed the writing and the decree.

Of course, in this signing of the decree that he was to be worshiped instead of Almighty God, Darius becomes a type of the coming Antichrist who also will command all men to receive his mark upon their hands and upon their foreheads, upon pain of death if they refuse. We shall treat with that in a subsequent chapter. But here we have the decree signed which made it illegal for anyone to pray to any god save to the king of Medo-Persia alone.

Daniel's Response

When Daniel had heard of this decree which struck at the very heart of his devotional life, he immediately resorted to prayer. Verse 10 relates for us that Daniel went to his room, and there with his face toward Jerusalem, he prayed unto God, undoubtedly for wisdom and for the deliverance of his people as well. Now we want to study very briefly this prayer of Daniel as a pattern for our own prayer life in order that we may receive the practical instruction which is so much needed in these days. Our own country was founded by men who knew the power and believed in the power of prayer, and today one of the greatest reasons for the straits in which we find ourselves is undoubtedly our failure to resort to this wonderful avenue of power, the direct line between heaven and the hearts of men. It is prayerlessness probably more than anything else in the lives of Christians which is responsible for the apathy and the awful conditions which are existing among us in these terrible days. Now there are a number of very interesting things about this little glimpse into Daniel's prayer life which I trust may be of real help to all of us.

First of all, you will notice that Daniel had some very definite convictions in regard to his attitude and his obedience to the government under which he lived, as well as to the law of Almighty God. Daniel was a man who believed in obeying the powers that be. He was a man who believed in being obedient to the laws laid down by the civil authorities so long as they did not come in conflict with his service of Jehovah. This is very evident from the fact that Daniel had been elevated to the high position as chief of the presidents under the reign of Darius. He could never have attained this high civic position were it not for the fact of his faithfulness to the civil authorities, but this faithfulness only went up to a certain point. When it began to interfere with his worship of Jehovah, he, like all Christians, believed that we must obey God rather than man. And because of this, as soon as he heard of the decree forbidding him to pray to Jehovah, he was the more determined to be faithful no matter what the result might be, and went immediately to his room. God give us men and women today of courage, like Daniel, daring to be like him, faithfully discharging our duties as citizens of the land whose liberties and privileges we enjoy, but realizing that our first obligation, our first duty and our first responsibility are toward the One upon whom all our blessings depend.

Regular Periods of Prayer

The second thing we notice from this brief verse in the sixth chapter of Daniel is that Daniel had a habit of prayer. He had cultivated regular daily periods which he set aside to look to the Lord Jehovah. No matter what the responsibilities of his high position and high office in the kingdom might be, nothing was allowed to interfere and so we read the very encouraging record that when Daniel knew the writing was signed, he went into his house and his windows being open in his chamber toward Jerusalem, he kneeled upon his knees three times a day and prayed and gave thanks before his God. Now notice the last phrase, "As he did aforetime." I do not know how I can emphasize enough the necessity of cultivating a regular habit of spiritual prayer. I do not mean by this that it must merely be a habit, that we must look at prayer as a sort of charm or fetish, or something that we have been brought up to do and so we pause several times a day to mumble a few words without our hearts being in it. I am speaking of that type of prayer which recognizes our utter dependence upon Almighty God for all of our material and spiritual blessings, and of the setting aside of a period for which we long and look forward to—a period when we can fellowship with God, when we can make our wants and petitions known to Him, and when we can praise Him and talk over with Him the problems of the day.

When I was a lad, we were taught to set aside a period each morning and evening, before and after each meal, to bow our heads, be it ever so briefly, and to recognize God as the Giver of all these gifts and all of these blessings which we had received. The old-fashioned periods of regular prayer have all but disappeared, and the practice so prominent a generation ago of asking grace at meals, in many cases before and after meals, has all but disappeared from the world, even from Christian circles today. Daniel was not ashamed to own his utter dependence upon the Lord God. Notice that Daniel did not only pray when he was in a tight place. It says here that he prayed, "as he did aforetime." Right now he was in danger and his life was being threatened, but it was only the regularity of his prayer that now sent him to his room facing toward Jerusalem at the appointed time.

Oh, that we might recognize the need and the necessity in our own lives of a regular daily habit of prayer before Almighty God! It would go a long, long way in solving the problems of our nation, as well as the problems of our churches and our individual lives today. Most men pray at some time or another, but a great deal of the prayer that we have been reading and hearing about in recent years is only the prayer of someone who found himself suddenly in a very tense and dangerous and difficult position. We have had examples of what has been known as "fox-hole religion" and "fox-hole prayers" where men, when they seemed to be at the very extremity and facing eternity, would cry unto God. Now, while we would not discourage or disparage this in any way whatsoever, that is not the kind of prayer Daniel indulged in. His was not an emergency prayer. His was a daily habit which he looked forward to and felt he needed as much as he did his daily food. To forget God when everything is rosy, and the sun shines brightly, and then to cry unto Him only when you are at your wit's end is at best only a very cowardly attitude and a very ungrateful devotion.

A Definite Object in Prayer

Then again, we notice from this record of Daniel's prayer that he had a very definite object. It is not without a purpose that the Holy Spirit has recorded for us that he opened his window toward Jerusalem. He was a captive in a strange land. He remembered the covenant that God made in his behalf, and the promises concerning his beloved people who were now in captivity. So he opened his window toward Jerusalem, and claimed the promise of Almighty God that when His people who are called by His Name, shall humble themselves, and pray, and seek His face, and confess their sins, the Lord will deliver them and send them back again into their own land. He had this object in prayer; he recognized that it was because of their sin that they were scattered and that only as they pleaded with God and met the conditions of God that they could again be restored.

And then notice that he had not only a definite object in prayer, but he had a definite place for prayer. It was not in the public eye, but it was in the secret of his chamber. Now the fact that these enemies of Daniel saw him praying and noticed him praying was not because Daniel had purposely opened the window, but it says very definitely in the verse, "his windows being open . . . toward Jerusalem." He had been praying here in private and in secret, and it was only because they were spying upon him that they found him praying to the Lord Jehovah. The Lord Jesus Christ said when He was here upon the earth that when we pray we are to go into our closets and shut the door, and He that heareth in secret will reward us openly. Daniel prayed in secret, even though the spies discovered him.

A DEFINITE ATTITUDE IN PRAYER

We have one other thing which is told to us about Daniel. We read in this tenth verse that he kneeled upon his knees three times a day. Daniel was a man who believed prayer was a sacred responsibility and privilege

—something that should not be hurried through and gotten over as soon as possible, but something that should be done deliberately and to which all the time necessary should be given. So he kneeled upon his knees—that is, he assumed a physical attitude that was a picture of his spiritual attitude when he approached Almighty God. It was the attitude of complete humility, of complete dependence. In olden times, when a conqueror would cause his prisoners to surrender, he would make them fall upon their knees in order that they might be utterly helpless, and this was the attitude Daniel assumed. He knelt upon his knees. Undoubtedly, although it is not said here, he bowed his head; he may have folded his hands and closed his eyes, but this thing is certain. Daniel teaches us here that in prayer we should assume an attitude by which we not only state our utter helplessness and humility and dependence upon the Almighty God, but seek to shut out all of the world and the disturbing influences which might hinder us from giving our whole heart and mind and soul to this most important exercise of the spirit, namely, prayer, when we approach unto God.

How little of this reverence we find today! When I was only a lad, I was taught to fold my hands when I prayed. This signified to Christ that I did not depend upon anything I did, but I ceased all my own work and all my own activity when I came to God. I was to bow my head as an expression of humility. I was to close my eyes in order that I might shut out everything else in the world and not let anything come in to disturb my fellowship with Almighty God. How we need a revival of a sense of the sacredness of prayer, of humility and of a turning again unto God!

May I ask you, at the conclusion of this brief chapter

on the prayer of Daniel, just what is your prayer life? Remember that it is not the loudness of your testimony, but it is the place which prayer has in your own private secret life that is the measure of your spirituality. Many a man and many a woman who are never heard in public are greater powers before Almighty God in the interest of others than some of the individuals who are constantly in the public eye because of the peculiar opportunities and talents which they may have received from God. So may I ask in conclusion, just what is your prayer life? Are you faithful to God? Have you regular periods for prayer set aside each day —periods with which you allow nothing to interfere? Do you have a definite object in your prayer, the salvation of others and the coming of the kingdom of our Lord Jesus Christ? Do you have a secret place for prayer, or is all your prayer in public, and do you, by the very attitude which you assume when you pray, show forth the attitude of your humble spirit before Him?

God help us to make our prayer today, "Lord, teach me how to pray." The disciples asked this of the Lord, and I want to ask it. I am sure that all of God's people today need to repeat that petition as we look at the prayer life of Daniel, "Lord, teach us to pray." We need not be surprised that God delivered Daniel from the mouths of the hungry lions when we recognize how he trusted God. God will deliver us, too, from the lions' den of affliction and trouble and persecution and doubt if we will put our trust in Him as Daniel did.

CHAPTER NINETEEN

The 144,000 Elect

Then the king commanded, and they brought Daniel, and cast him into the den of lions . . . And a stone was brought, and laid upon the mouth of the den; and the king sealed it with his own signet, and with the signet of his lords; that the purpose might not be changed concerning Daniel (Daniel 6:16-17).

> God moves in a mysterious way
> His wonders to perform;
> He plants His footsteps in the sea,
> And rides upon the storm.

God does not always make His purposes known immediately to His children, and deals with us in strange and difficult ways. It might seem from the record here in Daniel that something was radically wrong. Here was a man who had been faithful to the command of God and had lived a life of devotion and utter dependence upon God, a life of prayer, and yet for all his faithfulness, he is cast into a den of lions to be torn to shreds by these wild beasts. But God looks beyond the immediate and looks to the future, and out of every experience which He brings in providence upon His children, there is bound to come a greater blessing and a greater experience of His greatness and power to deliver. Surely if we would practice more faith in God, it would be the end of all our murmuring and all of our questions of God's dealings with us. If we could only put into practice the truth that we so often quote, that ''all things work together for good to them that love God, to them who are the called according to his purpose,'' it would drive the clouds away and give us songs in the night and cause us to praise Him even as Daniel in the midst of difficulty and of tribulation.

Probably no story in the Bible, except the story of Bethlehem and the manger, is more familiar to the average individual than the sixth chapter of Daniel, the intriguing and interesting story of this man who was cast into the den of lions and miraculously preserved and saved because of his faithfulness to Almighty God and because of the faithfulness of Almighty God. Previously we have been occupied particularly with the story of Daniel as a man of prayer in the midst of tribulation. Now we wish to remind you of the fact that when everything seems dark, we always have the open door of prayer and the avenue of deliverance in all our petitions. Now while we would not overlook the many moral lessons and the spiritual instruction contained in the story of Daniel, we must remember that Daniel is primarily a prophetic book. The Lord Jesus Christ Himself in speaking of the latter days labels Daniel as a prophet. Therefore, we turn again and again in these chapters to the prophetic interpretation of this prophetic book. In order to get the prophetic picture clearly before your mind, we must remind you again of the setting of this wonderful chapter. Darius, who had taken the kingdom over from Belshazzar, had appointed Daniel as one of the presidents over the group whom he had placed in authority over the land. These associates of Daniel had become very jealous and had laid a trap for him. They had caused the king to sign a decree that he alone should receive homage, he alone should be worshiped and anyone found worshiping any other God, or praying, or making a petition to any God except to the king, Darius himself, should be cast into the lions' den.

Now this incident immediately reminds us of another chapter in the Bible which is a fulfillment of the type which we have here. You will find the incident in Revelation 13, where we have the record of two beasts who are to rise up in the end time just before the setting up of the kingdom of the Lord Jesus Christ upon the earth. The first beast is called the beast of the sea, and will be a political ruler who will bear rule and dominion over the entire world. The second one is called the beast out of the land who will be a religious leader in connection with and in league with the political leader of the restored Roman Empire. Concerning this second beast, who will be a supernatural man, we have the following description:

> And deceiveth them that dwell on the earth by the means of those miracles which he had power to do in the sight of the beast; saying to them that dwell on the earth, that they should make an image to the beast, which had the wound by a sword, and did live. And he had power to give life unto the image of the beast, that the image of the beast should both speak, [now notice very carefully what follows, the last clause and the last phrase in this sentence] and cause that as many as would not worship the image of the beast should be killed. And he causeth all, both small and great, rich and poor, free and bond, to receive a mark in their right hand, or in their foreheads: and that no man might buy or sell, save he that had the mark, or the name of the beast, or the number of his name (Revelation 13:14-17).

I am sure that you see the striking similarity of this passage describing the Antichrist of the last days and his ability to perform miracles, and especially his demand of homage and worship from all the people of the world. We should note two things in this passage. One is that he made an image to the beast and all men were commanded to worship that image. That reminds us, of course, of Nebuchadnezzar who also made a great image; and because of their refusal to do so, the three young Hebrew children were cast into the fiery furnace and were supernaturally preserved. We saw at the time we studied that chapter that this was a picture of Israel in the Tribulation, in the fires of Jacob's trouble, but miraculously preserved by Almighty God. In the case of Daniel in the lions' den, we have a repetition of the same truth; we have here Darius demanding worship and homage and prayer from all of his people and those who refused were to be cast into the lions' den.

Now in the thirteenth chapter of Revelation we have the antitype, the fulfillment of the type of Darius, in the person of the Antichrist. We read concerning him "that as many as would not worship the image of the beast should be killed"; and then we have the mark of the beast placed upon those who are willing to follow the wicked king's command and all those who do not have this mark of obedience to the Antichrist are to be put to death. And so you see that, in perfect harmony with the fact that Daniel is primarily a prophecy, we have here another type, another picture, another shadow of the coming end time. At the end of this dispensation, after the Church of the Lord Jesus Christ has been caught away to meet her Lord, there will arise another great world ruler who is more particularly described in the chapters of Daniel which follow and which we shall take up in due time. This world ruler will be none other than the Man of Sin, the Antichrist, and he, too, will demand homage and worship; he will set himself up as God and claim that he himself is God; he will persecute and put to death all those who will seek to worship the true Jehovah. We know that the number of his name is ''Six hundred three score and six,'' and there is every reason to believe that when the mark of the beast is finally ushered in, it will consist of this number, six hundred sixty-six, tattooed or burned or in some other way placed upon the foreheads and upon the hands of all of his hapless servants. Those who do not have this mark, thereby declaring they refuse to worship the beast and the image of the beast, will be condemned to death. Now Darius, the king, was the one who here foreshadows the coming of this Man of Sin. He, too, had made a decree and signed it and sealed it with his own signet that anyone who would not worship him should be cast into the den of lions to be destroyed. But remarkably, marvelously, Daniel was preserved by the intervention of Almighty God. Here Daniel, then, becomes a picture of Israel in the Tribulation.

THE FAITHFUL REMNANT

For the fulfillment of this antitype of Darius, the king, and the record of God's care for His faithful remnant in the Tribulation Period as represented by Daniel in the lions' den, we can again turn to the book of the Revelation, where we read of a company, a faithful remnant of the twelve tribes of Israel, who were sealed by the Almighty and who refused to do homage to the wicked king inspired by Satan:

And after these things I saw four angels standing on
the four corners of the earth, holding the four winds of
the earth, that the wind should not blow on the earth, nor
on the sea, nor on any tree. And I saw another angel ascend-
ing from the east, having the seal of the living God: and he
cried with a loud voice to the four angels, to whom it was
given to hurt the earth and the sea, saying, Hurt not the
earth, neither the sea, nor the trees, till we have sealed
the servants of our God in their foreheads. And I heard the
number of them which were sealed: and there were
sealed an hundred and forty and four thousand of all the
tribes of the children of Israel (Revelation 7:1-4).

And then in verses 5 to 8 inclusive, we have a record
of the twelve thousand of each one of the twelve tribes
of Israel given in detail so that there may be no mistake
whatsoever in regard to this number. In the fourteenth
chapter we again meet this same company who are represented and typified by the faithful man of God, Daniel.

And I looked, and lo, a Lamb stood on the mount Sion,
and with him an hundred forty and four thousand, having
his Father's name written in their foreheads. And I heard
a voice from heaven as the voice of many waters, and as
the voice of a great thunder: and I heard the voice of harpers
harping with their harps: and they sung as it were a new
song before the throne, and before the four beasts, and
the elders: and no man could learn that song but the hundred
and forty and four thousand, which were redeemed from the
earth. These are they which were not defiled with women;
for they are virgins. These are they which follow the Lamb
whithersoever he goeth. These were redeemed from among
men, being the firstfruits unto God and to the Lamb. And
in their mouth was found no guile: for they are without fault
before the throne of God (Revelation 14:1-5).

Here we have the fulfillment of the story of Daniel in
chapter 6. Now will you please notice that concerning
this faithful remnant who had refused to bow their knee
to the image of the beast in the Tribulation Period,

it is said that in their mouth was found no guile, for they are without fault before the Throne of God. Very definitely you see the connection between this record and the record in Daniel, for Daniel was a man concerning whom the Bible records no fault, no blemish, no guile and no sin. To be sure, when we come to Daniel's prayer in the ninth chapter we find that he confesses his sin. He is the last one to claim that he is without fault, that he is without guile. He takes his place penitently with the rest of the nation of Israel in acknowledging his sin, but as far as the record of the Word goes he is one man, among all the characters of Scripture, of whom nothing evil is recorded.

That is probably because Daniel was to be the type of the faithful remnant, the hundred and forty-four thousand of the Tribulation Period, concerning whom it is said:

> And in their mouth was found no guile: for they are without fault before the throne of God (Revelation 14:5).

The Enemies Destroyed

There is a second matter in the sixth chapter of Daniel which must receive our attention, and that is the fate of those who had persecuted Daniel and had caused him to become cast into the lions' den. Here is the record:

> . . . So Daniel was taken up out of the den, and no manner of hurt was found upon him, because he believed in his God. And the king commanded, and they brought those men which had accused Daniel, and they cast them into the den of lions, them, their children, and their wives; and the lions had the mastery of them, and brake all their bones in pieces or ever they came at the bottom of the den (Daniel 6:23-24).

And then in the verses which follow we have the decree of Darius calling upon all men to worship the true

God of Daniel. I want you to notice that while Daniel was supernaturally preserved, the enemies who caused him to be cast into the lions' den were miserably destroyed. This will all find its complete fulfillment when the Lord Jesus Christ comes back again from heaven. Then He, too, will deliver the faithful remnant of those who had believed in God and refused to worship the beast, He will wreak vengeance upon His enemies and destroy those nations which have sought to destroy God's ancient covenant people. It is well that we know the program of God. Even today as we look around about us we see all of the signs and indications of the fulfillment of these very things. When we think of the turmoil in Palestine, when we think of the plight of God's people, Israel, and all of the uneasiness and strife which is going on, we can see the stage being set for the return of the Lord, for the deliverance of His people, for the judgment of the nations.

But there is one phrase with which I want to close this particular chapter. We read it in the twenty-third verse:

> So Daniel was taken up out of the den, and no manner of hurt was found upon him, because he believed in his God.

Please notice that expression, "Because he believed in his God." It is not said that Daniel was delivered because of his excellency, though he was a fine moral character; it is not said that he was delivered because of his goodness or because he belonged to that particular nation which was God's covenant people. The whole thing is in these words, "He believed in his God." Oh, how we need to emphasize today the fact that while judgment is coming and is certain upon all the wicked, for those who will believe in God and receive Jesus Christ, God's Son, as their own personal Saviour, there is salvation and deliverance. Listen, my friend! This time of Tribulation about which we are speaking is coming, and we believe it to be very, very near at hand. This will be a time when God will take off His restraining Hand from the nations round about, when the Antichrist will reign in fury and in fierceness, when hailstones weighing one hundred and twenty pounds will fall from heaven (Revelation 16:21), when pestilence and famine and disease and war and bloodshed and hatred and violence of a kind never before experienced by men will sweep through the world and cause millions upon millions untold suffering and death—and you may escape all this if you will simply follow the example of Daniel, and believe in God. Receive the Lord Jesus Christ today; accept His promise. Receive Him as your only hope of salvation, for the Scripture is still true, "Believe on the Lord Jesus Christ, and thou shalt be saved, and thy house."

CHAPTER TWENTY

The Four Beasts of Daniel

In the first year of Belshazzar king of Babylon Daniel had a dream and visions of his head upon his bed: then he wrote the dream, and told the sum of the matters. Daniel spake and said, I saw in my vision by night, and, behold, the four winds of the heaven strove upon the great sea. And four great beasts came up from the sea, diverse one from another (Daniel 7:1-3).

The prophecy of Daniel contains twelve chapters, evenly divided into two sections of six chapters each. We have so far been studying the first six chapters which contain the personal history of Daniel, the prophet, under Nebuchadnezzar, Belshazzar and finally king Darius of the Medes and Persians. That completed the first section of Daniel. Beginning with chapter 7, we have the second and closing section of the prophecy in which we have a series of visions which Daniel received from the Lord at various times during his career and which contain in their entirety a most graphic and comprehensive picture of history foreseen in advance from the time of Daniel until the setting up of the kingdom at the return of the Lord Jesus.

Now in the seventh chapter of Daniel we have the first

one of this series of visions. Notice first of all the introduction of the chapter. It was "in the first year of Belshazzar king of Babylon," so this goes back somewhat
beyond the sixth chapter which we have been studying.
Probably Daniel did not write down the records immediately, for some reason or another, but here we have it
just the same. He says, "I saw in my vision by night,
and, behold, the four winds of the heaven strove upon
the great sea." That gives us the setting for this particular vision. Now we have the four winds of heaven
referred to in the seventh chapter of the book of Revelation. There we are told that an angel commanded the four
winds to be held back from destroying the earth until
the faithful remnant of God had been sealed in their
foreheads. We believe that these four winds in the book
of Daniel have the same connection, that in the midst
of this coming conflict and the coming destruction under
these world empires, God is going to preserve His faithful people by sealing them, and keeping them even
through the storm of Tribulation.

THE GREAT SEA

Then we are told that these four winds strove upon
the great sea. Now symbolically the sea, in Scripture,
represents the nations of the world in turmoil, in all of
their unrest; but the expression, "great sea," in the
Bible always has one literal meaning. It refers to the
Mediterranean Sea. In general, there are only three seas
mentioned in the Scriptures: the Sea of Galilee, which
was really a lake, the Dead Sea and then the Great Sea,
which always refers to the Mediterranean. Now the setting for these four kingdoms described in the seventh
chapter of Daniel centers around this Great Sea, the
Mediterranean, at the eastern end of which is the land

of Palestine, the center of all human history and the center of God's government upon the earth when the Lord Jesus returns again.

In studying Bible prophecy, it is very important that we remember this fact, that Palestine, according to the Bible, is the geographic center of the globe. By this we mean that God deals with this country particularly, and the other nations are brought in and the other countries are mentioned only as they have some relationship with this land of Palestine. As a result, the directions mentioned in the Bible are always with reference to the land of Palestine. Please remember that. When the Bible speaks about the north country, it means north of Palestine. When it speaks of west, it means west of Palestine. And the same is true of the south. So, Scripturally, Palestine is the exact geographic center of the world in the program and plan of Almighty God for the nations. In the very same way, let me repeat, the Great Sea refers to the Mediterranean Sea, at the eastern end of which this land of Palestine is located. When we see the two beasts in Revelation 13 coming upon the scene, we are told that one of them comes out of the sea. Now symbolically, the sea means, of course, the nations. It also means that this political leader of the end time will arise from one of the countries surrounding the Mediterranean. The second beast comes out of the land, called the earth, and refers to the land of Palestine. So we have two great leaders of the end time, one arising from one of the countries around the Mediterranean, and the other definitely arising out of the land of Palestine. Now in Daniel 7 we see the four winds, which represent the power of God, striving upon the Great Sea; this gives us the introduction to the vision of Daniel which is to follow immediately. The great conflict of all the ages centers around the Mediterranean Sea and the Mediterranean countries. It is out of the Mediterranean area that all of these world kingdoms arise. In the third verse of Daniel seven we read:

> And four great beasts came up from the sea, diverse one from another.

Today, when we see interest centering around Palestine and the great problem of the Dardanelles and Gibraltar, the problem of Italy and all the nations round about, we can see the hand of history beginning to write again on the scroll which seems to have been interrupted but which is to be continued in the end time with a revival of the old Babylonian system of world power and dominion which, according to this chapter, shall be only destroyed at the return of the Lord Jesus Christ.

THE FOUR BEASTS OF DANIEL 7

The first one of these beasts which Daniel saw coming up out of the sea is described in these words:

> The first was like a lion, and had eagle's wings: I beheld till the wings thereof were plucked, and it was lifted up from the earth, and made stand upon the feet as a man, and a man's heart was given to it (Daniel 7:4).

Then follow descriptions of the other beasts: the second beast like a bear, the third beast like a leopard, then the unnamed beast of the last form of Gentile Babylonian world dominion. You notice immediately the similarity of this vision to the dream of Nebuchadnezzar's image. Nebuchadnezzar had seen the image consisting of four parts beginning with gold and degenerating finally until the feet were made of clay and of iron. It is the same period of time which is covered in this chapter. The lion corresponds to the nation of Babylon, the bear to Medo-Persia, the leopard to Greece and then the last one of these beasts, the monstrosity, once again to the Roman empire both in its historic form and in its prophetic form which it will assume at the end of this age. Now the lion, we are told, had eagle's wings, indicating the speed with which Babylon had carried on its conquest, but Daniel notices that the wings thereof were plucked, that its power had been taken away, lifted up from the earth and finally destroyed. All of this we have seen historically under the reign of Belshazzar.

Then we have the vision of the second beast:

> And behold another beast, a second, like to a bear, and it raised up itself on one side, and it had three ribs in the mouth of it between the teeth of it: and they said thus unto it, Arise, devour much flesh (Daniel 7:5).

This represents the conquering kingdom of Medo-Persia, which was a coalition between the Medes and the Persians. Persia was the more powerful and is represented by the bear being raised up on one side, one side being higher than the other; the three ribs indicate that it had overcome three great world powers of its day including Babylon.

Then the third of the beasts is described:

> After this I beheld, and lo another, like a leopard, which had upon the back of it four wings of a fowl; the beast had also four heads; and dominion was given to it (Daniel 7:6).

Here we have a prophetic vision of the third form of world empire and dominion from the day of Daniel on, in graphic description of the Grecian army under Alexander. The figure of a leopard is very descriptive; it speaks of the speed and the swiftness with which the Grecian armies overran the world in their day. We are told that the leopard had four heads, and we know that after Alexander's very brief, interrupted reign his kingdom was divided among his four generals, and for a time, until it was conquered by the Romans, was under four different heads and four different potentates. All of this has been historically confirmed.

Up until now we have only seen how these three first beasts correspond to the historic records of the Babylonian, the Medo-Persian and the Grecian empires, all of which can be checked by secular history and all of which harmonizes with the Word of God. But the chief interest is in the fourth beast, just as the chief interest in the second chapter of Daniel was in the feet and the toes of iron and clay. And so we read in the next two verses:

> After this I saw in the night visions, and behold a fourth beast, dreadful and terrible, and strong exceedingly; and it had great iron teeth: it devoured and brake in pieces, and stamped the residue with the feet of it: and it was diverse from all the beasts that were before it; and it had ten horns. I considered the horns, and, behold, there came up among them another little horn, before whom there were three of the first horns plucked up by the roots: and, behold, in this horn were eyes like the eyes of man, and a mouth speaking great things (Daniel 7:7-8).

Here again we have a description which sounds strangely familiar—familiar because we have practically the same thing in the second chapter of Daniel and a most graphic account of the same thing in the book of Revelation. This is the last form of Gentile world dominion upon the earth. It began with the ascendancy of the Roman empire; this was interrupted for a time but is the beast which was dead, and yet became alive again. It refers to that period of time in the very near future now, when the last form of Babylonianism shall again be

established and when there will be ten great kingdoms
who will unite in a confederacy to guarantee peace and
security to the world.

Now notice that this fourth beast had great iron teeth
corresponding to the iron of the legs of the image of
Nebuchadnezzar in chapter two; that it had ten horns,
horns meaning kingdoms in this particular case, so that
the confederacy of the end time will be the revived Roman
empire, the last form of Babylonianism, consisting of
the federation of ten horns. But we know from the feet
of Nebuchadnezzar's image, that the ten kingdoms will
be divided into two parts, probably an eastern and a
western, five nations in each lot, and that great difficulty
will be experienced in bringing these nations together
on a common basis and in a common program. And then,
finally, the solution seems to be found, for as Daniel
considered the horns (now notice this) there came up
another little horn by whom three of the first horns were
plucked up, and this horn was the one which is described
as having eyes like a man and a mouth speaking great
things. This little horn is the Man of Sin, the Antichrist,
the superman of the end time who will arise amidst the
confusion of the nations in their futile effort to bring
about peace and confederacy. For a brief time he will
succeed in uniting the nations together, in ruling them
and especially in rehabilitating the people of Israel in
the land of Palestine. After the Church of the Lord Jesus
Christ has been taken out of the world, an attempt will
be made, which we believe is already in progress at this
very time, to form a world federation which will be
headed up particularly by two blocks of five nations
each and these will be brought together for a little time
by a superman, by an international leader here called
the little horn, who will bring order out of disorder and

peace out of threatened war, and for a time will promise
to bring the long hoped for millennial rest and prosperity
upon the earth. However, his reign will be very, very
short, as we read in the verses which immediately follow:

> I beheld till the thrones were cast down, and the Ancient
> of days did sit, whose garment was white as snow, and the
> hair of his head like the pure wool: his throne was like the
> fiery flame, and his wheels as burning fire. A fiery stream
> issued and came forth from before him: thousand thou-
> sands ministered unto him, and ten thousand times ten
> thousand stood before him: the judgment was set, and the
> books were opened. I beheld then because of the voice of
> the great words which the horn spake: I beheld even till
> the beast was slain, and his body destroyed, and given to the
> burning flame . . .
> I saw in the night visions, and, behold, one like the Son of
> man came with the clouds of heaven, and came to the Ancient
> of days, and they brought him near before him. And there
> was given him dominion, and glory, and a kingdom, that all
> people, nations, and languages, should serve him: his domin-
> ion, which shall not pass away, and his kingdom that which
> shall not be destroyed (Daniel 7:9-11; 13-14).

The picture then becomes perfectly plain. We have
one kingdom after another arising, during the course of
human history, only to fall; we have all man's efforts
failing completely to bring about the desired prosperity
and peace and security for which man has longed in all
generations. And then, finally, the enemy of God, the
Antichrist, the superman, Satan incarnate, will make
one final attempt to bring together all of the disorganized
factions of the world, only to be destroyed by the coming
again of the Lord Jesus Christ. We are told of His
(Christ's) kingdom, that it is an everlasting dominion
which shall not pass away, and that His kingdom shall
not be destroyed.

As we look upon the world today in all of its turmoil,

we cannot help but be impressed with the fact that all of these things are even now in the process of fulfillment. When we think of the efforts being made, sincere efforts as far as man goes, to bring about a cessation of the ills and wars and strife that have vexed humanity, we realize that all of these efforts are in vain, that the only hopes that we have had, have already been dashed in pieces, and that there is only one thing for us to look for, the coming again of Him who said, "I will come again, and receive you unto myself." May the Lord help us to be ready for His appearing! The next event, we believe, will be the return of the Lord Jesus Christ in glory to put down His enemies, and set up His everlasting kingdom.

CHAPTER TWENTY-ONE

The Man of Sin

Then I would know the truth of the fourth beast, which
was diverse from all the others, exceeding dreadful, whose
teeth were of iron, and his nails of brass; which devoured,
brake in pieces, and stamped the residue with his feet;
and of the ten horns that were in his head, and of the other
which came up, and before whom three fell; even of that horn
that had eyes, and a mouth that spake very great things,
whose look was more stout than his fellows. I beheld, and
the same horn made war with the saints, and prevailed
against them; until the Ancient of days came, and judgment
was given to the saints of the most High; and the time came
that the saints possessed the kingdom (Daniel 7:19-22).

These verses contain the question of Daniel after he
had seen the vision of the four beasts described in the
seventh chapter. Daniel, although he had seen the vision,
was unable to interpret it himself, and had to receive
divine guidance and wisdom and light in order that he
might understand its meaning. Now it is much easier
for us, after all these centuries of history have corroborated the vision of Daniel for us, to understand the meaning, than for Daniel himself, because these things which
he saw had not yet come to pass. You will recall from

our previous chapter that Daniel saw four beasts, one like a lion, another like a bear, another like a leopard, and then this fourth beast about which he inquires in these verses—a beast which was an unnamed monstrosity. We have pointed out that the lion represented the head of gold of Nebuchadnezzar's image, the kingdom of Babylon; that the bear represented the Medo-Persian kingdom; that the leopard represented the Grecian kingdom which arose for a brief time only, to be divided into four different heads and then to be conquered by the Roman empire. Now Daniel wants to know about the kingdom which was to follow the kingdom of Greece. He said he would know the truth of the fourth beast which he had seen. We have already pointed out that this fourth beast had ten horns, and that these ten horns represented ten nations, ten kingdoms, which would be centered primarily around the Mediterranean Sea which is the center of God's dealings in the end time. Daniel's prayer for an interpretation did not go unheeded, for we have God's own answer beginning in verse 23:

> Thus he said, The fourth beast shall be the fourth kingdom upon the earth, which shall be diverse from all kingdoms, and shall devour the whole earth, and shall tread it down, and break it in pieces.

Now the fourth beast, of course, means the fourth kingdom from Daniel's time. There had been kingdoms before Daniel's time; the kingdom beginning with Nimrod way back in the eleventh chapter of Genesis, then Assyria and then Egypt. But with Daniel, the lion phase of world dominion began, with that of Babylon, followed by Persia and Greece; so this makes the Roman empire the fourth beast which is here described. However, the view is prophetic and looks forward to the time when the Babylonian system, the Roman empire,

after centuries of apparent inactivity, shall be revived
again at the end time. We are not confined for our
knowledge of this end-time revival of the Roman empire
to the seventh chapter of Daniel, but have it elaborated
upon in many other passages of Scripture, not only in
the Old Testament prophecies but in the New Testament
as well, and we know from these that at the end of this
dispensation there will be a revival of the Babylonian
system as it was seen in the days of the height of the
Roman conquest.

DANIEL AND REVELATION

The prophecy of Daniel occupies the same position
in the Old Testament as the Revelation occupies in the
New, and the two should always be studied together.
They complement each other and throw light upon each
other. In the Old Testament when Daniel gave his revelation, practically everything that he spoke of was still
future. In the book of the Revelation, however, we have
a backward look in which many of the things which
Daniel had prophesied had already come to pass. Now
this particular vision of the Babylonian system after
the Rapture of the Church and the raising up of the
Man of Sin was still future in John's day and to be sure,
is even future now. So I want to quote from the book of
Revelation a passage which I think will greatly help
us in understanding the seventh chapter of Daniel as well
as the rest of the prophecy of Daniel.

> And I stood upon the sand of the sea, and saw a beast
> rise up out of the sea, having seven heads and ten horns,
> and upon his horns ten crowns, and upon his heads the
> name of blasphemy. And the beast which I saw was like
> unto a leopard, and his feet were as the feet of a bear, and
> his mouth as the mouth of a lion: and the dragon gave him

his power, and his seat, and great authority. And I saw one of his heads as it were wounded to death; and his deadly wound was healed: and all the world wondered after the beast. And they worshipped the dragon which gave power unto the beast: and they worshipped the beast, saying, Who is like unto the beast? Who is able to make war with him? (Revelation 13:1-4).

You will notice that John here describes a beast which he does not name; he says that it had the similitude, first of a leopard, then feet as of a bear and the mouth of a lion. Now please remember that in Daniel we have exactly the reverse order, although he is talking about the same thing. In Daniel we have the lion first, then the bear and then the leopard. In Revelation we have it in exactly the reverse. We have the leopard the bear and finally the lion. Now the reason for this is in perfect harmony with the inspiration of the Scriptures. When Daniel spoke these things, he was looking forward, and the Babylonian lion kingdom was first, to be superseded by the Persian bear kingdom and then by the leopard of Greece; but when John wrote the Revelation, he was looking backward, and these things had been fulfilled in the interval, so that when he looks at this indescribable monstrosity, the beast of the end time, he sees first the Roman empire, the Grecian, the Medo-Persian and the Babylonian. What marvelous evidence of the harmony and the inspiration of the Word of God! But as in the case of Daniel, so here in Revelation we have two beasts. This first one, we are told, came up out of the sea, probably from one of the countries around the Mediterranean, and is a political leader who will be the head of the political combination of nations, here again represented by ten distinct nations. We have ten toes in the image of Nebuchadnezzar; we have seven horns upon the beast in Daniel seven. Here we have the beast with seven heads and ten horns, and upon his horns ten crowns, all speaking of this great confederacy of nations of the end time.

THE MAN OF SIN

But this effort on the part of the nations to bring about a world-wide federation, a World United Nations, will fail because of lack of adequate leadership. So, even today we are looking for a superman, a man who will be a statesman and a political power, one who will be able to smooth out all the differences of the nations and weld them together in one great commonwealth. Before we take up the revelation in Daniel seven as well as Revelation thirteen, concerning this superman, the Antichrist, we want to call your attention to one other verse:

And I saw one of his heads as it were wounded to death; and his deadly wound was healed: and all the world wondered after the beast (Revelation 13:3).

This undoubtedly refers to the Roman empire which for a time seems to be, at least outwardly, dead, but in the end time shall again be revived in very much the same form and covering very much the same territory as it had before its destruction and fall. Now over this revived confederacy of nations, there will arise, we said, a man, the Antichrist, who occupies such a large place throughout the Scriptures generally. It is not difficult to imagine what an immediate response there will be to the appearing of such an individual. Today we are witnessing the inability of the nations to come to any kind of an agreement as to the future of this world, and we find power politics still playing a part in keeping the nations apart and driving them farther and farther away from each other. If then a man shall arise who shall hold the key and solution to all of this vexing problem, we can easily understand how quickly he will be received and acclaimed as the liberator and saviour of the world.

This Man of Sin, this Antichrist, we believe, this little horn of Daniel seven, will be none other than Judas Iscariot, the betrayer of the Lord Jesus Christ, raised from the dead again. He will be Satan incarnate; Satan personally will enter into him and for a brief period of time, approximately seven years, he will reign upon the earth. During the first three and one-half years he will befriend God's ancient people, Israel, restore them to their land, rebuild their Temple and reinstate their Old Testament sacrifices, only to turn against them in the middle of that particular period. Everything in the world today seems to indicate that the time of the arising of this superman is very near at hand. Even though we have been dreaming and praying for peace and understanding among the nations as well as the people of the nations, there is today, we must candidly admit, more confusion, more strife, more misunderstanding, more selfishness, than ever before in the history of the world. While man is seeking frantically to bring about the solution of the world's troubles and to avert the plunging of the nations into a worse and a more terrible war then the one just recently past, we find that men are drifting farther and farther apart. If a man, therefore, could, and should arise, who would have a fool-proof solution whereby all these differences could be ironed out, it is easy to conceive that the world would bow at his feet and give him absolute dominion and power to go to the very limit. Well, this individual is going to arise. Thank God that he will not come until after the Church of Jesus Christ has been taken out!

Now turning again to Daniel seven, we have in the vision of Daniel a picture of some of the details which will bring forth this man. In verse 23 we read that the fourth beast shall be the fourth kingdom upon the earth. It will be the last form of world dominion, of world government, before the Lord comes. It will be different in that there will be an apparent success in bringing about a peace and understanding, but as a result of this brief peace, of this breathing spell, the Man of Sin will take advantage of the condition, suddenly reveal his true character and plunge the world into the greatest holocaust of all the ages. At that time remember there will be a revival of the Roman empire under the ten toes and the ten horns of Daniel seven, which are ten kingdoms which shall be grouped around the Mediterranean Sea, and out of that confederacy will arise this man. Now we are told something about the characteristics of this individual. We read the following:

> And he shall speak great words against the most High [he is going to be an atheist, an unbeliever], and shall wear out the saints of the most High [he will be anti-Christian and opposed to all of God's people], and think to change times and laws [he will bring about a great revolutionary change in the governments of the world, probably changing the calendar with the idea of eliminating everything that is based on Christianity]: and they shall be given into his hand until a time and times and the dividing of time (Daniel 7:25).

THREE AND ONE-HALF YEARS

We must stop to take time to study the last clause of this verse. It says that they, that is all this authority, all this power and all this blasphemy shall continue until a time and times and the dividing of time. Now this is usually linked with the twelve hundred and sixty days of Revelation, the forty-two months of the Great Tribulation, here called the time, one year, and times, probably two years, and the dividing, or one-half of time, which gives us the exact time of the latter part of the Antichrist's reign. Now right here let me remind you of the order of events. We believe the next thing which will happen will be the coming of the Lord Jesus Christ to take His Church out before the Tribulation. Then the Man of Sin, according to Scripture, will arise; he will reign for exactly seven years corresponding to the seventieth week of Daniel still unfulfilled. The first three and one-half years he will befriend God's ancient people, Israel, will succeed in building up a great world power and a great world system of government which men will hail as the very solution of all men's problems. Then in the middle of that Tribulation Period, after three and one-half years, he is going to march upon the city of Jerusalem, he is going to desecrate the newly rebuilt Temple, he will set up the image of the political head of this government, the image of the beast, will give to it the power to speak, and will command all men, particularly the nation of Israel, to pay homage to this imposter and this intruder in the very holy place of the Temple of Almighty God. For three and one-half years this thing will continue until it seems that humanity will be annihilated from the face of the earth, and then we have the great event for which the Church and the world are longing today, suddenly happening. In verses 26 and 27, we read this:

> But the judgment shall sit, and they shall take away his
> [that is, this beast's] dominion, to consume and to destroy

it unto the end. And the kingdom and dominion, and the greatness of the kingdom under the whole heaven, shall be given to the people of the saints of the most High, whose kingdom is an everlasting kingdom, and all dominions shall serve and obey him [that is the One who comes, the Lord Jesus Christ].

This is the same thing we see in verse 13, where we read:

I saw in the night visions, and, behold, one like the Son of man came with the clouds of heaven, and came to the Ancient of days, and they brought him near before him.

And there He also received the kingdom. That "but" at the beginning of verse 26 is probably the most important and most encouraging word in the entire seventh chapter of Daniel, for we have the picture very briefly given; this age will end in apostasy and terrible calamity, in wars and rumors of wars and pestilences and distress of nations. Then the Church will be taken out and the Man of Sin will be revealed; he will promise to lead the world out of its maze of difficulty, but only to plunge it into the greatest war of all history which shall end at the time of the end of the Tribulation in the battle of Armageddon centered in the land of Palestine. This battle will come to an end only when the Lord Jesus Christ, the Son of man, returns again and destroys His enemies and sets up His glorious millennial kingdom. So we believe the next event in the program of God is the return of the Lord Jesus Christ for His own.

My friend, may I ask you if you are ready for that event? It is the surest thing in all the world. God says it and God cannot lie. The most important thing for each one of you to do, is to decide right now what you will do with the Lord Jesus Christ, the One who may be here at any moment. God help you to make the decision and make it now, before it is forever too late.

CHAPTER TWENTY-TWO
The Little Horn

> Then I lifted up mine eyes, and saw, and, behold, there stood before the river a ram which had two horns: and the two horns were high; but one was higher than the other, and the higher came up last. I saw the ram pushing westward, and northward, and southward; so that no beasts might stand before him, neither was there any that could deliver out of his hand; but he did according to his will, and became great. And as I was considering, behold, an he goat came from the west on the face of the whole earth, and touched not the ground: and the goat had a notable horn between his eyes (Daniel 8:3-5).

These verses record for us a part of the second vision which Daniel had and related for us in the eighth chapter. Before going on to the interpretation given in this chapter concerning the ram and the he goat as representing the nations of the world, we want to say a few things by way of explanation concerning the peculiarities of the book of Daniel. Remembering that Daniel is a prophetic book according to the Lord Jesus Himself, and remembering that there is a great deal of misunderstanding in the interpretation of this book, we want to point out a few of its characteristics. The great part of this book, of course, was written by Daniel who, like most of the other writers of the Old and New Testament, was a Hebrew inspired by the Holy Spirit, but Daniel contains one entire chapter written not by a Hebrew but written by a Gentile, by a king of Babylon, containing the testimony of the conversion of Nebuchadnezzar in his own words. We have spent some time in studying this testimony, because of its value, in a preceding chapter. Now there is another important characteristic of the prophecy of Daniel, namely, that it has been written in two different languages, in the Aramaic and in the Hebrew. Please note this carefully. All of chapter one and the first three verses of chapter two of the book of Daniel are written in the Hebrew tongue. Then a new section of Daniel begins and from chapter 2, verse 4, up to chapter eight, we have it written in the Chaldean, the popular language of that day in Babylon. It might be well to quote here the verse which begins the Aramaic portion of this wonderful book:

> Then spake the Chaldeans to the king in Syriack, O king, live for ever: tell thy servants the dream, and we will shew the interpretation (Daniel 2:4).

Then from chapter 8 through chapter 12, to the end of the book, we again have the Hebrew tongue used by Daniel.

EVIDENCE OF INSPIRATION

We call attention to these details because they constitute another among the thousands of evidences of divine and supernatural inspiration of the Scriptures. If this book had not been inspired by the Holy Spirit, we would not find these characteristics. Now there is a very definite reason for this change in language found in the book of Daniel. Remember that Daniel deals with two things: first, it deals with the history of God's ancient covenant people, Israel; and then it deals with the time of the Gentiles, this present age, during which the nation has been set aside and the kingdom has been postponed. In the first chapter of Daniel we have the personal history of four Hebrews, Belteshazzar (Daniel), Shadrach, Meshach and Abed-nego, in the court of the heathen Babylonian king, Nebuchadnezzar, and as such, in perfect harmony with the structure of Daniel, it is written in the Hebrew tongue. But beginning with the fourth verse of the second chapter and running through chapter 7, we have a series of visions and revelations, through king Nebuchadnezzar and interpreted by Daniel, which deal with the history of the nations during the time that Israel has been set aside, and again in perfect harmony with this purpose, it is written in the popular language of that day, the Syriack or the Aramaic. Then beginning with chapter 8 we have the resumption of the history of Daniel's people particularly in the end time of the Tribulation Period when, after God has taken the Church out, He will begin to deal again very definitely with the nation of Israel. And so we have, in perfect harmony with all that which has gone before, the Hebrew tongue resumed in the record beginning with Daniel 8. All of this, we say, is a wonderful evidence of divine inspiration, and, added to the thousands of other evidences within the Book itself, makes this Bible beyond all controversy to the open mind, a supernatural Book, supernaturally inspired by a supernatural Holy Spirit.

The Second Vision of Daniel

With this background in mind will you consider carefully the second vision which Daniel received as recorded in the eighth chapter. You will notice from the first verse that it was two years after the first vision as related in

the seventh chapter; we are told that it was in the third
year of the reign of king Belshazzar. Now Daniel had a
very peculiar vision. He was at Shushan in the palace
in the province of Elam and he saw a vision of a ram
which stood before the river, undoubtedly the river referred to in the previous verse, the river Ulai. This ram
was peculiar in that it had two horns, but one horn was
larger, that is higher, than the other horn, and the one,
the higher one, came up after the first one had made
its appearance. Then he saw this ram pushing westward,
that is, it came from the east pushing west and north
and south, and conquering everything that lay in its
path. Now, we are not left in doubt as to the interpretation of this particular vision, for Daniel inquires of the
Lord as to the meaning of all these things, and a man's
voice comes to him and says:

> Gabriel, make this man to understand the vision (Daniel
> 8:16).

God sent Gabriel, His angel, to make known unto
Daniel the meaning of this vision. Then we read in verse
17:

> So he came near where I stood: and when he came, I was
> afraid, and fell upon my face: but he said unto me, Under-
> stand, O son of man: for at the time of the end shall be
> the vision.

Now verse 19:

> And he said, Behold, I will make thee know what shall
> be in the last end of the indignation: for at the time ap-
> pointed the end shall be.

Before taking up the interpretation of this vision of
the ram, we must call your attention to two phrases
found in the verses we have just quoted. The first phrase
is from verse 17:

> O son of man: for at the time of the end shall be the vision.

And the second phrase is from verse 19:

And he said, Behold, I will make thee know what shall be in the last end of the indignation: for at the time appointed the end shall be[or the end shall come].

So we are immediately reminded that, while this vision of the ram and the he goat had a historic fulfillment in the kingdoms of Greece and of Medo-Persia, nevertheless, it looks beyond all this to the time of the end, that is the end of this present dispensation, the end just before the Son of God will return to set up His kingdom. So we are told, "For at the time of the end shall be the vision." And then the expression, "last end of the indignation," is the expression which is very commonly used for the time of the Tribulation Period. It is called the time of the indignation of the Lord and refers to that period of time we have mentioned so many times before, when the Church shall be taken out, and a period of seven years shall intervene between the Rapture and the Second Coming of Christ, called the day of indignation, the day of vengeance, the day of Jacob's trouble, the day of the wrath of Almighty God and the day of the Tribulation. So bear in mind very carefully that while we have here a prophecy concerning some events which were to transpire very shortly after the vision was given, they are typical of the end time and look forward to the end of this particular age.

MEANING OF THE RAM

As we said, we are not left in any doubt as to the interpretation of Daniel's vision, for we read:

The ram which thou sawest having two horns are the kings of Media and Persia (Daniel 8:20).

Now everything is clear. At the time in which Daniel wrote, he was still living in the days of Belshazzar and the kingdom of Babylon had not yet fallen to the kings of Media and Persia, but soon after we have the fall of Babylon as we learned when we studied the impious feast of Belshazzar on that night when the fingers of a man's hand wrote his doom upon the wall, and he was conquered by the kingdom of Media and Persia. Now the Medo-Persian kingdom was a coalition of two great powers, Media and Persia. Media was first and Persia was second, but as time went on Persia became the stronger of the two and gained the ascendancy. This is represented by the ram with the two horns which here are called the kings of Media and Persia. But we are told in the third verse that the second horn was higher than the other and this one came up last, and history stands as mute evidence to the infallible accuracy of the Word of God when it tells us that Media first was the stronger of the two powers, but gradually Persia gained the ascendancy and became the real power in the Medo-Persian kingdom.

Interestingly also, we have the statement here that it was a ram which he saw, which came and devoured and destroyed the kingdom of Babylon. Now history records for us, and we are glad to relate it, that the national symbol of the Medo-Persian empire was a ram. It was a figure of a ram which they carried upon their banners as they went into battle; just as the symbol of the United States is an eagle and we associate England with a lion, Russia with a bear, and so forth, so the symbol of the Medo-Persian empire was a ram. We have here a complete picture in these few verses of the history of this dominating empire which for a short time after overthrowing Babylon occupied the center of the stage of the nations of the world. We have here, then, a coalition of two powers, one of which became more powerful than the other, and for a time overran the entire world.

VISION OF THE HE GOAT

The next event in the vision of Daniel is now recorded:

And I was considering, behold, an he goat came from the west on the face of the whole earth, and touched not the ground: and the goat had a notable horn between his eyes. And he came to the ram that had two horns, which I had seen standing before the river, and ran unto him in the fury of his power. And I saw him come close unto the ram, and he was moved with choler against him, and smote the ram, and brake his two horns: and there was no power in the ram to stand before him, but he cast him down to the ground, and stamped upon him: and there was none that could deliver the ram out of his hand. Therefore the he goat waxed very great: and when he was strong, the great horn was broken; and for it came up four notable ones toward the four winds of heaven. And out of one of them came forth a little horn, which waxed exceeding great, toward the south, and toward the east, and toward the pleasant land. And it waxed great, even to the host of heaven; and it cast down some of the host and of the stars to the ground, and stamped upon them. Yea, he magnified himself even to the prince of the host, and by him the daily sacrifice was taken away, and the place of his sanctuary was cast down (Daniel 8:5-11).

All of this would be greatly confusing, I am sure, to most of us, were it not for the fact that the Holy Spirit has again seen fit to give us the exact interpretation, and looking at this interpretation in the light of subsequent history we can see the accuracy of Daniel's prophecy, for we are told in verse 21 who this rough or hairy goat was.

And the rough goat is the king of Grecia: and the great horn that is between his eyes is the first king. Now that being broken, whereas four stood up for it, four kingdoms shall stand up out of the nation, but not in his power. And

in the latter time of their kingdom, when the transgressors
are come to the full, a king of fierce countenance, and understanding dark sentences, shall stand up (Daniel 8:21-23).

Here, then, we have the answer of the Holy Spirit
Himself. This he goat which came rapidly without touch-
ing the ground and put to naught the ram in vision is
none other than the kingdom of Greece. Now we know
from history that Greece was the kingdom which over-
threw the kingdom of Medo-Persia and took its place,
for a time at least. When we remember that all of this
was written by Daniel when he was still in the kingdom
of Babylon and before the Medo-Persians had even made
a threat to overthrow the kingdom of Babylon, we begin
to recognize the accuracy of all which Daniel wrote.
Now in regard to this he goat, we are told that he ran
and smote the ram which was Medo-Persia, and broke
his two horns, that is, completely subdued his power,
and there was no power in the ram to stand before him.
History corroborates all this and tells us how Alexander
the Great at the height of his power swept across the
world with incredible speed and there was nothing which
could stand before him; in an unbelievably short period
of time he had conquered practically the whole world,
and, as you remember, he wept because there were no
more worlds to conquer.

All of this was literally fulfilled in the kingdom of
Greece. Alexander, usually called Alexander the Great,
moved with his army for the first time from the west
into the east. All the other conquests had begun in the
east and had moved on to the west and the north and the
south, but here for the first time we have the current
of conquest reverted, and we find the kingdom of Greece
spreading eastward over the entire face of the earth.
Now the notable horn between the eyes which is men-

tioned is very evidently a reference to the Grecian leader, Alexander. We are told of him that he waxed great, and when he was strong the great horn was broken. Greece, in the height of its power, came to an ignominious end, for Alexander, still a young man, broken down by licentiousness and drunkenness, died at a very early age, and the Grecian kingdom was thrown into great confusion and split into four different kingdoms, a different ruler ruling over each one of them. All of this is given to us in the eighth verse where we are told that after the great horn is broken, four notable horns came up toward the four winds of heaven. Here again we have history corroborating everything that Daniel saw, for we are told that after Alexander the Great died, confusion broke out and his kingdom was divided. Syria came under the leadership of Seleucus; Greece came under the leadership of Lysimachus; Thrace came under the dominion of Cassander; and Egypt under Ptolemy. These four kingdoms were the divisions of the Grecian kingdom and they continued until about 50 B.C., when Rome swept down with its sword and conquered the world, and we have the fourth great world empire since the days of Daniel taking its place upon the scene of action among the nations.

In our next chapter we shall consider the little horn which came out of one of these four divisions of the Grecian empire as recorded in verse 9 where we read:

> And out of one of them came forth a little horn, which waxed exceeding great, toward the south, and toward the east, and toward the pleasant land.

We shall have occasion to point out how this, too, was literally fulfilled in the person of Antiochus Epiphanes who became the great type of the coming desecrator of the holy things of God, the Man of Sin in the Great Tribulation Period. But now before closing this message, we want to remind you of the inerrancy of the Word of God. We hope that this message has in some way impressed you with the truthfulness of this marvelous Word. Not only is the Bible absolutely unquestionable in the matter of prophecy but also in the matter of salvation, and according to this unbreakable Word, you, my friend, are a sinner and are on the way to eternal destruction and doom, for God is a just and holy as well as a loving and merciful God. God has provided a way of salvation whereby you may be saved by looking to the Lord Jesus Christ and trusting Him before the awful conflict which we shall study in the next chapter breaks upon this world. Will you not receive Him now? "Believe on the Lord Jesus Christ, and thou shalt be saved."

CHAPTER TWENTY-THREE

The Two Thousand Three Hundred Days

And I heard a man's voice between the banks of Ulai, which called, and said, Gabriel, make this man to understand the vision. So he came near where I stood: and when he came, I was afraid, and fell upon my face: but he said unto me, Understand, O son of man: for at the time of the end shall be the vision. Now as he was speaking with me, I was in a deep sleep on my face toward the ground: but he touched me, and set me upright. And he said, Behold, I will make thee know what shall be in the last end of the indignation: for at the time appointed the end shall be (Daniel 8: 16-19).

In this eighth chapter of the prophecy of Daniel we have the second vision which God gave His servant. In it he beheld a ram which we have already identified as the kingdom of Medo-Persia, the two horns representing the two divisions of this kingdom. Then we saw a he goat which is interpreted for us as the kingdom of Greece. And this he goat had a very notable horn between his eyes which was none other than the historic character, Alexander the Great, before whose victorious army none were able to stand. In a very short time he had conquered the then known world, but in the midst of his pride and in the midst of his strength, because of licen-

tiousness and drunkenness, he was soon cut off and died
an untimely death. And then there was a squabble
among the generals in his army and the Grecian kingdom was divided into four separate parts which we
told you were ruled over by four of his generals. This
continued until about 50 B.C. when the Roman legions
came down and overran not only the land of Palestine
but the entire Grecian empire. The interesting thing in
this chapter is the mention of a little horn which came
out of one of the four divisions into which the empire
of Greece had been divided. Let me quote this verse
again:

> And out of one of them [that is, out of one of these four
> divisions into which the Grecian empire was divided] came
> forth a little horn (Daniel 8:9).

Then in verses 11 and 12 we are told:

> He magnified himself even to the prince of the host, and
> by him the daily sacrifice was taken away, and the place
> of his sanctuary was cast down. And an host was given
> him against the daily sacrifice by reason of transgression,
> and it cast down the truth to the ground; and it practised,
> and prospered.

Again there need be no doubt as to whom this little
horn represents, for we read concerning the rough goat
with the great horn, as follows:

> Now that being broken, whereas four stood up for it,
> four kingdoms shall stand up out of the nation, but not in
> his power. And in the latter time of their kingdom, when
> the transgressors are come to the full, a king of fierce coun-
> tenance, and understanding dark sentences, shall stand up.
> And his power shall be mighty, but not by his own power:
> and he shall destroy wonderfully, and shall prosper, and
> practise, and shall destroy the mighty and the holy people.
> And through his policy also he shall cause craft to prosper
> in his hand; and he shall magnify himself in his heart, and

by peace shall destroy many: he shall also stand up against the Prince of princes; but he shall be broken without hand. And the vision of the evening and the morning which was told is true: wherefore shut thou up the vision; for it shall be for many days. And I Daniel fainted, and was sick certain days; afterward I rose up, and did the king's business; and I was astonished at the vision, but none understood it (Daniel 8:22-27).

We are amazed at the detail and accuracy with which this vision gives us a picture of that which was about to come to pass. Now please remember that while this was a prophecy of certain events which were to take place during the term of the Grecian empire, it also looks far beyond to the time of the end of which this little horn is but a type and a shadow. According to Daniel, after the fall of Alexander the Great and the splitting up of his kingdom into its four divisions, there was to arise a very strange individual who is called here "a king of fierce countenance, and understanding dark sentences." He would persecute the people of God and would bring about the setting up of the abomination of desolation in the city of Jerusalem. Now it is a historical fact that Antiochus Epiphanes came out of Syria, one of the four notable kingdoms into which Alexander's empire was divided. We know also that he first made many, many promises to the people in the land of Palestine, only to disregard them all. We know that in the height of his power he went into Jerusalem, desecrated the Temple, abused and killed the priests of the Lord Most High, went to the altar upon which only holy things and clean animals were to be sacrificed, and instead, as an insult to the God Jehovah of Israel and the Temple and all of its holy worship, he slaughtered a swine, a pig, and sacrificed it upon the altar which was reserved only for the holy sacrifices of the Almighty. This was the setting up of an abomination and becomes a type and a picture of the Man of Sin who also in the middle of the Tribulation Period after the Church has been caught away will once again desecrate the Temple by setting up an image of the political beast of Revelation 13, and demand that all people shall pay homage to and worship the image of this beast.

The Lord Jesus Christ, in Matthew 24 warns His people concerning this particular vision. It may be well at this very point to turn for a moment to this chapter. Here the Lord Jesus Christ answers a question of the disciples when they asked Him what should be the sign of His coming and the end of the age. He then gives a long list of signs which were to happen before His Second Coming: deception, wars, rumors of wars, famine, pestilences, earthquakes, violence and racial strife in various places; people shall betray one another, there will be false prophets, the love of many shall wax cold—a great list of indications which have been fulfilled in the main, even during these last days. Then after having given them this long category of signs of His return and of the end time, He says:

> When ye therefore shall see the abomination of desolation, spoken of by Daniel the prophet, stand in the holy place . . . Then let them which be in Judaea flee into the mountains: Let him which is on the housetop not come down to take any thing out of his house (Matthew 24:15-17).

Then in verses 21 and 22 He gives us the key:

> For then shall be great tribulation, such as was not since the beginning of the world to this time, no, nor ever shall be. And except those days should be shortened, there should no flesh be saved: but for the elects sake those days shall be shortened.

And so we have here another instance in Daniel of

a double prophecy. First of all these words concerning the horn which came up as this man of fierce countenance were literally fulfilled in the coming of Antiochus, the enemy of God's ancient people, the defilement of the Temple and the ushering in of the time of great suffering and sorrow for those who were faithful unto the service of the Lord. He took away the daily sacrifice, and profaned the Temple in many, many different ways. Then after a short reign of this awful terror we have a deliverer arising to save Israel. We do not have the record in the Bible but from contemporary history and from the book of the Maccabees, one of the Apocryphal books, we know that Judas Maccabeus and his brother arose about three and one-half years after this desecration of the Temple and of the altar and delivered the nation of Israel, at least temporarily and partially, from the awfulness of this king of fierce countenance, the type of the coming Antichrist.

Twenty-Three Hundred Days

In order that there may be no mistaking the literalness of the fulfillment of this prophecy, in the person of this terrible man, Antiochus Epiphanes, we read in Daniel 8:14:

And he said unto me, Unto two thousand and three hundred days; then shall the sanctuary be cleansed.

Here we have the verse which mentions the much discussed and much misunderstood, "two thousand three hundred days," until the sanctuary should be cleansed. Now this was the answer which Daniel overheard in the conversation between two saints who were speaking concerning the length of time of the defilement of the Temple and the sacrifice and the altar. The setting here, you will remember, is the prophecy concerning this man

who was to come out of one of the divisions of the
Grecian empire and was to be an enemy of Israel and
was to desecrate the Temple of Jehovah at Jerusalem.
We read these words in Daniel 8:13:

> Then I heard one saint speaking, and another saint said
> unto that certain saint which spake, How long shall be the
> vision concerning the daily sacrifice, and the transgression
> of desolation, to give both the sanctuary and the host to be
> trodden under foot?

The question was, "How long will this desecration of
this enemy of God's people last?" And the answer was,
"Two thousand three hundred days." Now a great
deal of misunderstanding has resulted from this number
because of a very unscriptural theory called the "year,
day" theory by which some would have us believe that
we are to count one year for every day, and according
to that reckoning, of course, it would mean that the
sanctuary would be trodden under foot for twenty-three
hundred years. Well, that period of time has already
passed, and evidently nothing has happened, so we go
to the record itself and we find that from the time that
the Temple was desecrated and Antiochus slaughtered
a swine upon the altar in Jerusalem up until the time
of the deliverance of Jerusalem under Judas Maccabeus
was exactly two thousand three hundred days. So we
have a fulfillment of the prophecy, and it therefore cannot lie in the future except only in type and in shadow.

To make a day mean a year leads us into all sorts
of folly and misunderstanding. If we are to take that,
then, of course, we also have to take the fact that the
Creation was not in six literal days, but that it took six
literal years instead. Then we are to suppose that the
madness of Nebuchadnezzar, which was to last seven
years, would, if we are to multiply that by three hundred

and sixty-five, still be going on today. All sorts of misunderstandings result when we depart from the simple, literal interpretation of the Word of God. So we have in this verse in Daniel the simple statement that the reign of terror by the little horn who would arise out of the Grecian empire would last for exactly two thousand and three hundred days, which is a matter of history that cannot be denied.

THE GREAT TRIBULATION

But when we have seen the historic fulfillment we have only touched upon the real teaching of this particular chapter, for, as we said, this vision looks to the time of the end. We have already pointed out from verses 17 and 19 that it deals with the end time and in verse 19 we are told that it deals with the last end of the indignation. So Antiochus becomes a type of the Antichrist who will also for a time befriend the nation of Israel, but then in his wrath and fury, he will descend upon the Holy Land, will capture Jerusalem, desecrate the Temple and set up his image in the place where God alone was to be honored; and as a result of this we find that exactly three and one-half years are determined until he shall be brought to an ignominious end. This corresponds to the twelve hundred and sixty days in Revelation, the time, the times and the half a time; it corresponds to the forty-two months, and exact period of time during which Israel shall pass through the fires of the Great Tribulation in fulfillment of this type, then to be ended by the return of the Lord

A great deal of misunderstanding concerning the twenty-three hundred days comes from the fact that it has not been literally translated from the original. The word "day," in Daniel 8:14, is literally "evening morn-

ing," the same expression which is used in the first
chapter of Genesis where we read "And the evening
and the morning were the first day," and "the second
day." Now this is significant, for it is God's own commentary on the fact that these are literal days. If they
are not literal days, then the days of Genesis, chapter
one, are not literal either. So we have the record here
of the literal days. This is borne out by Daniel 8:26,
where we read:

> And the vision of the evening and the morning which was
> told is true.

That is, these were two thousand three hundred even-
ings and mornings, the Biblical expression for a literal
day of twenty-four hours, and it is corroborated and em-
phasized again in the twenty-sixth verse.

All of this is history and stands as mute evidence to
the infallible testimony and accuracy of the Word of
God. But, my friend, these are typical prophecies. We
believe that we are on the very threshold now of the
return of the Lord Jesus Christ, when He Himself will
come to take His Church out, and then we shall have
the fulfillment of all of this prophetic picture in the day
of the Tribulation which we take up in greater detail
when we come to the ninth and the tenth chapters of the
book of Daniel. Before closing this particular chapter,
may I again ask you, "Are you ready to meet the Lord
Jesus Christ when He comes?" All of these things have
been written in order that we may know that God has
a plan and a program. We believe that the next thing
in the program of God is the return of the Lord Jesus
Christ, to take out every believer unto Himself, and then
to pour out His wrath and indignation upon a Christ-
rejecting and God-dishonoring world.

CHAPTER TWENTY-FOUR

Daniel's Prayer of Repentance

> Seventy weeks are determined upon thy people and upon
> thy holy city, to finish the transgression, and to make an
> end of sins, and to make reconciliation for iniquity, and to
> bring in everlasting righteousness, and to seal up the vision
> and prophecy, and to anoint the most Holy (Daniel 9:24).

The ninth chapter of the book of Daniel contains
first the prayer of Daniel to the Lord in regard to His
people, Israel, who were at that time in captivity, away
from their land and away from the city of the Lord,
Jerusalem. The second part of the chapter contains
the answer of God to the prayer of confession which is
in the first part, and in this answer we find that God
gives Daniel what probably constitutes one of the most
important prophetic revelations found in the entire
Bible. Nowhere do we find a key to the program of God
which is so clear and so fool-proof as we have in this
revelation of God to Daniel concerning the seventy
weeks, determined upon the nation of Israel and the
holy city of Jerusalem. Someone has called this seventy
weeks the framework of all Bible prophecy. If we have
this framework established properly, then we shall have

no difficulty in fitting in all the details and putting in all the rest of the parts as revealed in the different passages of Scripture.

But, before taking up the wonderful teaching of the seventy weeks of Daniel's prophecy, we must give some attention to the background and the foundation as found in the first part of this chapter, that we may better understand and appreciate the prophetic part when we come to it. You will notice from the first verse that this vision was given sometime later than the vision which we studied in chapter 8. It is declared to be in the first year of Darius, the son of Ahasuerus, that is, very soon after the fall of the Babylonian empire and the ascension of Darius, the king of the Medes and Persians. Now Daniel, by this time, was an old man. He had survived the reign of Nebuchadnezzar, and of his son Belshazzar, and was now in the reign of Darius. Daniel was probably a man past seventy years of age and during all of this time he had not denied the Lord. It is interesting to note that Daniel himself was a great student of the Scriptures, and this in itself will account for much of the revelation which God was pleased to give to him, for it is an inviolable principle that the more we study God's revelation, the more God gives us of His revelation. The more we exercise ourselves in knowing His will, the more He reveals His will to us. So we read this most interesting notation:

> In the first year of his reign I Daniel understood by books the number of the years, whereof the word of the Lord came to Jeremiah the prophet, that he would accomplish seventy years in the desolations of Jerusalem (Daniel 9:2).

Daniel, in all of these years, had been very diligently studying as much of the Word of God as was written at that time. In particular he had been studying the proph-

ecy of Jeremiah, and there he had found something
very encouraging and exceedingly interesting. In his
study of the prophecy of Jeremiah he had come to read
the eleventh and twelfth verses of the twenty-fifth chapter of the prophecy, where it states:

> And this whole land [referring to the land of Palestine]
> shall be a desolation, and an astonishment; and these nations
> shall serve the king of Babylon seventy years. And it shall
> come to pass, when seventy years are accomplished, that
> I will punish the king of Babylon, and that nation, saith
> the Lord, for their iniquity, and the land of the Chaldeans,
> and will make it perpetual desolations.

Here was a definite prophetic statement made a long
time before it was really accomplished, that after seventy
years of captivity the Lord would return Judah again
unto their own land. This was in confirmation of another
prophecy given way back in the book of Leviticus even
before Israel had entered the land. This passage was
undoubtedly one which Daniel had also read and had
taken note of very carefully. In this interesting passage
given by Moses, we have the following prophecy:

> And I will scatter you among the heathen, and will draw
> out a sword after you: and your land shall be desolate, and
> your cities waste. Then shall the land enjoy her sabbaths, as
> long as it lieth desolate, and ye be in your enemies' land:
> even then shall the land rest, and enjoy her sabbaths (Levit-
> icus 26:33-34).

Now it is a matter of history, a matter of record, that
the children of Israel had been in the land of Palestine
from the occupation of the land up until the time of the
captivity, "exactly four hundred and ninety years."
That was seventy sevens, a number which will be well
for us to remember in our study of the seventy weeks
of Daniel. The Lord had commanded Israel that one

year out of each seven should be holy unto the Lord; it
was a year in which they were not to sow any of their
fields, but were to allow that which grew up of itself
to come forth, and the Lord promised that He would
give them enough from the first six years to carry them
over the seventh year, and into the eighth. That was
God's purpose concerning the sabbatic year. Every
seventh year was to be a sabbatic year unto the Lord.
But the nation, in its greed and in its unbelief, refused
to observe this sabbatic year, and for four hundred and
ninety years they did not allow the land to rest one
year out of seven, but cultivated it continuously, with the
result that at the end of the four hundred and ninety
years the land had become drained of its fertility and
had become more or less desolate, and God said He would
carry away the children of Israel into a strange land
until the seventy sabbatic years which they had neglected
should have been made up. That is the meaning of the
passage in Leviticus 26:34:

> Then shall the land enjoy her sabbaths, as long as it lieth
> desolate, and ye be in your enemies' land: even then shall
> the land rest, and enjoy her sabbaths.

It is well to bear this in mind. Undoubtedly Daniel
recognized that these seventy long years were now coming to an end. That this is the reason is evident from
Leviticus 26:35 where we read:

> As long as it lieth desolate it shall rest; because it did
> not rest in your sabbaths, when ye dwelt upon it.

So Daniel knew from the study of the Scriptures that
seventy years were determined upon Jerusalem, and
that at the end of this seventy years it would be time for
them to return again to the Promised Land and to the
worship in Jerusalem.

I am glad we have this record in Daniel concerning his study of the Word of God, because in these days when the Bible is so neglected and ignorance is so widespread concerning the will of Almighty God, we need to be reminded that Daniel's God still lives. God knows all things beforehand, and therefore could predict and reveal just what would happen. Daniel believed this. He believed that after seventy years Israel would return, and nothing could prevent it, for God had said it, and God cannot lie.

But there is another thing which is evident here, and that is that even though Daniel believed in the sovereign program and purpose of God, that at the end of seventy years God would fulfill His promise, he was not a fatalist. He did not sit down and say that whatever is to be is predestinated and, since everything has all been planned, it makes no difference what I do whatsoever. But when Daniel saw the program, even though he believed it to be the unchangeable program of God, he immediately began to do something about it. He began to pray, and so we read:

> And I set my face unto the Lord God, to seek by prayer and supplications, with fasting, and sackcloth, and ashes: and I prayed unto the Lord my God, and made my confession (Daniel 9:3-4).

Something we need to emphasize is our part in response to God's program. God's program *is* fixed, and unchangeable, but we have a responsibility nevertheless. Failure to accept both God's sovereign will, and man's responsibility, has caused a fatalistic outlook upon life, even among those who profess to be following the Lord Jesus Christ. There are those who see only God's sovereignty and not man's responsibility, but both are in the Bible. We may not be able to understand it, but we are expected to believe it. To see only God's part, and ignore our own, can only lead to an unscriptural fatalism. We who recognize that God is sovereign in all His dealings must also recognize the fact that, though we might not be able to reconcile it, we do have a personal responsibility to the Lord God in all of these matters. And so when Daniel recognized the fact that the time was almost up according to God's Word for the deliverance of Jerusalem as he had read in the prophecy of Jeremiah, and had studied from the book of Leviticus, he immediately begins to do something about it so that He may be in God's will and be in a position where God can reveal Himself to him and he may receive the maximum of blessing. As a result of his study of the Word of God, God first of all revealed to Daniel the cause of the plight of his nation, namely, sin. Then God revealed to him a plan of redemption for the nation according to that which He had said through the prophets of old. First of all, please notice that Daniel had a revelation of his sin, and as a result of that he began to pray.

Daniel's Confession

Daniel was a sinner, and no one knew it better than Daniel himself. Daniel was not a man who claimed for himself holiness and infallibility, but was the first to acknowledge that he, though one of the most wonderful characters in the entire Scriptures, was a sinner who deserved the wrath of Almighty God and could only throw himself upon the mercy of the Almighty. Let me remind you that this record of Daniel's prayer and Daniel's confession is his own record and is part of his own acknowledgment of sin in which he takes his place together with the rest of the nation of Israel as being utterly unworthy in the sight of Almighty God. In this fact the Bible is different from any other book which has ever been written, for the Bible is the only book in the world that treats every one of its characters without bias, without prejudice and without favor. Each character is fairly dealt with. God does not shield His saints, nor does He justify the sinners, but He gives us the picture of each man as he actually is. While the Lord tells of the faith of Noah, He also tells us of his drunkenness toward the end of his life. While God tells us of the wonderful faith of the man Abraham, He does not hesitate to relate to us the lack of faith and trust of Abraham, and his many mistakes as recorded in the book of Genesis. While the Lord tells us that David was a man after God's own heart, He does not fail to tell us also of his sin and immorality and the murder he committed, all of which are blots upon the record of the history of this man. That is characteristic of the Word of God. It gives a fair and an unbiased picture of all its characters.

It is quite different with the biographies and autobiographies of men. I read just recently a biography of a very great Christian man whom the Lord used in a wonderful, marvelous and unusual way, but from the beginning to the end of that book, the biographer had not related one single fault or flaw in the character of the person whose life he was relating for us. As far as that biography was concerned, this man was perfect, this man was without flaw, and according to this record did not need the grace of God, for he himself could stand upon his own merits and upon his own works. I am sure that the person whose biography this author was setting down would be the last one to claim anything of the kind and would probably be very angry that

such a one-sided picture had been presented--a picture
wherein only his virtues and his success and his goodness and his good works had been magnified. The Bible
is not such a book. We find that the Bible deals
thoroughly and fairly and even gives the devil his due.
The record in Daniel 9 is a striking example of this.
Daniel is often pointed to by Bible scholars as the one
man in Scripture concerning whom no evil is recorded.
He and Joseph were probably the only two heroes in
the entire Bible about whom very little or nothing of
evil is recorded. And yet the statement that nothing is
recorded concerning Daniel as derogatory to him or
which records any fault or flaw or sin is quite wrong and
without any foundation. Daniel himself has given us the
record as we have it in this chapter. Let me repeat, that
Daniel would have been the last person in the world
to claim for himself any perfection or holiness. On the
contrary, his prayer is filled with confession and repentance and in it he identifies himself with the people
of God in their sin. Read his own words:

> And I prayed unto the Lord my God, and made my con-
> fession, and said, O Lord, the great and dreadful God, keep-
> ing the covenant and mercy to them that love him, and to
> them that keep his commandments; we have sinned, and
> have committed iniquity, and have done wickedly, and have
> rebelled, even by departing from thy precepts and from thy
> judgments: neither have we hearkened unto thy servants the
> prophets (Daniel 9:4-6).

And then in the eighth verse:

> O Lord, to us belongeth confusion of face, to our kings,
> to our princes, and to our fathers, because we have sinned
> against thee.

The tenth verse:

> Neither have we obeyed the voice of the Lord our God,
> to walk in his laws.

And again in the eleventh verse he cries out:

> We have sinned against him.

Again we read in the thirteenth verse:

> . . . this evil is come upon us: yet made we not our prayer before the Lord our God, that we might turn from our iniquities.

Also in the fifteenth verse it says:

> We have sinned, we have done wickedly.

And all through Daniel's prayer the bulk of it has to do with confession of sin and his humiliation. I am glad that this record is here, because Daniel is probably the outstanding saint of the Old Testament. Apart from this ninth chapter which contains his own personal confession, Daniel seems to have been outwardly perfect in his moral and business life, in his personal and domestic life, in his civil life and in his obedience to the powers that be. Daniel was the last man to claim any merit of his own because he lived so close to God that he recognized what an unworthy creature he was, and could only throw himself upon the mercy of Almighty God.

The more holy a man is, the more he will be conscious of his unholiness. The more a man realizes his awful sin, the more humble he will be in the sight of God. What we need today, if we are to know the will of God and be ready for His revelation and for the coming of His Son, is a sense of our own unworthiness. It will not do for us to strut and claim our perfection and exalt our goodness and in pride lift up ourselves as being better than others. Our only hope lies in facing the fact of our own sin, our national sin and our personal sin, and in confessing it faithfully and humbly before the Lord.

God grant that we may learn the lesson which Daniel had learned so well, after studying the Word of God. Daniel knew that he was absolutely unworthy and that God's mercy was his only hope, and so he concludes his prayer with these words:

O Lord, hear; O Lord, forgive; O Lord, hearken and do; defer not, for thine own sake, O my God: for thy city and thy people are called by thy name ((Daniel 9:19).

God help us to learn the great secret of confession of sin and cleansing.

If we confess our sins, he is faithful and just to forgive us our sins, and to cleanse us from all unrighteousness (I John 1:9).

CHAPTER TWENTY-FIVE

How God Answers Prayer

> Seventy weeks are determined upon thy people and upon thy holy city, to finish the transgression, and to make an end of sins, and to make reconciliation for iniquity, and to bring in everlasting righteousness, and to seal up the vision and prophecy, and to anoint the most Holy (Daniel 9:24).

The ninth chapter of the prophecy of Daniel has frequently been referred to as the very backbone and skeleton of all Bible prophecy, by which we mean that it contains the framework, the general outline, around which all other prophecy is built. If we err in our understanding of the seventy weeks, we shall err in all the rest of prophetic truth. If we have the proper interpretation of the seventieth week of Daniel, we shall have no difficulty in fitting all the rest of prophetic revelation into the general scheme and pattern which God has laid down throughout the Scriptures. We are, therefore, going to give considerable time to the study of the revelation concerning the seventy weeks which, according to our key-verse, is determined upon Daniel's people, Israel.

You will recall that in the first part of the chapter we have Daniel's lengthy prayer of confession and humilia-

tion before Almighty God. He recognizes the fact that
the sad plight of his people, including himself, is due to
their sins and the righteous judgment of God upon the
nation. But Daniel not only recognized the fact that sin
was the cause of all their distress, but he recognized
another thing, and that is that God is merciful, slow to
anger and of great pity, and is willing to forgive those
who in humility come and confess their sins. It will do
no good to try to justify ourselves. It does not help to
alleviate the troubles that beset us to claim our own merit
and boast of our own holiness. Our hope, like Daniel's
hope, lies only in this: we must confess our sin, admit
our own unworthiness, and cast ourselves completely
and wholly and unreservedly upon the mercy and the
long-suffering of God.

It is refreshing to note that Daniel pleads on the basis
of the promises of Almighty God. This is a point that
we cannot overemphasize. As we have reminded you before, Daniel had been studying the Scriptures and he
found in them the promise that after Israel had been
sent away captive into the land of Babylon, at the end
of seventy years their captivity would end and they would
be returned again to the land of Palestine. All of this
was recorded not only in the book of Leviticus, but was
very definitely stated in the term "seventy years" used
repeatedly by Jeremiah the prophet. When Daniel found
these promises of Almighty God in the Word of God, he
immediately began to claim them, and began to insist
that God, who cannot lie, must keep His promise to him,
and in his confession he again and again refers to this
promise which God Himself has made. Oh, how we need
to learn that lesson today! We must base our pleas
on the promises of God, not on our righteousness, not
on our goodness, not on our merits, not on our religion,

not on our good works—but only on the promises of God. This is evident from the very outset of the prayer of Daniel. In the opening sentence, we read:

> And I prayed unto the Lord my God, and made my confession, and said, O Lord, the great and dreadful God, keeping the covenant and mercy to them that love him, and to them that keep his commandments (Daniel 9:4).

That was the plea, the basis, on which Daniel made his petition to the Lord; not in self-righteousness, not in bitterness, but in humble confession of his unworthiness, he pleaded for the mercy in the promises of Almighty God. We have the same thing again in the close of his prayer. He says in the eighteenth verse:

> . . . for we do not present our supplications before thee for our righteousnesses, but for thy great mercies.

And so we have the interesting and valuable lesson that Daniel, though he recognized his unworthiness, found comfort in the fact that God keeps covenant and keeps His word.

Maybe some of you who read these words are discouraged because of your sins and failures and probably, because of your misunderstanding of the love of God, imagine that there is no hope for you. Then remember that God's mercy is everlasting, that His longsuffering and His kindness are still extended to you and that, if you are willing to meet His conditions, believe on His promises and trust His Word, you too may find the deliverance for which Daniel prayed and which the nation received, and which is open to every child of God. Not in vain has the Lord told us in I John 1:9 that "if we confess our sins, he is faithful and just to forgive us our sins, and to cleanse us from all unrighteousness." I believe that is a verse which ought to be repeated over and over and over again in the ears of God's people everywhere. There are no conditions laid down at all, no strings tied to this promise, except that we confess our sins. And may I repeat, though it may seem that we repeat it too often, that our hope is not in trying to justify ourselves, not in claiming our own holiness, not in going about boasting about our righteousness, but in confessing our sin in humility, acknowledging our utter unworthiness, and then pleading only on the promises of God that if we confess, He forgives and cleanses from all unrighteousness.

This is very humiliating for the natural man. Man likes to exalt his own goodness, he likes to boast of his own good works, he likes to strut about telling about his own achievements, but the closer we walk with God, the nearer we come to understanding the heart of Almighty God, the more we feel our complete and utter unworthiness in His sight. We shall see in our subsequent studies of Daniel, how this thing was further illustrated in his life, that when he met the revelation of the holiness of God, he became as a dead man. John, too, when he saw the Lord Jesus Christ, fell down as one dead (Revelation 1:17). Isaiah, when he stood before the flaming holiness of Almighty God, called out, "Woe is me . . . because I am a man of unclean lips, and I dwell in the midst of a people of unclean lips." It is a good rule to be remembered at all times that the more we understand holiness, the more we abhor and admit our sin. The more we understand true holiness, the more we will recognize our own sinfulness and unworthiness and the more eager we will be to cast ourselves upon the mercy of God and plead for His holiness and not our own.

God Answers Prayer

In response to Daniel's humble confession of sin, and his petition to the Almighty, God sent the angel Gabriel in a swift answer to the prophet Daniel. We have the record in Daniel 9:20:

> And whiles I was speaking, and praying, and confessing my sin and the sin of my people . . .

I want to stop here for a moment and show you that Daniel was not confessing only the sin of his people and losing himself in the crowd. It says here, ''I was speaking, and praying, and confessing *my* sin and the sin of my people Israel.'' It is very easy for us to admit that we are sinners, that all have sinned, that we are a sinful people, that we are a fallen race, that we are a sinning nation, but when it comes to a personal confession, that is not always so easy. Daniel, who stood head and shoulders above all of us, I am sure, as far as the record of his life is concerned, could say that he was confessing *his own* sin, and we need to put the personal pronoun into *our* confession, not into our boasting, and to say, ''I have sinned.'' I believe these three words are the hardest three words in any language for anyone ever to say—to say, ''I have sinned. I was wrong. I have done wrong. I was in the wrong.'' These, I repeat, are difficult words for any individual to say. Yet I am convinced, that 95 per cent and probably more, probably 100 per cent of all the spiritual troubles of God's people could be alleviated if men would only learn to say, ''I have sinned before Almighty God.'' And I am also convinced that practically all of the ills of humanity which vex people and which separate men and women, nations and communities and churches, husbands and wives, fathers and sons, mothers and daughters, brothers and sisters could be corrected immediately if they were only willing to say, "*I am to blame. I was wrong*. It was all my fault. I have sinned." Let me leave this with you as a very practical instruction. Probably you are having difficulty now. Probably there is a great rift between you and a loved one, probably your home is threatened with disruption, probably calamity is threatening in your domestic life or in your business life. Let me give you this remedy as a spiritual physician. Learn to say, "It is my fault. I was wrong. I was to blame." You will see that many of the difficulties which now cause you such heartache and distress would be immediately removed and peace and joy and tranquillity would be restored. God help us to learn to say, "It was my fault. I made my confession. I have sinned." We have many examples of this truth throughout the Word of God.

Among the many examples that we might cite, we take the case of king David. His record, that is his moral record, does not make very good reading. He was a man who stretched forth his hand to take another man's wife, and then to cover up his sin, committed murder. Now certainly we would hardly expect such a man as David to be called a man after God's own heart, and yet that is exactly what he is called in the Scriptures. It was not because he had done these things—God never condones evil; God punishes evil and God punished David in a very, very definite way—but David was called the man after God's own heart because he had learned to say, " I *have sinned*." Let us take another example from the New Testament. You remember the story of the prodigal who left his father's house and spent everything that he had in riotous living. He was restored and received again into the fellowship and the wealth of his

father's home only when he had learned to say just
three words, "I *have sinned.*" I trust we have not
occupied too much time in emphasizing this truth. We
have done so only because we are convinced from the
depth of our heart that many of you who read this message can solve the problems which right now are vexing
you more than anything else, if you are willing to humble
yourselves, go to the loved one, friend or member of
your family, and say the thing that you have been too
proud to say all the time, "I was wrong. It was my fault.
I have sinned. Will you forgive me?" Try it, my friends,
and see if it works. Then, if it does not work, I have
been wrong in what I have been preaching to you, but I
am sure that if you are willing to follow this formula
which Daniel had learned, and by which he had become
the object of God's unusual favor and revelation, you
will find that it will work in your own life as well.

But what is true of your relationship with your fellow
man and with your loved ones, in your home and among
your friends, is especially true of your relationship to
Almighty God. If there is a breach in your fellowship,
and you have lost your joy and your power and your
fruitfulness and your testimony, and you are not happy
as you used to be in the service of the Lord and your
song is gone, then listen, my friend, when I tell you that
it is no one else's fault but your own. There is sin in
your life, whatever that sin may be. Certainly it is not
God's fault, and what someone else does should not in
any way interfere with your fellowship with your Lord.
Your only solution is to make a frank diagnosis and
confess your sin, and say "I have sinned." Then make
your plea on the promise of Almighty God that "if we
confess our sins, he is faithful and just to forgive us
our sins, and to cleanse us from all unrighteousness."

How God Answers Prayer

When we meet God's condition, even as Daniel did, the answer of God is not only sure, but it is also very, very swift, for we read:

> Yea, whiles I was speaking in prayer, even the man Gabriel, whom I had seen in the vision at the beginning, being caused to fly swiftly, touched me about the time of the evening oblation. And he informed me, and talked with me, and said, O Daniel, I am now come forth to give thee skill and understanding (Daniel 9:21-22).

While Daniel was speaking, the angel Gabriel was there. Now we know from the preceding chapters that it takes time for angels to travel. They are not omnipresent as Almighty God is; they are still creatures. And so Gabriel had been sent long before Daniel had finished his petition. Daniel never finished his prayer at all; he had to interrupt it and stop it. There is no "Amen" at the end of Daniel's prayer because, before he was through, God was already there with the answer.

There is another little touch in verse 21 which I would like to mention in passing, and that is that the angel Gabriel touched Daniel at about the time of the evening oblation. That was the time of the regular daily sacrifice. Of course, there was no sacrifice being offered in Babylon where he was. The sacrifices in Jerusalem had been discontinued, but Daniel, even though there was no actual sacrificing going on, still observed the time that God has instituted, the time of day when the sacrifice was to be offered. During that time he was upon his face before Almighty God, still continuing his regular habit of prayer and still spiritually sacrificing unto the Lord God, and it was at this time that the angel Gabriel came. Now notice the message that the angel brings:

At the beginning of thy supplications the commandment
came forth, and I am come to shew thee; for thou art greatly
beloved: therefore understand the matter, and consider the
vision (Daniel 9:23).

And then follows the vision of the seventy weeks of
Daniel which, as we said at the beginning of this chapter,
is the very backbone and the skeleton of prophecy. Before reading the next chapter in which we shall deal
with these seventy weeks in detail, it might be well to
read again, very, very carefully, the ninth chapter of the
book of Daniel, and to acquaint yourself thoroughly and
completely with all of its particulars so that you will
have the facts clearly in mind. But now, before we close
this chapter, may I again emphasize what I have been
trying to say in regard to the prayer life of Daniel,
that probably no greater evil has ever beset any of
God's people than the evil of spiritual pride. Not only
by that do I mean that we are not conscious of our sin,
but that we are too proud to confess our sin. And I
would like to press home again, though it may seem like
needless repetition, the necessity of examining our lives
at this very moment and finding what it is that is hinder-
ing the fellowship and the joy and the communion not
only with God, but with God's people, and then taking
the onus and the blame ourselves, and being willing to
say, "I have sinned." Try it, my friend, and see what
a blessing will come into your life as you confess your
sin and trust God to forgive your sin.

CHAPTER TWENTY-SIX

The Seventieth Week of Daniel

Seventy weeks are determined upon thy people and upon thy holy city (Daniel 9:24).

In considering the important subject of the seventieth week of Daniel's prophecy we want to call your attention to the first part of the twenty-fourth verse of the ninth chapter, "Seventy weeks are determined upon thy people and upon thy holy city." The first thing that I want you to notice before we take up the actual meaning of the weeks is that this is a prophecy concerning something that is coming to pass which cannot be changed. The weeks are "determined"; they are all set and fixed and planned by Almighty God and therefore there can be no changes. The second thing I want you to notice is that whatever this seventy weeks means, it has to deal with the people of Israel, the city of Jerusalem and the land of Palestine. That is very definite, for we are told that these weeks are determined upon "thy people," referring to Daniel, Daniel's people, the nation of Israel; and upon "thy holy city," referring to the capital of the land of Palestine, the city of Jerusalem.

Now if you will bear these two things in mind, I think it will help you a great deal in understanding the expression, "seventy weeks." What God says here through the angel Gabriel, is that His dealings with the children of Israel, His covenant nation, will cover a period of seventy weeks until the setting up of the kingdom, or as it is put up in verse 24, "to finish the transgression, and to make an end of sins, and to make reconciliation for iniquity, and to bring in everlasting righteousness." So we have the definite statement here, whatever the meaning of these seventy weeks may be, that it is the period of time in which God is going to deal with the nation of Israel and with the land of Palestine up until the time of bringing in everlasting righteousness, which is, of course, the establishment of the Messianic kingdom at the Second Coming of the Lord Jesus Christ.

The expression, seventy weeks, means literally "seventy sevens" and has reference to years. It was customary in oriental language among the children of Israel to speak of seven years as a week. That was a common expression among them. And so we have the weeks of years, and taking that interpretation here we find that Daniel is told that seventy sevens, or seventy periods of seven years each, are determined upon the nation of Israel, until the Lord Jesus Christ will set up His glorious kingdom upon the earth. The word translated as "weeks" may be translated either as sevens or as weeks, since a week consists of seven days and is called a week and therefore the same expression is used.

However, we find in other passages of Scripture that a period of seven years is also called a week. Notable among these passages is one which is found in the twenty-ninth chapter of the book of Genesis. In this chapter, you will recall, Jacob, who had been working for Laban, his uncle, falls in love with Rachel, the daughter of Laban. He had made a bargain with Laban that he was to work for seven years and at the end of the seven years he was to receive Rachel as his wife. But the scheming Laban had other plans, and so when the wedding day came, he gave Leah, the sister of Rachel, to be the wife of Jacob, instead of Rachel for whom he had been laboring. This was a very clever ruse because Laban knew that Jacob loved Rachel more than anything else. And so he makes a bargain with Jacob and says, ''Why don't you just continue to work another seven years for me here, and I will give you Rachel immediately to be your wife?'' Concerning this bargain we read this account:

> And Laban said, It must not be so done in our country, to give the younger before the firstborn (Genesis 29:26).

Now notice very carefully:

> Fulfil her week [seven years], and we will give thee this also for the service which thou shalt serve with me yet seven other years (Genesis 29:27).

Here we have a striking example of the fact that a period of seven years is called a week. Now with that in mind, notice that the angel Gabriel reveals to Daniel that seventy weeks, seventy periods of seven years, are going to be needed to fulfill God's program with His people Israel. That makes exactly four hundred and ninety years. Remember that figure; from the time of the return of the captivity at the decree to build the Temple at Jerusalem, until the setting up of the millennial kingdom, God's dealings with Israel will cover a period of four hundred and ninety years. Now if you will recall that this prophecy was given over twenty-five hundred years ago and everlasting righteousness has not yet been brought in, and the millennial kingdom has not been ushered in, you will have the key to the understanding of God's dispensational dealings.

THREE DIVISIONS OF TIME

It is a very important fact to remember that God in His dealings with the children of Israel deals in seventy weeks of years; from Abraham to Canaan, interestingly enough, was four hundred and ninety years; from Joshua, that is the possession of the land, to the setting up of the kingdom of Israel in Palestine, was four hundred and ninety years; from the beginning of the kingdom to the captivity was four hundred and ninety years; and from the return of the captivity until the end of God's dealings with His nation Israel will be, according to Daniel 9:24, another four hundred and ninety years. This is the last seventy weeks of God's dealings with Israel before the setting up of the long promised Levitic kingdom. Now this last period of four hundred and ninety years began very soon after Daniel wrote this prophecy, but strangely enough, only sixty-nine of these weeks have been fulfilled. The last one still lies in the future. At the end of the sixty-nine weeks, or four hundred and eighty-three years, the program for Israel was interrupted at the Cross of Calvary, the setting aside of the nation occurred, and the program has been postponed during this entire dispensation, to be resumed only when the Church of the Lord Jesus Christ, the interim purpose of God, has been accomplished and taken to be with her Lord in heaven. Let me repeat that statement. Four hundred and eighty-three of the four hundred and ninety years determined upon the nation of Israel and Jerusalem have been fulfilled and were terminated at the crucifixion of the Lord Jesus Christ.

Then God began to deal with the Church, and Israel as a nation was set aside and the kingdom postponed until God's purpose for the Church has been fully accomplished, and she shall be taken out and God will begin dealing with Israel for the last and the closing week of the seventy weeks of Daniel. Now you will notice that the seventy weeks are divided into three parts: the first section lasted for seven weeks, or forty-nine years; the second part of it lasted for sixty-two weeks, or four hundred and thirty-four years; that leaves the last one of these weeks, the seventieth week, seven years, still unfulfilled, even up to this present time. You will find it recorded as follows:

> Know therefore and understand, that from the going forth of the commandment to restore and to build Jerusalem unto the Messiah the Prince shall be seven weeks, and threescore and two weeks: the street shall be built again, and the wall, even in troublous times. And after threescore and two weeks shall Messiah be cut off, but not for himself (Daniel 9:25-26).

Please notice that we have first of all a period of seven weeks, or forty-nine years. Now we know exactly when the four hundred and ninety years began, when the seventy weeks of Daniel began, for we are told in this verse that from the going forth of the commandment to restore and to build Jerusalem unto the Messiah Prince shall be seven weeks, and threescore and two weeks. In other words, from the going forth of the commandment to rebuild Jerusalem, until the time of the crucifixion of the Lord Jesus Christ will be exactly four hundred and eighty-three years. History confirms this, that from that time until the crucifixion of Christ was exactly four hundred and eighty-three years.

Now if you will turn to Nehemiah 2:1, you will have

the exact date given to the very year, when the command to rebuild Jerusalem was made. Nehemiah, one of the captives of Israel, had been employed in the service of the king in the palace of Shushan; note his words carefully:

> And it came to pass in the month Nisan, in the twentieth year of Artaxerxes the king, that wine was before him: and I took up the wine, and gave it unto the king.

Now here we have Nehemiah serving in the palace of the king, and we are told it was in the month of Nisan, which was April, and that it was the twentieth year of Artaxerxes the king. The record goes on to show how Nehemiah made a request of the king that he might be permitted to go to the city of his fathers, Jerusalem, the land of Palestine, and there rebuild the Temple and the wall and again set up the glory and splendor of the Temple worship. A decree was issued by Artaxerxes as recorded in this second chapter of Nehemiah, and he with a company of others left to rehabilitate the city of Jerusalem and to rebuild the Temple. Now history fixes the date of the twentieth year of Artaxerxes' reign as 445 B.C., so that it corresponds exactly, to the very year, with the seventy weeks of Daniel's prophecy. The first seven weeks, or forty-nine years of the seventy, were to be occupied in rebuilding the temple under Nehemiah and Zerubbabel and Ezra, the priest. This is given in Daniel 9:25:

> . . . the street shall be built again, and the wall, even in troublous times.

It is a matter of history that the rebuilding of the walls of Jerusalem and the Temple and all of the streets, and so forth, took exactly forty-nine years, fulfilling the first division of the seventy weeks of Daniel which was up to the completion of the Temple in the city of Jerusalem. Then, from that period on, we are told there would be sixty-two weeks, or four hundred and thirty-four years, and we know also from the record that this takes us up to the crucifixion of the Lord Jesus Christ. The record states, "And after threescore and two weeks shall Messiah be cut off, but not for himself," that is, after four hundred and thirty-four years from the rebuilding of the Temple, the Messiah, which refers of course to the Lord Jesus Christ, shall be cut off; that is, He was crucified, but not for Himself, for His death was in the place of others. And then after the crucifixion of the Lord Jesus Christ the city of Jerusalem was to be destroyed and trodden under foot, and the verse goes on to say:

And the people of the prince that shall come.

Now the prince that shall come is the Antichrist. Of course, he did not come at that time, but it says here, the *people* of the prince; that is, those who represented world dominion and power, the spirit of this age which entered the nations in their rebellion against Almighty God, would come and destroy the city and the sanctuary. This, too, is a matter of history. In 70 A.D. we know that Titus, the Roman, swept down upon the land of Palestine and destroyed the city and the sanctuary, and carried away the rest of the children of Israel as captives into all the lands of the world. God stopped His dealings, naturally, with the nation at the crucifixion of the Lord Jesus Christ, and we are told that from the time of the destruction of Jerusalem, "the end thereof shall be with a flood," and unto the end of this age, until the seventieth week shall be resumed, wars and desolation are determined.

So we notice that two things are determined. First in verse 24, seventy weeks are determined upon Israel, and it is also determined that until the end of this dispensation wars and desolation, and not a Utopian millennium, will be ushered in. The picture, then, becomes perfectly plain. Sixty-nine weeks have been fulfilled from the commandment to restore and rebuild Jerusalem up until the crucifixion of the Lord Jesus Christ. Then God began to deal with the Church, calling out a Bride for His Son, the Lord Jesus Christ; Israel, as it were, is sidetracked for the present and then God will resume His national dealings in the last week still unfulfilled, when the Church of the Lord Jesus Christ is raptured. Now all of this is corroborated by the rest of the Scripture. We read, for instance, concerning the prince that shall come, that is the Antichrist:

> And he shall confirm the covenant with many for one week: and in the midst of the week he shall cause the sacrifice and the oblation to cease, and for the overspreading of abominations he shall make it desolate (Daniel 9:27).

Now here we have the statement that the Antichrist will make an agreement and a pact and a covenant with the nation of Israel to last one week, or a period of seven years which corresponds to the Tribulation Period, but in the midst of that period he will set up the abomination of desolation which we have already pointed out will be when he sets up the image of the beast as we see it in Revelation thirteen, in the Temple of Jerusalem, and tries to force all to pay homage to and bow in worship before this image of the beast. Moreover, the Lord Jesus Christ tells us without a question of doubt that this shall take place in the Tribulation Period. In referring to it, He says in Matthew 24:15:

When ye therefore shall see the abomination of desolation, spoken of by Daniel the prophet, stand in the holy place.

Here we have the Lord Jesus Christ referring to this same incident in the middle of the week, and then follows the instruction of the Lord for them to flee into the mountains and to be ready for the time of the Great Tribulation. Now, if this abomination is set up in the middle of the week, it means that three and one-half years precede its setting up, and three and one-half years will follow its setting up, and that is exactly what the Word of God tells us. In Revelation 11, concerning the two witnesses which shall testify during the last half of the Tribulation Period, we are told that Jerusalem is given unto the Gentiles and the Holy City shall be trodden under foot "forty and two months," that is a half a week, three and one-half years. Then in the third verse we read:

And I will give power unto my two witnesses, and they shall prophesy a thousand two hundred and threescore days [three and one-half years].

In the twelfth chapter of Revelation we are told that Israel will be protected by the Lord during this time for a time, and times and half a time, again three and one-half years, the last half of the Tribulation Period. Concerning the beast, Revelation 13:5 states:

And there was given unto him a mouth speaking great things and blasphemies; and power was given unto him to continue forty and two months.

Now with all this evidence of the Scriptures I trust that you will be able to see what God meant to reveal to Daniel. There are seventy weeks during which God will deal with Israel; the first sixty-nine expired at the crucifixion of the Lord Jesus Christ; at the Rapture of the Church, God will continue the last week, and this week we call the Tribulation Period. The last part of it, the last half of it, is called the Great Tribulation.

May I again ask you if you are ready to meet the Lord Jesus Christ? If He should come today, would you be prepared to meet Him in the air? If your answer is "yes," you will escape the terror and suffering of the Great Tribulation.

CHAPTER TWENTY-SEVEN

Angels and Demons

Then I lifted up mine eyes, and looked, and behold a certain man clothed in linen, whose loins were girded with fine gold of Uphaz: His body also was like the beryl, and his face as the appearance of lightning, and his eyes as lamps of fire, and his arms and his feet like in colour to polished brass, and the voice of his words like the voice of a multitude (Daniel 10:5-6).

The tenth chapter of the prophecy of Daniel is an interlude just preceding the final revelation which God was to give Daniel concerning the history of His own beloved people, the nation of Israel, during the end time, and especially during the period of the Great Tribulation. Daniel, as we have seen, had been doing a great deal of thinking and studying concerning the Word of God and the promises which He had made concerning His ancient people, and so we find in the first part of this chapter that Daniel is greatly exercised. The time is the third year of Cyrus the king of Persia. That was after Darius had been the king of Medo-Persia for some time, and as Daniel was thinking and meditating upon these promises of God as given in the other prophecies, we are told that he was mourning three whole weeks. As we have pointed out, Daniel was a man of humility, a man who knew how to confess and recognize his utter unworthiness in the sight of Almighty God. And so during a period of three whole weeks Daniel was exercised concerning the things that God had revealed to him. We read in the third verse:

> I ate no pleasant bread, neither came flesh nor wine in my mouth, neither did I anoint myself at all, till three whole weeks were fulfilled.

And then at the end of those three weeks God begins to reveal Himself to Daniel through the agency of an angelic being. This angelic being who is described in the verses with which we began this chapter was an angel of very, very high rank and order. He is described as a most glorious person clothed with fine gold, his body like a beryl, his face as the appearance of lightning, his eyes as lamps of fire, his arms like the color of polished brass. This immediately reminds us of the description of the Lord Jesus Christ as it is given to us in the book of the Revelation by John, but evidently this was not a theophany, that is, an appearance of the Lord Jesus Christ, which we have in many other parts of the Scriptures, but rather an angel of exceeding beauty and marvelous power and station. That this personage was an angel and not the Lord Jesus Himself is evidenced by verse 13, where we read:

> But the prince of the kingdom of Persia withstood me one and twenty days: but, lo, Michael, one of the chief princes, came to help me; and I remained there with the kings of Persia.

From this passage we learn that the angel who had been sent from heaven to speak to Daniel was opposed in his passage through the realm of the demons, which is the upper atmosphere, and for twenty-one days was hindered so violently and vigorously that he was unable to get through until God dispatched Michael, the archangel, to assist this heavenly messenger in gaining passage through the domain of the evil spirits of Satan, so that he could come with his message to the prophet Daniel.

When this angelic being appeared to Daniel, those who were with Daniel, his companions, did not see the vision of the angel or hear the words and understand that which this angel spoke to him. We read this account:

> And I Daniel alone saw the vision: for the men that were with me saw not the vision; but a great quaking fell upon them, so that they fled to hide themselves. Therefore I was left alone, and saw this great vision (Daniel 10:7-8).

Then after a period of great amazement on the part of Daniel, with his face toward the ground, the heavenly messenger touched him and strengthened him and gave him the message which he was to put down for these latter days for our instruction. We read this record:

> Then said he [that is, this heavenly messenger], Knowest thou wherefore I come unto thee? and now will I return to fight with the prince of Persia: and when I am gone forth, lo, the prince of Grecia shall come. But I will shew thee that which is noted in the scripture of truth: and there is none that holdeth with me in these things, but Michael your prince (Daniel 10:20-21).

Before taking up the revelation of the vision which is recorded for us in the two closing chapters of Daniel, we want to spend some time on the ministry of the angels, both the work of the angels of God, as well as of the fallen angels, and primarily of that fallen archangel, Lucifer, who became Satan, and whose activity is so evident in the closing vision of the prophecy of Daniel. The ministry of angels is very much misunderstood by the average individual. Of course, the world does not believe at all, like the Sadducees of old, in the ministry of angelic beings, of the spirit beings, of which the Bible has so much to say, but even among Christians we find that there is much confusion, misunderstanding, haziness, concerning the ministry of these spirit beings—a ministry which, I repeat, occupies such a tremendously large place in the Word of God. And so we believe that it will be profitable to spend some time, considerable time if need be, in studying what the Word of God has to say concerning these angelic beings, those who are today attending the work and the ministry of God and the Lord Jesus Christ, as well as those who have sinned and today are fallen angelic beings, usually known as demons, over which Satan, the prince of these demons, is ruling supreme.

We can gain considerable information concerning the ministry of the angels by reading this tenth chapter of the prophecy of Daniel in which we have some very interesting and rather startling information concerning their activity and power and ministry, their station and rank, and the particular purpose for which God uses them. To treat the revelation concerning the angels of God in the Scripture fully would take a great many books, so in the limited space that we have in this book we want to give you rather a sort of an outline which will aid you in studying the subject for yourself. We shall try to condense the teaching of the Word of God as to the main truths and revelations concerning the spirit beings. We shall look at their origin and their number, at the ranks of the various angels and their nature, at their ministry and work. We shall learn how

He guards His own and delivers His saints; how angels are set as watchers to watch over the history of the world. Then there is the comforting truth of the angelic ministry in carrying us home when the time of our departure comes and in gathering God's own people at the Second Coming of the Lord Jesus Christ. And we shall look particularly at the practical aspect of angelic ministry in their present dependence upon God's people as they assemble for worship, as well as in their personal and private lives.

THE ORIGIN OF ANGELS

The Bible is clear in telling us that these angelic spirit beings, invisible to the human eye, were created before God created anything else in the universe. Before the record of the book of Genesis, we have these beings already in existence. When we read in Genesis 1:1, "In the beginning God created the heaven and the earth," we find from the rest of Scripture that the angels were already present, probably before any of them had fallen or had become demons. They were already present and they beheld the grandiose spectacle as God created matter out of nothing and created the world and the stars and the systems and the constellations of the sky. In the book of Job we read concerning these angelic spirits being present at the time of creation:

> Where wast thou when I laid the foundations of the earth? declare, if thou hast understanding. Who hath laid the measures thereof, if thou knowest? or who hath stretched the line upon it? Whereupon are the foundations thereof fastened? or who laid the corner stone thereof; when the morning stars sang together, and all the sons of God shouted for joy? (Job 38:4-7).

Now it is an accepted fact that the morning stars refer to the angels of God and that the expression, "sons of God," in the Old Testament refers to angelic beings. There are many other evidences in the Old Testament concerning this truth. The expression, "sons of God," in the Bible has two meanings. It speaks first of all of the angels who are the sons of God by their first creation. Then we, who have believed on the Lord Jesus Christ, are sons of God by a new creation, by the new birth, by the creation which the Holy Spirit performs within the hearts of those who trust the finished work of the Lord Jesus Christ. It is well to remember and bear this difference in mind. This does not mean that we become by conversion angelic beings, but rather that we become members of the family of Almighty God. So we see that the angels were present at the creation, and were created before the rest of the worlds, as we know them today.

NUMBER OF ANGELS

Although angels are invisible to the human eye, the Bible teaches very definitely that they not only exist, but that they exist in tremendous numbers. We have many, many mentions of them throughout the Scriptures. These references give us some idea of the innumerable company of the angels which had been created by God, not only to attend Him and His Throne, to glorify Him and to sing His praises, but to act as ministers, as servants for those who shall trust and believe on the Lord Jesus Christ as their own personal Saviour. In Daniel 7:10, we read:

> A fiery stream issued and came forth from before him: [of course, this refers to the Lord Jesus Christ Himself, and then we read] thousand thousands ministered unto him, and ten thousand times ten thousand stood before him: the judgment was set, and the books were opened.

Here we have the statement that the number of angels runs into millions and countless millions. There is no word in the Hebrew language for million. They expressed it by saying a thousand thousand, so the expressions here, "thousand thousands," and "ten thousand times ten thousand," mean many, many millions of angelic beings. In Revelation 5:11, we read:

> And I beheld, and I heard the voice of many angels round about the throne and the beasts and the elders: and the number of them was ten thousand times ten thousand, and thousands of thousands.

And Hebrews 12:22 tells us this concerning the numbers of the angels:

> But ye are come unto mount Sion, and unto the city of the living God, the heavenly Jerusalem, and to an innumerable company of angels.

These are also called the armies of heaven. So we have the Bible revelation that around the Throne of God, and undoubtedly circulating throughout the earth in their ministry toward the Church and the people of God, there is an innumerable company of hundreds of millions and millions of angelic beings whose purpose and whose work we want to study.

RANKS OF ANGELS

A further revelation in the Scripture concerning these interesting angelic beings is that they are not all on the same order or on the same plane. There are higher angels and there are lower angels. This is not a matter of perfection, but it is rather a matter of ministry and of work. As there are stars of the first magnitude and stars of the second magnitude, so there are angels who, because of their ministry and work and because of their creation and their calling by God, hold higher positions, different positions, and carry out a different ministry from that of the other angels. Ranks and positions of angels are suggested by a number of passages of Scripture, one of the most clear probably being that which is found in Colossians 1:16:

> For by him [that is, by Christ] were all things created, that are in heaven, and that are in earth, visible and invisible, whether they be thrones, or dominions, or principalities, or powers: all things were created by him, and for him.

The same truth is expressed in Ephesians 1:21, where the same distinction in rank among the angelic beings is suggested. Now some of the angels are called archangels because of the importance of their mission, probably because they have been set over other companies and other ranks of angels. We read, for instance, about Michael, the archangel; Gabriel is considered by a great many to be one of the higher archangels whose business it was particularly to bring messages from heaven to God's people upon the earth. Lucifer himself before he fell and became Satan was one of the angels who had been given a very high position as the guardian of the Throne of God in heaven, as recorded for us in the prophecies of Ezekiel and Isaiah, and then this high angel fell, rebelled against Almighty God, and became Satan and the devil, instead, and with him in his revolt a great host of lesser angelic beings followed and became demons.

It is well to remember that Lucifer is a fallen angel, and that he himself is called Satan because there was only one as highly exalted as he was, but other fallen angels are called demons. They are creatures who at one time were the attendants of the Throne of God, were without sin, and then rebelled and fell from their high position, and today have become the enemies of Christ and are reserved in the blackness and darkness of night forever and ever. To each one of the angels God had given a specific and a definite task. To the angels of high order were reserved duties of great importance, such as bringing messages to the prophets of old, heralding the coming of the Lord Jesus Christ, and also ruling over the other angels that had been placed underneath them.

We also know that in the end, when we shall meet the Lord Jesus Christ, these very beautiful, wonderful angelic beings shall become our servants according to the Word of God, but we ourselves will be higher than the angels. It says in the Bible that we shall judge the angels, and that they are "all ministering spirits, sent forth to minister for them who shall be heirs of salvation." What a wonderful thing it is to be a Christian! What a wonderful thing it is to be a child of God, a member of the family of God, a part of the Bride of the Lord Jesus Christ, so that even these previously created angelic beings will become our servants, and their business throughout eternity will be to minister unto those who do belong unto Him who said, "Come unto me, all ye that labour and are heavy laden, and I will give you rest." At the close of this chapter, may I ask you if you belong to that company who shall be redeemed? Are you a member of the body of Christ? Have you trusted His finished work? Then these angelic beings, denied to be sure, by the world today, nevertheless are God's reserved army for your happiness, your joy and your protection. "Believe on the Lord Jesus Christ, and thou shalt be saved."

CHAPTER TWENTY-EIGHT

The Ministry of Angels

According to the Bible heaven is the place where God dwells. Upon His Throne He is ministered unto by innumerable companies of angels, created spirit beings of great power, great wisdom and great beauty, arranged in various ranks as to the ministry which they are to perform. But the angels are not confined to heaven; their ministry seems to be as wide as the universe itself. What ministry the angels may have on other planets and other bodies of the universe we do not know, but we do know that according to Scripture they have been from the beginning of man's history upon the earth, very, very active in the affairs of men, and in carrying out the purpose and the program of God. The teaching concerning angels, although denied by those who do not believe the Word of God, occupies a very large part of the Scriptures.

It is well for us to remember that round about us in the atmosphere, observing our behavior and conduct and standing ready to help those who belong to the Lord Jesus Christ, are great myriads of angelic beings. It is our ignorance of their existence that causes us untold trouble and loss of much joy and happiness. If we could understand better the teaching of the Scripture concerning the ministry of angels in our own personal and individual life, it would bring us untold comfort. You Christians as you face the problems of life, as you lie upon your bed of illness, do you realize that at your disposal God has placed a great company of these angelic spirit beings whose business it is not only to watch over you but to reveal God's will to you and to be at your beck and call at any time whatsoever?

In our previous chapter on angels as suggested by the tenth chapter of Daniel where Daniel receives his final revelation concerning the end time through the ministry of one of these angelic beings, we have studied a number of truths, to be sure in outline form, concerning the ministry of these created beings. We have seen that they were created by God even before the foundations of the world. We have noted that their number is incalculable. It is called an innumerable company of angels. Then we saw that there are various ranks and stations among these angels, that they have different ministries to perform in the carrying out of God's program and the revelation of His will to the children of men. We saw that even Satan was one of these high angels at one time, but because of his rebellion against the Throne of God he fell, and Lucifer became Satan, the devil, an enemy of God instead of the minister of God. It is utterly impossible within the scope of this book to give in detail the great volume of revelation contained in the Scriptures concerning angelic beings. It is our purpose, rather, to give merely an outline which may be used by you in your own further private study on this interesting subject.

THE NATURE OF ANGELS

We have already stated that angels are created beings. Although they are very wise, they are not omniscient; although they are very powerful, they are not omnipotent; although they move swiftly from place to place, probably with the speed of lightning, they are not omnipresent; that is, they are created beings and, therefore, are limited in their wisdom, in their ministry and in the speed with which they can move from place to place. It is well to remember these facts, for there is a great deal of misunderstanding concerning the nature of these angelic beings. Now the Bible is quite clear that these angels have bodies. By this we do not mean material bodies, for there are spiritual bodies as well as material bodies. God is not limited or confined to material bodies, but may have many, many other bodies in His created plan which may not necessarily be visible or tangible or observable by the human eye. But the Bible does seem to indicate very clearly that the angels have bodies and that without these bodies they are relatively helpless in the performance of their duties. In Luke 24, we have a passage which at least suggests this truth. The Lord Jesus Christ in His glorified body, after the resurrection, stands among His disciples, and this is the record:

> But they were terrified and affrighted, and supposed that they had seen a spirit. And he said unto them, Why are ye troubled? and why do thoughts arise in your hearts? Behold my hands and my feet, that it is I myself: handle me, and see; for a spirit hath not flesh, and bones, as ye see me have (Luke 24:37-39).

That is, the bodies of these angelic beings, these spirits, are not material bodies, are not even like the resurrection body of the Lord Jesus Christ with flesh and bones, but are of an entirely different nature. Then in the First Epistle to the Corinthians where Paul writes about the resurrection bodies of the redeemed after the coming again of the Lord Jesus Christ, we read this interesting account concerning these new resurrection bodies:

> But God giveth it [that is, the example of the grain] a body as it hath pleased him, and to every seed his own body. All flesh is not the same flesh: but there is one kind of flesh of men, another flesh of beasts, another of fishes, and another of birds. There are also celestial bodies [that is, heavenly bodies], and bodies terrestrial [that is, earthly bodies]: but the glory of the celestial is one, and the glory of the terrestrial is another (I Corinthians 15:38-40).

Here we have the definite statement made that there are celestial or heavenly bodies; undoubtedly these angelic beings are invested with these heavenly bodies. Sometimes these angels appear in human form and then are called men. They have the ability when God so desires to take on human bodies in order to reveal themselves unto men. So in the tenth chapter of Daniel we have Daniel seeing a man, and then describing him as an angelic being.

The Scriptures seems to indicate very clearly that angelic beings are dependent, in a measure at least, upon some kind of a body in the exercise of their ministry. It is generally conceived that the angels when they sinned, lost these celestial bodies, and they became disembodied spirits as part of the curse pronounced upon them. Now these fallen beings, Satan and his angels, as disembodied spirits, are helpless and powerless without their bodies, and so whenever they seek to exercise their power and their dominion they must enter into some kind of a body.

Lacking their celestial body, they have to enter into any kind of a body they can find.

It is for this reason, undoubtedly, that when Satan tempted Eve he did not tempt her as a spirit but he entered into the body of the serpent, because without a body he was powerless. In the days of Noah we read of the sons of God intermarrying with the sons of men, the children of men. Of course, there the sons of God again refer to angelic beings, and in order to carry out their pernicious program they had to assume a body. Even in the New Testament we find that when these demons were cast out of a man possessed, by the Lord Jesus Christ, they requested Him and pleaded with Him that they might not be sent back into the pit as disembodied spirits but might enter into the herd of swine. You know the record; the swine were taken possession of by these demons, they rushed down a steep place and were choked in the sea. The demons would rather be in the bodies of swine than be disembodied spirits. As we come to the end of this age we find that when Satan is preparing for his master stroke against the Lord Jesus Christ he will again embody himself in a man. That man will be the Man of Sin, the personal Antichrist, the son of perdition, who will be none other than a man, a superman to be sure, indwelt by Satan personally, as the prince of demons, in his last effort to overthrow the kingdom of the Lord Jesus Christ.

The Ministry of Angels

Concerning the ministry of angels in the Scriptures, the Holy Spirit has a great deal to say. First of all we believe the primary ministry of these angelic beings is to worship God, to attend Him as the Supreme Creator of the universe; and so we read continuously and re-

peatedly that all the angels of God worshiped Him, and
the Throne of God is represented as being surrounded
by these angelic beings, singing their praises, "Holy,
holy, holy, Lord God Almighty." The second ministry is
to herald good news to the children of men. It was an
angel who spoke to Mary and to the father of John and
angels attended the birth of the Lord Jesus Christ and
made known the good news to the shepherds as they
gathered upon the hills of Galilee.

Then the angels had a ministry of delivering messages
of a very personal nature as we have learned in the tenth
chapter of Daniel which we are studying. Answering
prayer, the answer to Daniel's prayer, was by angelic
ministry. We find, too, in the Scripture, that the angels
were active in the ministration of the giving of the law,
that great message of the perfect will of God as expressed in the Ten Commandments given to Moses. Then
also we find that they are the special attendants of the
Lord Jesus Christ, not only at His birth as we saw, but
in the temptation angels came and ministered to Him.
In Gethsemane angels ministered to Him; it was an angel
who spoke to Joseph and instructed Him to flee with
the young child into the land of Egypt. Then we are
told that the angels have a particular ministry of guard-
ing God's own people in times of danger. Undoubtedly the
expression, "guardian angel," comes from this revelation of the Word of God. We have an example of this
very thing in this book which we are studying. In Daniel
6:22, when Daniel was in the lions' den, he said to the
king:

> My God hath sent his angel, and hath shut the lions'
> mouths.

Certainly there is a great comfort for all of God's
people in the knowledge that His angels are at our dis-

posal in times of danger and in times of trial. Then not only does He guard His own, but He delivers His own as well. In the book of Acts we read that the enemies of the Gospel in the early church laid their hands on the apostles and put them in the prison, and then we read:

But the angel of the Lord by night opened the prison doors, and brought them forth (Acts 5:19).

Angels delivering God's prophet! In Daniel 4 we are told that they are watchers over the affairs of men, for in the vision of Nebuchadnezzar we saw that a holy one and a watcher came down from heaven with orders to cut down the tree. In Hebrews 1:14, we read that they have a special ministry to all the saints of God. The angels, we are told, are ministers sent forth to minister unto them that shall be the heirs of salvation.

CARRY US HOME

But not only do these angels have a ministry during the days of our life, a fact which should be encouraging to us, but even at the hour of death they have a special ministry which God has designated them to do. From the story of Lazarus and the rich man we learn that when Lazarus died the angels of God carried him into Abraham's bosom. God sends a special detachment of His heavenly troops at the hour of a Christian's death in order to take his spirit and to carry it safely and gently home to the Saviour, there to be with Him forever and ever. What a wonderful, marvelous provision, taking away not only the fear of life's problems but even the fear of death! When that time comes when we shall have to walk through the dark, dark valley, He will have His angels to carry us home. And not only that, but He will use the angels to gather His own at His coming again. In Matthew 13:49, we read:

> The angels shall come forth, and sever the wicked from among the just.

In the same chapter the Lord Jesus Christ, in speaking about the second mystery of the tares among the wheat, tells us this interesting truth:

> The field is the world; the good seed are the children of the kingdom; but the tares are the children of the wicked one; the enemy that sowed them is the devil; the harvest is the end of the world; and the reapers are the angels (Matthew 13:38-39).

What a marvelous ministry God has reserved for these creatures!

But now before we bring this chapter to a close, we want to call your attention to a very practical aspect of this angelic ministry as found in First Corinthians. Paul is speaking of the conduct of God's people in the assembly of the church and concerning the order in the assembly. He tells us that a woman ought to pray and prophesy with her head covered, that is, without her hair being cut. I realize that this is very unpopular in these days, and yet here it is in the Word of God. The reason Christian women should not cut off their hair, which is their glory, is given very significantly. Here it is:

> For this cause ought the woman to have power on her head because of the angels (I Corinthians 11:10).

Since Adam was a type of the Lord Jesus Christ and is the head of the woman, so Christ is the Head of the Church, and as a symbol of our humility and submission to our Head, the Lord Jesus Christ, we are to put it into practice even in our assembly worship and in our daily life. One of the ways was the humility of the wife in submission to her husband as indicated by her refusal to cut off the glory which is the woman's, even her hair. And then we have the added information, "because of the angels." Now literally it means, because of the angels who are looking on, and to me it is a comforting thought to know that in our worship, in our assembling together, in our fellowship together with the people of God, we are attended by these angels who are watching over us, ready to direct, ready to bring the message of God and witnessing our worship. Because of their presence all of our life should be spent in humility and love and submission to Him who has made all this possible.

Now we have not been able to exhaust or even to treat in detail all of the wonderful revelation concerning the angelic ministry in the Scriptures. In the succeeding chapters we shall speak about the ministry of fallen angels, Satan and his demons especially. But now before we close this message, will you not bow your head and praise God for the wonderful provision He has made for us while we walk through this vale of tears and shadows until we meet Him face to face?

CHAPTER TWENTY-NINE

The Personal Antichrist

> He shall enter peaceably even upon the fattest places
> of the province; and he shall do that which his fathers have
> not done, nor his fathers' fathers; he shall scatter among
> them the prey, and spoil, and riches: yea, and he shall
> forecast his devices against the strong holds, even for a
> time (Daniel 11:24).

This verse in the very middle of the eleventh chapter
of Daniel is part of the description of the coming Man
of Sin, the superman, the Antichrist. While the first
35 verses of this chapter describe for us in detail
the history of the nations after Daniel's time, and particularly the history of the little horn described in Daniel
8 whom we identified as Antiochus Epiphanes, the
historical character who defiled the Temple at Jerusalem
and brought about the desecration of the holy place,
it is nevertheless a type of the coming Man of Sin who
shall arise after the Church has been taken out and who
shall for a brief period of time cause consternation and
destruction within the world.

In the previous chapter, we studied angelic beings
and were occupied almost exclusively with a considera-

tion of the unfallen angels who today in innumerable hosts surround the Throne of Almighty God to worship Him and stand ready to do His bidding in regard to the history of the world and particularly to minister to the Church of the Lord Jesus Christ. We realize that we merely scratched the surface of the great mass of revelation contained within the pages of the Bible concerning the ministry of the angels, but we must not ignore the fact that there are not only these unfallen angelic beings in all of their beauty, but that the Bible also has a great deal to say about fallen angels.

The leader of these fallen angels we know best by the name of Satan, and the devil, while the lesser subjects of this great leader are called in Scripture, demons. Now Satan's plan and purpose is to thwart and to prevent, if possible, the program of the Lord Jesus Christ. As we have repeatedly pointed out, the Lord Jesus Christ has a kingdom and He has a Bride. The kingdom is the millennial kingdom which will be established upon this earth at His Second Coming, and until His Second Coming, He is calling out a Bride, which is His Church, from every nation, tongue, tribe and people. Satan, being the enemy of the Lord Jesus Christ, will seek to produce an imitation christ whom we know best by the term of the Antichrist. He will seek in every way to undo the program of God and, in opposition to the program of God, to set up a kingdom of his own and a church of his own. From what the Bible tells us, these demon beings over whom Satan reigns are very powerful beings, although they are not omnipotent. Some knowledge of the power of these beings may be gained from the testimony of the angel who comes to Daniel in response to his prayer. He tells Daniel that he was hindered for a period of three whole weeks and was

unable to break through the hosts of these demon beings
with the message which God had given him for Daniel.
We have the record in Daniel 10:12-13:

> Then said he unto me, Fear not, Daniel: for from the
> first day that thou didst set thine heart to understand,
> and to chasten thyself before thy God, thy words were
> heard, and I am come for thy words. But the prince of the
> kingdom of Persia withstood me one and twenty days.

From this passage we learn that the prince of the
kingdom of Persia, who was one of these fallen demon
beings, was so powerful that even this celestial messenger
was not able to overcome him; and it took three weeks,
at the end of which time Michael, the archangel, had
to be sent in order to overcome the hosts of the evil
one. This gives us something of a picture of the power
of Satan. If one of his angels was able to withstand one
of God's own messengers and hold up the message for
a period of three weeks, then we can realize to a degree
the tremendous power of the enemy which is against us.

THE PERSONAL ANTICHRIST

We have already pointed out that Satan and his angels
seem relatively harmless and powerless without being
incarnated in some kind of a body. So the Bible teaches
that at the end of this age, Satan, in preparing his master
stroke against the kingdom and the Church of the Lord
Jesus Christ, will enter into a man and will be incarnated
in a human being, and as the personal Antichrist, the
superman, the Man of Sin, of the end time, will seek
to give the final stroke which will defeat the entire
program of the Lord Jesus. This man, we said, is known
by many names in Scripture. He is called the bloody and
the deceitful man, he is called the Man of Sin, he is
called the son of perdition and probably best known by

the name of the Antichrist. After the Church of the
Lord Jesus Christ is taken out, this man will appear
upon the scene. We have a great body of Scripture which
describes both the program as well as the personality
of this man.

First of all, notice that his rise will be very sudden.
This is in imitation of the true Christ. You remember
that Christ for thirty years remained in obscurity in his
home in Nazareth and the silence of those years was
broken only once in Luke 2. Then when His time had
come, He was baptized in the River Jordan, and after
the temptation He at once revealed Himself in the miracle
of the making of water into wine at Cana of Galilee,
and we read that many disciples believed on Him. So,
too, the Antichrist will remain in obscurity until the
Spirit takes away the Bride and then, according to
II Thessalonians 2, "shall that Wicked be revealed."
He may even now be in the world. He may be in the
process of preparation for his hellish and devilish
work. Then when his time shall come and the restraint
and the hindrance of the Holy Spirit is removed, he
shall suddenly appear. He will come with the baptism
of hell and announce himself by miracles and lying
wonders. His reign will be for a time and times and a
half a time, or approximately three and one-half years
according to the Scripture, the identical length of time
of the active ministry of Christ on the earth.

Jesus said, "I am the light of the world." This man,
too, will come claiming himself as the light, but instead
he will be the minister of darkness. We read this description of him and his powers:

> Even him, whose coming is after the working of Satan
> with all power and signs and lying wonders, and with all
> deceivableness of unrighteousness in them that perish; be-

cause they received not the love of the truth, that they might be saved. And for this cause God shall send them strong delusion, that they should believe a lie (II Thessalonians 2:9-11).

Undoubtedly one of the elements of his marvelous success in gaining the hearts of the people lies in the fact that he will come promising the very thing which is uppermost in the hearts of men all over the world today, namely, *peace.* This old world is sick and tired of war and is looking for peace, looking for a leader who will be able to bring a lasting peace. Now we know that Christ is the Prince of Peace, and that when He comes He will come bringing in everlasting peace, but the devil also knows this and will try to steal a march on the Prince of Peace by getting in, as it were, on the ground floor. He will offer peace to the nations before the coming of Christ and thus steal away the hearts of men, only to set the stage for the most terrible war and slaughter the world will ever experience. In Revelation 6:1-2, we read:

> And I saw when the Lamb opened one of the seals, and I heard. as it were the noise of thunder, one of the four beasts saying, Come and see. And I saw, and behold a white horse: and he that sat on him had a bow; and a crown was given unto him: and he went forth conquering, and to conquer.

Here is the white horse of peace upon which the wicked one ushers in that short period of the Tribulation Period. It is an imitation of the real Prince of Peace who is seen in Revelation 19:11. When the Antichrist comes, it will be with a promise of peace upon the earth. Now referring to our chapter, Daniel 11, notice how clearly it is given in type and prophecy:

> And in his estate shall stand up a vile person, to whom they shall not give the honour of the kingdom: but he

shall come in peaceably, and obtain the kingdom by flatteries (Daniel 11:21).

And after the league made with him he shall work deceitfully: for he shall come up, and shall become strong with a small people. He shall enter peaceably even upon the fattest places of the province (Daniel 11:23-24).

His first move is to gain the confidence of the people, and especially the nation of Israel which up until that time has been persecuted and scattered throughout the world. He needs their wealth to carry on his program and his first attempt will be to gain the favor of God's downtrodden covenant people. He will aid them in their return to the land of Palestine and restore it to them and in general show them many favors. We read in Daniel 11:24-25:

. . . He shall scatter among them [that is particularly among the nation of Israel] the prey, and spoil, and riches: yea, and he shall forecast his devices against the strong holds, even for a time. And he shall stir up his power and his courage against the king of the south with a great army; and the king of the south shall be stirred up to battle with a very great and mighty army; but he shall not stand: for they shall forecast devices against him.

Now here is a very important passage in the light of present-day current events. Here we have the cleverness of Satan through the Man of Sin, the Antichrist. He will take up for the Jews their cause against their old enemy, the Ishmaelites, here called the king of the south, the North African tribes. Trouble is even now brewing between these two old enemies, and it is in the headlines every day, between Isaac's children, the children of Israel, and Ishmael's children, the enemies of the nation. Just recently the powers of the south caused a massacre of hundreds of Israelites in the land of Palestine. This has been going on but will become intensified as we reach the end of the age. This is according to Scripture, "the beginning of sorrows," but when this Antichrist shall come, his master stroke will be to guarantee peace to Israel and to promise to give them back their land in totality by offering to subdue their enemy and those who now, according to the promise made to Abraham, are occupying the land contrary to the Scripture. But this peace and these favors which he will promise will be but for a short time, long enough only to gain his point and influence; then he will turn upon those he has pledged to protect with all the fiendish and hellish hatred that Satan himself is able to raise. In Daniel 11:28, we read:

> Then shall he return into his land with great riches; and his heart shall be against the holy covenant; and he shall do exploits, and return to his own land.

And then in verse 31:

> And arms shall stand on his part, and they shall pollute the sanctuary of strength, and shall take away the daily sacrifice, and they shall place the abomination that maketh desolate.

It is this abomination that Christ speaks of when referring to the abomination of desolation in Matthew 24. So you see this peace will be only for a little season, soon to be followed by the last great war. The white horse of Revelation six is soon followed by the red horse:

> And there went out another horse that was red: and power was given to him that sat thereon to take peace from the earth, and that they should kill one another: and there was given unto him a great sword (Revelation 6:4).

The world has been looking for such a master statesman and leader for centuries and ages, one who would be able to weld a government of the world which would be invincible and undefeatable. In the restored ten-toed

Babylonian Roman empire, which is even now in the process of formation, in league with the nation of Israel, there will be a league of nations which will continue until the King Himself comes and destroys them with the brightness of His appearing. This political head of the restored Babylonian system will be only a figurehead. He will be called the political head, but the Antichrist will be the power behind the throne. He will work through, and use as a tool, this political head, and carry out his own ends and purposes through him. We have the record in Revelation 13:11-12, where we are told that the Antichrist is the real power behind the throne.

THE ANTICHRIST'S RELIGION

Religiously, this Man of Sin will be the consummation of all ungodliness and atheism and lawlessness; he will deny all authority except his own. He is called in Scripture the lawless one, and in the heyday of his power will attempt to dethrone God from His seat as he did in the beginning. This is always the spirit of the Antichrist. It was this that caused him to be cast out of heaven; because the anointed cherub in Ezekiel 28:14 exalted himself against God, he was cast from his position of power. Again, this was the bait with which he beguiled our first parents, for he promised them that they would be as God, and in the last demonstration of his power, he will again assume the same form. As Christ claimed He was God, so, too, we see Satan again imitating the Lamb by making the same claims which He made. In II Thessalonians 2:3-4, we read:

> ... the son of perdition; who opposeth and exalteth himself above all that is called God, or that is worshipped; so that he as God sitteth in the temple of God, shewing himself that he is God.

And in Daniel 11:36:

> And the king shall do according to his will; and he shall
> exalt himself, and magnify himself above every god, and
> shall speak marvellous things against the God of gods, and
> shall prosper till the indignation be accomplished: for that
> that is determined shall be done.

I trust that from these few remarks taken from
Daniel and other parts of the Scriptures concerning the
coming of this superman, you will see how the world is
being prepared for the coming of such an individual.
The stage is even now being set. The world is suffering
because of a lack of adequate leadership, lack of adequate
unity and adequate understanding to bring about the
desired peace for which men have been longing and praying. When this man comes, this Antichrist, and will
give the formula, the apparently fool-proof formula, for
an abiding peace, we can easily understand that the
leaders of the world will immediately align themselves
with him, only to be deceived in the end. Now, my friend,
as we come to the close of this chapter, remember that
there are only two masters, Christ and Satan. There are
only two leaders, the seed of the woman and the seed
of the serpent, and you must pledge allegiance to one
or the other. Very soon the time will be here when Christ
will come and then it will be forever too late to make
your decision. Now, before it is too late, "believe on the
Lord Jesus Christ, and thou shalt be saved."

CHAPTER THIRTY

The Approaching End

And at that time shall Michael stand up, the great prince which standeth for the children of thy people: and there shall be a time of trouble, such as never was since there was a nation even to that same time: and at that time thy people shall be delivered, every one that shall be found written in the book (Daniel 12:1).

Thus does Daniel begin the final chapter of the prophecy which was given to him concerning the end time. Now you will notice that this very rich and illuminating verse begins with the expression, "and at that time." The conjunction "and" of course immediately links it with that which has been given before, and the expression, "and at that time" refers us to the events which are related and which we studied briefly in the eleventh chapter of the prophecy. Now the eleventh chapter of Daniel has to do very largely with the activities of a certain individual who is the enemy of the Lord Jesus Christ and is known in Scripture as the Antichrist, from the prefix "anti," which means "to be against." Volumes could be written concerning that which the Bible has revealed about this terrible person, but we are seeking

in this book to bring only in brief outline a skeleton of
the teaching of the Word of God as suggested in Daniel
in order to stimulate you to study these things for yourselves in greater detail.

We have in the past chapters been pointing out the
political policy of the Antichrist, his religious program
as outlined in the Word of God, and we want to take a
moment to see the attitude which the world will assume
when this man appears. We have previously pointed
out that when he comes he will be received for a brief
period of time, immediately after the Rapture of the
Church, to bring peace upon the earth and among the
nations, and he will be hailed and acclaimed as the
saviour of the world and the great world leader for
whom men have been looking so long. To the nation of
Israel he will proclaim himself as the promised Messiah.
So clever will be this imitation that the nation will be
restored to their own land in peace. They will put their
trust in him only to have their faith broken off in the
middle of the Tribulation.

> And he shall confirm the covenant with many for one week:
> [remember this is the last week of the seventy weeks of
> Daniel] and in the midst of the week he shall cause the sacri-
> fice and the oblation to cease, and for the overspreading of
> abominations he shall make it desolate, even until the con-
> summation, and that determined shall be poured upon the
> desolate (Daniel 9:27).

This one, then, will come and will promise peace, and
after only a few years he will show his true colors and
will desecrate the Temple, turn upon God's ancient
people and become their bitter enemy. And yet while
he is promising peace, they will believe in him. It is
this one that Christ Himself meant when He said:

I am come in my Father's name, and ye receive me not: if another shall come in his own name, him ye will receive (John 5:43).

The nation of Israel today is ready for someone who will promise them relief from their suffering and from their dispersion and who will bring forward an acceptable plan whereby they may be restored to the Promised Land given to them through Abraham, their father. But not only will the nation be ready to receive such a man with such claims but the world in general will be ready also. We are living right now in a very, very weary, war-torn world. Although the conflict has been over for some time, the results are still here, the scars do not seem to heal, and we seem to be farther from the time of peace than we have ever been before. There can be no question whatsoever that when a man will arise who will be able to put forward his formula for lasting and abiding peace, it will not take him long to gain the confidence of the nations of the world.

And the religious world today, too, is looking for just that kind of an individual. The Bible tells us that when this Antichrist appears not only will he bring together the political factions of the world in a great superempire, but he will also be able to promise to bring together all of the dissenting factions of the different religious beliefs and faiths that today plague the world, into one great federation of religion. Already there are many indications that a desire for this very thing is springing up within the hearts of men. Men in general are sick of the heckling and the splitting which have characterized so much of organized religion throughout the ages. And from every quarter of the globe we read about and hear about movements which are already on foot— movements which look toward organic union of the various religious groups of the world. The evident aim and purpose is not only to bring about a one-world kingdom, but a one-world church as well, to do away with all the differences which now separate the people, and to bring about a man-made millennial unity and peace. We can read in almost any newspaper any day, or hear over the air, an account of some form of an attempt to bring together man in one great world church and one great world kingdom.

In our succeeding chapter we shall try to point out how this leader who will be the power behind the political as well as the religious program of that time will succeed in almost realizing the dream of mankind. But now we want to say a word concerning the destiny of this man, the Antichrist. The prophecy given in the third chapter of Genesis that the seed of the woman should bruise the head of the serpent will find its fulfillment in the coming again of the Lord Jesus Christ. In this early prophecy we are told that God will put enmity between the seed of the woman and the seed of the serpent. Now practically all Bible students agree that the seed of the woman is a direct reference to the coming of the Lord Jesus Christ. It is called the *prot-evangelium* and refers to the coming of God in the person of His Son in the form of a man as we have it celebrated, of course, in the birth of the Lord Jesus Christ; but as there was a seed of the woman, so we read of the seed of the serpent, and while the serpent symbolizes Satan himself personally, the seed of the serpent will also be an incarnation of the spirit of Satan and will be this Man of Sin whom we are discussing. Now the battle between the seed of the serpent and the seed of the woman will continue for six thousand years during man's day, and then at the end of that period of time the prophecy which we find in

Genesis 3:15 will find its fulfillment; the seed of the woman will finally crush the head of the serpent.

There are two bruisings mentioned in that verse; one, where the seed of the serpent will bruise the heel of the seed of the woman. This, we believe, was fulfilled and accomplished on the Cross of Calvary where He was bruised for our iniquities and smitten for our transgressions, but that was not victory for Satan. That was part of God's revealed program, and when the end of the age shall come, then shall the seed of the woman crush the head of the serpent. This is given in many, many passages of Scripture, that Satan shall finally and forever be cast into the lake of fire, but the personal Antichrist who is the human tool of the devil will meet his fate a thousand years earlier. Let me repeat that. Satan will not be cast into the lake of fire until after the millennium, but the Antichrist who is the incarnation of Satan will be cast into the lake of fire before the millennium, a thousand years earlier than Satan himself. We must distinguish, of course, between Satan and the Antichrist. The Antichrist is the incarnation of Satan and so the Antichrist becomes merely the tool of the devil for the carrying out of his purpose, and when that purpose fails Satan will forsake him. And so we find that while Satan will not be cast into the lake of fire until after the millennium, according to Revelation 20:10, the personal Antichrist, the tool of the devil, will meet his fate a thousand years earlier and will be cast together with the political head of the revived Babylonian empire into the lake of fire after the Tribulation and before the Millennium Period.

> And then shall that Wicked be revealed, whom the Lord shall consume with the spirit of his mouth, and shall destroy with the brightness of his coming: even him, whose com-

ing is after the working of Satan with all power and signs
and lying wonders (II Thessalonians 2:8-9).

And the beast was taken, and with him the false prophet
that wrought miracles before him, with which he deceived
them that had received the mark of the beast, and them that
worshipped his image. These both were cast alive into a
lake of fire burning with brimstone (Revelation 19:20).

And he shall plant the tabernacles of his palace between
the seas in the glorious holy mountain; yet he shall come
to his end, and none shall help him (Daniel 11:45).

In this closing verse of the eleventh chapter of Daniel
we have in a few brief words what the Holy Spirit has
to say concerning the ultimate destiny of the Man of Sin,
the Antichrist. We know from the book of Revelation
that at the same time the Antichrist is cast into the lake
of fire, the devil who was the real incarnator of the
Antichrist, will be cast into the bottomless pit for one
thousand years during which period Christ reigns here
upon the earth with His saints while Israel receives all
of the Lord's covenant blessings in the land.

Before we continue we should like to gather up the
events as we have had them thus far. We have found in
our contact with believers that a great many of God's
dear children who are interested in the return of the Lord
are tragically mixed up as to the chronology of the events
preceding the coming of the Lord, that is, the order of
things from this very day on until the Lord returns
again, and so we are going to give you very briefly and
as clearly as we can the events as they are chronicled in
the Bible for us that we may be among those who are
intelligently watching for their Lord.

We believe that we are living at the very end of this
dispensation and that the next event will be the coming
of the Lord Jesus Christ to take the Church unto Himself.

The Bible clearly teaches that at the close of this dispensation of grace the Church will be caught up and the Spirit who indwells the Church today and is the One who hinders the revelation of the Man of Sin, will be taken out of the way. And then when this hinderer, the Holy Spirit dwelling within the Body of Christ, is taken out of the way, Satan will reveal or unveil his masterpiece, his incarnation, the Antichrist, the Man of Sin. Then will follow the period of the Great Tribulation which corresponds to the last week of the seventy weeks of Daniel 9, but this week will be shortened for the sake of those saved during this particular period, especially the saved among the nation of Israel; and at the end of that seven-year period which is shortened because of the elect who are upon the earth, we will have the Battle of Armageddon, which we shall study in the next chapter. Then the nations of the world will gather for the last great battle of all time with all the modern weapons and equipment of war in the battleground to the north of Palestine, only to come to a dismal and miserable end. The climax will be the coming of the Lord Jesus Christ with His saints and then the Antichrist shall be destroyed and cast into the lake of fire and Satan himself will be cast in the bottomless pit. The reign of terror will end at this Battle of Armageddon when the king of the south, the king of the north and the king of the east will meet on that great historic battleground. This battle will make the last World War look like child's play with tin soldiers, but more about that in a later chapter.

Before we close this chapter may I ask you a question? Do you realize how near this event may be? And are you of that company who will be spared the Tribulation of those days? If you have not accepted peace, the peace that God made through Christ, will you not do it now? There is still time as you are reading these very words, but no one can give you the assurance that you will ever have another opportunity. No one can even promise that you can do it tomorrow. The Spirit of God is even now gathering out a people for His Name, and when the last one of the number that He has already determined has been brought in, then shall that long looked for day break upon us. Those who are washed in the blood will be caught up to be with Christ and those who have rejected Him will pass through the darkest period in the history of this world. And remember that "God shall send them strong delusion, that they [that is those who are left behind], should believe a lie: that they all might be damned who believed not the truth, but had pleasure in unrighteousness." O friend, flee from the wrath to come before it is too late! The Saviour still waits and He offers you His salvation full and free. He paid the price. God was in Christ reconciling the world unto Himself, and now we do beseech you, "be ye reconciled to God." Oh, come, ere it is too late!

CHAPTER THIRTY-ONE

Armageddon

He shall enter peaceably even upon the fattest places of the province; and he shall do that which his fathers have not done, nor his fathers' fathers; he shall scatter among them the prey, and spoil, and riches: yea, and he shall forecast his devices against the strong holds, even for a time (Daniel 11:24).

And the king shall do according to his will; and he shall exalt himself, and magnify himself above every god, and shall speak marvellous things against the God of gods, and shall prosper till the indignation be accomplished: for that that is determined shall be done. Neither shall he regard the God of his fathers, nor the desire of women, nor regard any god: for he shall magnify himself above all. But in his estate shall he honour the God of forces: and a god whom his fathers knew not shall he honour with gold, and silver, and with precious stones, and pleasant things. Thus shall he do in the most strong holds with a strange god, whom he shall acknowledge and increase with glory: and he shall cause them to rule over many, and shall divide the land for gain (Daniel 11:36-39).

The eleventh chapter of the prophecy of Daniel divides itself into two parts. The first 35 verses comprise the first part and are occupied with a description of the reign of Antiochus Epiphanes who spoiled the land of Palestine, betrayed God's ancient people, Israel, and set up the abomination of desolation. All this has become a matter of history, and can be confirmed by historic accounts. Then in the second part, from verse 36 through 45, we have a description of the Man of Sin of the end time, of whom Antiochus Epiphanes was merely a type and a shadow among many other types of the Antichrist which we have in the Scriptures. It is well to remember this division, because in Daniel we have not only history, but a picture of the future as well.

We learn a great many things about this personal Antichrist in the second part of the chapter and something about the program which he will institute, and then, of course, the facts concerning his dismal end. A number of things, I believe, are worthy of note. We find that he is associated with the political head of the revived Roman empire of the end time who corresponds to the beast out of the sea in Revelation 13. In co-operation with this beast out of the sea, this head of the revived Roman empire, this Antichrist who will come out of the land, probably from the tribe of Dan, will seek to set up a government which will completely dominate the world and revive the old Babylonian dream of a world-federated empire with one religion, one governmental head, one capital, one language and with all nations subjected to this new form of government.

An Atheist

From Daniel 11:37, we notice that he will be an atheist. He will be anti-Christian, for he will not regard the God of his fathers; that is, the God Jehovah of the nation of Israel, nor the desire of women, which in Scripture is the way of designating the Lord Jesus Christ. Every devout mother in Israel had within her heart the desire and the prayer that she might become the mother of the Messiah who was to deliver Israel, and the expression, "the desire of women," refers, of course, to the Messiah who was to come. So we see that this Man of Sin is anti-Christ, that is, "against the Christ." We are further told in verse 37 that he shall not regard any God, for he shall magnify himself above all. He will seek to establish himself above God. That has been the dream of Satan since time began. The original sin of Satan was pride; he sought to dethrone God and set himself up as the king of the world, and so this Man of Sin who will be the reincarnation of Satan himself will be anti-Christian, anti-God; he will be the great atheist.

Then in verse 38 we are told that he will be a materialist. He shall honor the god of forces; that is, literally, the god of nature. And in this atomic age we can readily understand how this Man of Sin will hold up the discoveries of science, especially the release of atomic energy, as the hope of the world which he will probably rule and dominate at that particular time. Now this god of forces he will honor with gold and silver and precious stones and pleasant things. He will be the greatest spender the world has ever seen, in his attempt to convince men and women that he is their only hope and their only saviour. Then the final mistake that this Man of Sin will make is given in the last part of verse 39, where we are told that he will rule over many, for a time at least, and apparently conquer the entire world, but then will make the great error of dividing the land for gain. Now remember, the expression, "the land," always refers to the land of Palestine, the geographic center of the world as far as Bible prophecy is concerned. We have already covered this in one of the pre-

vious chapters, but we call your attention to it again.
That great final sin of this Antichrist will be when he
stretches out his hand to the land of Palestine and seeks
to divide it in order that he may promote and further his
own greedy end. Now that act of the Antichrist in seeking to divide the land will be the signal for his destruction, and so we have a second great power mentioned.
We read in verse 40:

> And at the time of the end shall the king of the south
> push at him: and the king of the north shall come against
> him like a whirlwind, with chariots, and with horsemen,
> and with many ships; and he shall enter into the countries,
> and shall overflow and pass over.

Please notice, first of all, that it is at the time of the
end when these two other great powers, the king of the
south and the king of the north, will come against this
federated revived Roman empire over which the Antichrist is reigning and ruling. It is at the time of the end.
Since it follows immediately upon the reference in the
thirty-ninth verse to the dividing of the land for gain,
we see that this is his final act—when he does this, the
time of the end has come. Now please notice that the king
of the south shall push at him. We have already reminded
you many times, that directions in Scripture are always
with reference to, and in relation to, the land of Palestine,
the geographical Biblical center of the world; therefore,
the king of the south refers to a federation of nations and
peoples who live to the south of the land of Palestine.
We know that they are none other than the bulk of the
Arab tribes, the descendants of Ishmael, who was the
son of Abraham by Hagar, the Egyptian woman. When
the Antichrist goes into the land of Palestine and begins
to divide the land for gain, there is a sudden activity
on the part of the Arab nations, and they organize to

oppose this attempt on the part of the ruler who has taken over Palestine.

Then there is a third power mentioned in this same verse:

> . . . and the king of the north shall come against him like a whirlwind, with chariots, and with horsemen, and with many ships; and he shall enter into the countries, and shall overflow and pass over.

After the Antichrist has made his bid to take over Palestine and to divide the land in order to keep peace, the Arab nations rise up in revolt and at the same time there is a threat that comes down from the north. Now this northern confederacy is described in detail in the thirty-eighth and thirty-ninth chapters of Ezekiel, which of course, are beyond the scope of our exposition here. However, we recommend that in this connection you read them very carefully. Here Ezekiel describes the great northern army of the end time, called Gog and Magog, and tells us that associated with Gog will be a large number of satellite nations, including Gomer and his bands. Now among Bible students it is almost generally agreed that Gog refers to the land of Russia, we have the description very graphically given in chapter 39, and associated with Russia will be the Germanic peoples. We shall see Poland and Czechoslovakia and the northern part of Germany and Yugoslavia and those nations that today are already being formed into the Russian bloc. They shall push down from the north, and we are told they will be very successful for a time and will enter into the country and overflow and pass over. The destiny of this northern confederacy is given in the thirty-ninth chapter of Ezekiel.

We have a fourth power mentioned here, one which

is confirmed and corroborated in the book of the Revelation. We read in Daniel 11:44:

> But tidings out of the east and out of the north shall trouble him: therefore he shall go forth with great fury to destroy, and utterly to make away many.

Now the tidings out of the east refer, of course, to the countries to the east of the land of Palestine, not only the near east, but particularly, we believe, the Chinese and Japanese nations who shall constitute the fourth great army of the end time—an army which shall be destroyed at the coming of the Lord. In the book of the Revelation we are definitely told that God will dry up the bed of the Euphrates River in order to make a great national transcontinental highway through which the kings of the east shall descend with their armies and hosts to take part in the last great battle, the Battle of Armageddon.

Then we have one other statement concerning the Antichrist:

> He shall plant the tabernacles of his palace between the seas [that is, between the Mediterranean and the Dead Seas] in the glorious holy mountain [that is, Mt. Zion where Jerusalem is located]; yet he shall come to his end, and none shall help him (Daniel 11:45).

That will be the end, and the twelfth chapter of Daniel, which we shall study next, tells us of the coming of the Lord Jesus Christ at the time of the end to destroy these nations.

THE LAST GREAT BATTLE

Now we have given you in barest outline the picture in the eleventh chapter of Daniel concerning the last great war of this age, the Battle of Armageddon. We saw first that there will be a revival of the Roman empire. This will be a combination, a federation of nations, including most of the countries formerly occupied by the Roman empire, those that ring the Mediterranean Sea—probably Britain and France, the southern part of Germany, Greece, Italy, Palestine and the countries in the northern part of Africa—and these will seek to set up a world bloc which will be headed by the head of the revived Roman empire, and, of course, will be energized by the Man of Sin who will be the power behind the throne. At the same time there will be the formation of another bloc called the king of the north, headed by Russia, by Gog, as described in the Bible, and consisting of the Russian nation together with its satellite powers, a movement which is taking place right now.

Simultaneously with the organization of this northern bloc, we have the organization of the southern federation of the Arab nations as a protest against the dividing of the land of Palestine in order to keep peace between the nation of Israel and the nation of Ishmael. Then the fourth one, the kings of the east, the yellow races, will come down, and these four, according to Scripture, will meet in the hills of Meggido, in the valley of Jehoshaphat, described in the Bible as the Battle of Armageddon. They will be struggling there for possession of the land of Palestine and the wealth of the nation of Israel, and this battle which would result in the complete annihilation of civilization and mankind from the face of the earth in this atomic age will be suddenly interrupted and come to a tragic end by the appearance of the Lord Jesus Christ. He will come down from heaven and in flaming fire take vengeance upon these enemies of the Lord, destroy them, set up His glorious millennial kingdom in the land of Palestine and reign over the house of Jacob forever.

SIGNS OF THE TIMES

We have given you a skeleton of events as they are related for us in the eleventh chapter of Daniel. We have not gone into all the detail we would like to, but have tried to summarize the events because those whose eyes are open to the truth of the Word of God will see that the very things which Daniel prophesied 25 hundred years ago or more, are being enacted in the world at this very, very moment. We see in Europe the formation of the two great power blocs, the one consisting of territory corresponding almost exactly to the old Roman empire. Then there is the formation of Gog under the leadership of Magog, and the formation of that great group of nations with their tremendous resources standing in the way of the ideals of the democratic nations. We have also seen the tremendous unrest among the Arabian peoples, the Ishmaelites, over the problem and the question of the land of Palestine. And then we are seeing, too, great activity in the regions of the east, China and even Japan, all of which has been described by Daniel.

Surely we are living in the latter days, and the Lord Jesus Christ, who castigated the Pharisees for being able to discern the sky and predict the weather, and then not being able to discern the signs of the times because of their spiritual blindness, might well castigate God's people today. They are more occupied with the restoration of material things and with a world conversion and a world program than they are with the signs of the times which indicates beyond a shadow of doubt to the spiritually enlightened mind that we are living in the very last days, and that the next event will be the return of the Lord Jesus Christ to take out His Bride first of all, then to put in motion the final preparation for the destruction of His enemies and finally to set up His kingdom. Surely as we look upon the unrest in Europe and Africa, the problems of Palestine, the revival of the nations which once constituted the Roman empire and the tremendous speed with which Russia is bidding for power, we can see that Daniel was speaking of the very days in which you and I live.

What a challenge to be alive today! What a challenge to those who are Christians to be busy for the Lord in the last few days which remain! What a tremendous challenge to those who are unsaved to flee from the wrath to come! We close this chapter with a prayer that God will use it by His grace, and through His Spirit show many of you the need of receiving the peace of God before the awful judgment breaks upon this wicked earth. May God grant it! "Believe on the Lord Jesus Christ, and thou shalt be saved."

CHAPTER THIRTY-TWO

The End Time

> But thou, O Daniel, shut up the words, and seal the book, even to the time of the end: many shall run to and fro, and knowledge shall be increased (Daniel 12:4).

In the last part of the twelfth chapter of Daniel we have the final message through the Holy Spirit to the prophet concerning the time of the end. In Daniel 12:1, we have, as we stated before, a brief but yet marvelously complete picture of the time of the end. Now the time of the end is usually, in Daniel, an expression which refers to the end of this particular dispensation, although it includes also all the events from the rejection of the Lord Jesus Christ up until this time. In this verse we therefore have a picture of the coming Great Tribulation. It is called the time of Jacob's trouble because it will be during this Tribulation Period that Israel shall pass through the last great fire of affliction and persecution. It is called the time of trouble such as never was since there was a nation, even to that same time, and at the time of the end, now notice carefully, it says "thy people shall be delivered." That is, the nation of Israel shall find its deliverance at the end of the Tribulation Period,

"every one that shall be found written in the book."
Then in verses 2 and 3 we have an elaboration of this
truth:

> And many of them that sleep in the dust of the earth
> shall awake, some to everlasting life, and some to shame
> and everlasting contempt. And they that be wise shall
> shine as the brightness of the firmament; and they that turn
> many to righteousness as the stars for ever and ever.

Now these two verses, of course, must be studied in
the light of the first verse where the nation of which
Daniel is speaking is the nation of Israel, and this
resurrection which is spoken of here is a national resurrection. It tells us that the nation which has been scattered throughout the world for twenty-five hundred
years and has been buried among the nations, as it were,
in the dust of the earth, will be revived and saved as is
stated in the first verse, "thy people shall be delivered."
Some who have accepted their Messiah, the Lord Jesus
Christ, shall go on into the kingdom glory; those who
have worshiped the beast and have rejected the offer
of the Messiah, shall awaken, as it were, to everlasting
shame and contempt. And then the rewards will be
handed out and "they that be wise shall shine as the
brightness of the firmament."

SEALING THE BOOK

Now in Daniel 12:4, he received a command to shut
up the words, that is, not to reveal them immediately,
and to seal the book even to the time of the end. The
time of the end really begins with the New Testament
with a new revelation of truth which we have after the
Cross of Calvary through the Holy Spirit, and so what
God really says to Daniel is that these words which he
has written will not be understood until after the coming

of the Lord Jesus Christ; then these words will become
intelligible and understandable. That is quite evident
from what John has to say in the book of the Revelation.
John, you remember, at the close of the last book of the
Bible, records this:

> And he saith unto me, Seal not the sayings of the prophecy
> of this book: for the time is at hand (Revelation 22:10).

The things, therefore, which Daniel saw in his vision
could not be understood except in the light of the New
Testament revelation. That is not only true of the
prophecy of Daniel; it is true of much of the Old Testament that it is unintelligible without the light of the
New Testament. Someone has very aptly said,

> The New is in the Old concealed,
> The Old is by the New revealed.

So while these words could not be understood in the
days of Daniel himself, we are living today in the age
wherein the light of revelation makes clear the mystery
of the Old Testament.

Then we have the closing phrase of the fourth verse
which is one of the most important statements in the
last chapter of Daniel:

> Many shall run to and fro, and knowledge shall be in-
> creased.

Now please notice carefully that this is what the
Holy Spirit has to say concerning the time of the end.
He says that in the time of the end, that is toward the
fulfillment of these prophecies of Daniel and the Second
Coming of the Lord Jesus Christ, many shall run to
and fro and knowledge shall be increased. It has already been pointed out that these two expressions have

to do with an age of speed and of cultural and intellect-
ual development. Many shall run to and fro. It means
that it will be an age of greatly increased speed; as we
look round about us we are amazed at the development
and progress which has been made during only one
lifetime, during one generation. Many of us can remember the old horse and buggy days, when automobiles and
airplanes and fast ships were utterly unknown, when
the ox teams were still seen upon our village streets
and when progress was by the slow means of walking
or by horses or animal-drawn carriages. Yet within the
span of one brief lifetime all of this is changed. We have
seen the automobile come, and the fast ships; we have
seen the development in the airplane industry. Today
airplanes travel upwards of five hundred miles an hour;
they can span the Atlantic Ocean in a few hours and the
Pacific in less than a few days. Even the vehicles for
the transportation of the ordinary civilian have been
geared up to where they attain almost unbelievable
speed. Right now they are working on the matter of
jet-propelled missiles with which they even hope to
reach the moon within a reasonable period of time.

If there is one description which fits the days in which
we are living, it is that it is an age of almost unbelievable
speeds on every hand. Scientists tell us that this is only
the beginning of things; they are even now working on
missiles and airplanes which will be able to attain
speeds of thousands of miles an hour, faster than sound.
These missiles and airplanes have been developed for
a considerable length of time, but scientists seek to increase the speed to incredible astronomical figures.

The second sign of the times which Daniel gives here
is that "knowledge shall be increased." Never before
in the history of the world has there been such a rapid

increase of knowledge as seen in all of the developments in literature, in inventions, in science, in medicine, in surgery and in every realm of human interest and endeavor. We think as we study these words, "knowledge shall be increased," about the radio which is just a matter of the last 25 years; we think of television, of jet-propulsion, of the numerous scientific miracles which are being developed today; we think of the increase in literature, books being available to everyone; we think of the advance in medicine, in the treatment of disease and in surgery. Our colleges today are jammed to their capacity and thousands upon thousands seeking an education are waiting, unable to be admitted. Not only is knowledge being increased, but there is an increase in the methods of communication in every realm of human endeavor, an almost unbelievable increase of science so that we have, within a lifetime, come out of the dark ages into an age of illumination of knowledge. And then, to top it all, man by the knowledge which God has permitted him, has finally tapped the secret of the universe. Within the last few years he has been able to answer the question of the composition of matter in the discovery of atomic energy, has been able to break it up and release that unbelievably powerful energy which we know as the basic force of all matter. This was discovered and perfected in the atomic bomb which by one explosion killed one hundred thousand men, women and children in one single city in Japan. Scientists tell us that the discovery of the atomic bomb is the most revolutionary, single development that any man has ever made or is ever likely to know even in the future and that we ought to be thoroughly alarmed at the possibilities of man's own discovery. Well, turning to the book of Daniel, we find that this was predicted over two and one-half millenniums ago. Let us read Daniel 12:4 again—it can bear repeating:

> But thou, O Daniel, shut up the words, and seal the book, even to the time of the end: many shall run to and fro, and knowledge shall be increased.

Now a close study of this verse will reveal that the time of the end, while it is often generally applied to this entire dispensation as the last time, or the last dispensation, before the setting up of the kingdom, also has a narrower meaning, and when the context indicates it, it means the very end of this dispensation. That seems to be the implication in this fourth verse, for he says that he is to seal the book, even to the time of the end, and then he puts in the phrase to make it a little clearer, "many shall run to and fro, and knowledge shall be increased." In other words Daniel is saying that his book will be largely a sealed book and little understood by the readers until the time of the end which will be characterized by many running to and fro and by knowledge being increased. Well, we have reached that exact period in the history of the world; of no other age in history can it be said that man has attained such speed and that knowledge has increased. Even though much of this knowledge is used for the purpose of destruction and preparation of war, yet it is true that knowledge has increased at a rate so great that it is almost unbelievable. That this is the meaning of Daniel is very evident from the rest of the chapter. In Daniel 12:9-10 we read these words:

> And he said [that is, this heavenly messenger who was speaking to Daniel], Go thy way, Daniel: for the words are closed up and sealed till the time of the end. Many shall be purified, and made white, and tried; but the wicked

shall do wickedly: and none of the wicked shall understand; but the wise shall understand (Daniel 12:9-10).

Now here we have additional information that at the time of the end one of the indications of the nearness of the return of the Lord Jesus Christ—in addition to the age of speed which all of you must admit is here right now, for you are a part of it, and in addition to the great increase of knowledge and education—is that it will be a time of wickedness. We read, "Many shall be purified, and made white, and tried." It will be a time when many will see the signs of the times and separate themselves and prepare to meet their Lord and be purified. It will be an age of separation among God's people from the world, and as a result of this, they shall be tried, that is, they will suffer for the stand which they are willing to take. Surely I am convinced, and you must be convinced, that we are living in an age of that kind today. The lines between atheism and faith in God are being very tightly drawn. The lines between those who still believe in the old-fashioned Gospel of the Book and the blood and the substitutionary atonement of the Lord Jesus Christ, and His physical resurrection and His personal coming again, and those who deny all these truths are becoming more and more evident. On every hand we see the signs of God's true people separating themselves from those things which are not according to His Word and the promises of His Book.

While there is a great deal of activity on the part of those who deny the truths of God's Word, who unite and federate and get together to smooth out their differences, at the same time there is going on a tremendous movement among God's people to come out from among them and to be separate and to touch not the unclean thing and to be willing to walk alone and stand alone for the faith once for all delivered unto the saints. That is the experience of many of us today, who, because of the stand we are willing to take for that which we believe to be verily the very Word of God, are discredited and often times separated from the company of those whom we had even learned to love, and the time is here when we should be willing to take our stand for the truth because we are living in the day of the revival of Babylonianism of which God says "come out from among them." If ever there has been a time when Christians who are really born again should assert themselves, have no fellowship with the unfruitful works of darkness, it is these days in which we live. And so as a third sign of the times we are given in the twelfth chapter of Daniel these words:

Many shall be purified, and made white, and tried.

But at the very same time that God's people are being separated and prepared for the Second Coming of the Lord Jesus Christ, wickedness will increase and become more and more rampant; violence on every hand will be evident, and so the tenth verse continues:

But the wicked shall do wickedly: and none of the wicked shall understand; but the wise shall understand.

In the light of the rest of revelation, this is a very significant statement, for as we have before pointed out, this world will end in apostasy, not in world-wide revival, not in world conversion, but wickedness and violence and immorality and war and hatred and divisions and strife will increase toward the end of the age until the Lord Jesus Christ comes again. That is what Daniel says, "The wicked shall do wickedly." What it really means is that the wicked shall do more wickedly, because they do not understand. They do not know the program, they do not know what God is doing, they do not believe that the end is near; somehow they feel that they are going to pull themselves up by their bootstraps, that everything is going to come out all right, that finally man will learn his lesson and bring in the man-made Utopian millennium of peace. They are deluded by Satan who has blinded their eyes, but then the closing phrase of the verse says:

The wise shall understand.

And surely there has never been an age in history when more light has been shed upon the truth, when there has been more understanding on the part of those who really want to know God's will concerning the truth of the Second Coming of the Lord Jesus Christ. The very interest which you yourself are showing in the truth of the imminent return of the Lord Jesus is the evidence of the inspiration of this Word.

And so in closing may I again emphasize the fact that the most certain and imminent thing is the return of the Lord Jesus Christ before He lets judgment break loose upon this earth. May I again plead with you to "prepare to meet thy God." Are you ready? Are you prepared? If He should come today, are you ready to meet Him with joy because you have heeded His admonition, "Believe on the Lord Jesus Christ, and thou shalt be saved"?

CHAPTER THIRTY-THREE

The Signs of the Times, Part One

But thou, O Daniel, shut up the words, and seal the book, even to the time of the end: many shall run to and fro, and knowledge shall be increased (Daniel 12:4).

In this fourth verse of the twelfth chapter of Daniel we are told what to look for at the time of the end. We have been studying some of the signs of the times as suggested by this chapter, but we are not confined to it, for the entire Bible is an elaboration of these same words, and according to the Lord Jesus Christ, there has been another age in the history of man when knowledge was greatly increased. Contrary to common belief, the early days of man's habitation upon this earth were not days of ignorance, but soon after the Fall, man, who had been created in the image of God and perfection, reached and attained a height of knowledge and development in every conceivable line—a height which will be equaled only in this day in which we are living. It is a significant and important fact to remember that the Lord Jesus Christ when speaking of the events which would precede His Second Coming, referred us again and again to the days immediately before the Flood, the days which were the days of Noah. Although this fact is not recognized by a great many people, the days of Noah were characterized by the same things which will characterize the days immediately preceding the coming again of the Lord Jesus. One of these characteristics was that it was an age of rapid increase of knowledge, temporarily halted by the coming of the Flood which wiped out all but eight of the inhabitants of the world. Because of its tremendous significance we want to refer you in this connection to the record of it in the book of Genesis:

> And Cain knew his wife; and she conceived, and bare Enoch: and he builded a city, and called the name of the city, after the name of his son, Enoch . . . And Lamech took unto him two wives: the name of the one was Adah, and the name of the other Zillah. And Adah bare Jabal: he was the father of such as dwell in tents, and of such as have cattle. And his brother's name was Jubal: he was the father of all such as handle the harp and organ. And Zillah, she also bare Tubal-cain, an instructer of every artificer in brass and iron . . . And Lamech said unto his wives . . . I have slain a man to my wounding, and a young man to my hurt. If Cain shall be avenged sevenfold, truly Lamech seventy and sevenfold (Genesis 4:17, 19-24).

Now in this brief and seldom read and little understood passage in Genesis, we have a number of things which the Lord Jesus Christ must have referred to when He said, "As it was in the days before the flood." There are six things which characterize the days before the Flood, as given to us in this passage, and I trust you will read and study them carefully. Notice, therefore, that it was:

1. An age of city building. Cain built the first city (verse 17).

2. An age of polygamy. Lamech was the first polygamist (verse 19).
3. An age of development in agriculture. The beginning of cattle raising (verse 20).
4. An age of the development of music. Jubal was the first to handle the harp and the organ (verse 21).
5. An age of metallurgy. It was the early antediluvian iron and steel age (verse 22).
6. An age of crime. Lamech follows Cain's suit and kills two men (verses 23-24).

Now note each one of these indications carefully in the light of what we have read in Daniel, that knowledge shall be increased, and in the light of the rest of the Scriptures concerning the end of the age.

City Building

In Genesis 4:17 we read for the first time about the building of cities, and these were the creation of man. When God created man, He did not place him in a city, but in a garden. Cities were invented by wicked men, and have ever since been the very symbol of wickedness and corruption. In the concentrations of populations, sin develops at a rate utterly unknown in rural districts. Someone has said, "God lives in the country; the devil reigns in the city." Now space does not permit us to point out the dangers of city life, morally and spiritually —dangers unknown and impossible in many other districts. Well, it all began there before the Flood. It was the first great city-building boom of history and was followed by all the evils which are peculiar to the urban districts and city life. The past generation or two has been a repetition of the days of Noah, and today we are in the greatest city-building, house-building boom of all history.

Fifty years ago about 75 per cent of all people lived on farms and in small rural communities. Then came the industrial revolution with its machinery and labor-saving farm implements so that millions employed on the farms were no longer needed, but as the door of labor closed in the country, the newly built factories which sprang up in the cities were engaged in building the very labor-saving machinery which had called the workers from the farm. New and better machinery was built throwing more and more men out of work on the farms while demanding more and more men in the factory to build more labor-saving machines to throw more men out of work on the farms to seek employment in the city to build more machines to throw more men out of jobs, and so on indefinitely until today the ratio has been reversed and some 75 per cent of the population lives in the city with the corresponding increase of wickedness and crime which always characterizes city life. Therefore, if we would apply the words, as given in Genesis four, that Cain knew his wife and she conceived and bare Enoch and he builded a city, we would know that the city-building of today is another indication of the coming of the Son of Man.

POLYGAMY

The second characteristic of the antediluvian days was polygamy, the breakdown of the home. Lamech was the first to break God's rule of creation, and began a sin which culminated in the Flood. It was undoubtedly this that Jesus spoke of when He said that in the last days they would be marrying and giving in marriage. He was not referring to any condemnation of marriage, for that was a God-given institution; God Himself brought together the first man and woman in the Garden of Eden. The reference is to the abuse of marriage. God made one man, Adam, to be the husband of one wife, Eve, and said, "Therefore shall a man leave his father and his mother, and shall cleave unto his wife [not wives]: and they shall be one flesh." Today we have a repetition, therefore, of Noah's day.

I remember when, as a boy, we heard of a divorce, we thought it the greatest of shame. When a divorce was obtained, which was seldom, the parties concerned were often so ashamed that they left the community to begin life anew where they were not known. Divorces were hard to obtain, but better still, were seldom sought. Churches refused fellowship to the guilty parties and discouraged it violently. But today, thanks to a modern philosophy and enlightenment and our modern civilization, all of this is changed. Divorce is now glorified, and made a means of lucrative popularity.

The rate of divorce in the last fifty years has doubled, trebled, quadrupled and doubled again, while our land is becoming flooded with a generation of children who have never known the blessing of a happy home, and this has been the greatest single contributing factor to the juvenile delinquency problem. If all the committees and societies now working to solve this problem of juvenile crime would begin at the root, they should start with the divorce evil, for it is the basis of the whole matter. Statistics show that by far the greater majority of all juvenile crime cases come from broken homes. Divorce is an evil cancer, contrary to God's Word, and should never, never even be mentioned among believers. Yet, in some states, there are as many as six divorces annually for every ten marriages and they are still on the increase, and while the Scripture only recognizes one ground for divorce, the courts today

grant divorces on almost any ground whatsoever. God
help us in this day of crisis, for when the home deterio-
rates, the nation is doomed, no matter what other meas-
ures may be taken. As it was in the days of Noah, so
shall it be.

AGRICULTURE

Just a few words about the third sign of the end of
the age as given in Genesis 4. It was an age of great
development in agriculture and animal culture. Jabal,
in Genesis 4:20, was the first raiser of cattle mentioned
in history. The fact of the development of this branch
of modern civilization is too well known to need much
comment. What advancement has been made in farming
and agriculture with the new machinery, and in the
science and progress of cattle breeding as well as of
poultry and sheep! We have gone ahead by leaps and
bounds. The milk production of dairy cattle has been
pushed to unbelievable heights; in the development of
beef cattle, careful breeding and discoveries for pre-
vention of disease have done veritable miracles. Artificial
insemination of cattle with the seed of carefully selected
males has made prize stock available to all. The pedi-
greed seed of a prize-winning sire can be flown across
the country and even across the seas to introduce this
superstrain in herds abroad. Surely it is the age of
miracles in agriculture, horticulture and animal hus-
bandry. Well, Jesus said, "As it was in the days of
Noah."

THE MUSICAL AGE

And now a word about the fourth characteristic mentioned in this chapter. In Genesis 4:21 we have the name
of the first musician mentioned in history, Jubal. He was
the father of those, we read, who handle the harp and

organ. It was, therefore, an age of the development of
music. Little need be said about present-day music and
musical instruments. Never was there more music in the
air than there is today. We have but to tune in the radio
to learn that music is the basis of the great percentage
of programs, and *such music*. This is the age of jazz,
swing, syncopation, the development of pagan tintinnabu-
lations which defy all efforts at description. Music, music,
music, so-called music, squeaks, squawks, baby talk and
monkey calls until we read of people going almost completely crazy by the very influence of music. Yes, Jesus
knew what these days would be like when He compared
them to the days of Noah.

The Steel Age

Another important characteristic of the pre-Flood
days, one mostly overlooked by people who read the
Bible, was the development in the metallic arts. Tubal-
cain, we are told in verse 22, was an instructor in the
art of metallurgy, "an instructer of every artificer in
brass and iron." How tremendously striking is the
similarity to the age in which we live when we remember
the words of our Lord, "As it was in the days before
the flood"! This may, indeed, be called the metal age,
the steel age, and is often referred to in that way. The
steel industry today ranks at the very top of all in-
dustries. As the supplies of wood decreased, man developed the products of metal to an amazing degree.
Through alloys and compounds unbelievable strength
and durability have been developed; rust-proof and
corrosion-resisting compounds have revolutionized industry, agriculture, our domestic life and even our warfare. Steel products and products of other metals have
been developed until our locomotives and cars can

thunder along on two thin strips of steel in almost
perfect safety and at unbelievable speed. Trains have
been made one of the safest means of travel in the
world by the substitution of steel coaches and Pullman
cars for the old-fashioned combustible wooden coaches
of recent memory. Warships, airplanes, tanks and all
the equipment of war shriek the truth of Jesus' words
when He said, "As it was in the days of Noah." Tubal-
cain, "instructer of every artificer in brass and iron,"
has been resurrected in tens of thousands of men engaged today in the industry of ancient Tubal-cain before
the Flood. Think back twenty years when you bought
your first car with wooden frames and wooden bows
across the top and wooden running boards and dash-
boards and compare this car with the millions of automobiles which are on our highways today. Yes, Jesus
knew when He said, "As it was in the days of Noah."

VIOLENCE AND MURDER

And now we must consider the sixth and last of the
signs of the times given in this fourth chapter of Genesis in the light of Daniel 12. This man Lamech had
killed two men, and then boasted of it. He glorified the
business of murder. Instead of being ashamed of his
dastardly act he boasted of the fun he had had, and
gloated over the fact that he had killed two men. If we
were to use one single word to describe this age, it
would again be the word, "violence." Think of the war
which is named by the descriptive title, global war, and
the atrocities and violence in the world today. Think of
the crime and the destruction, and then remember that
man, instead of being smitten with repentance and sorrow, is still boasting of his achievements, and glories in
his iniquities. Men are glorified because of the number

of persons whom they may have killed. And so as we turn again to the twelfth chapter of Daniel where the Lord tells us that the last days shall be characterized by great increase of knowledge and great increase of speed, we find that the unregenerate human heart is only using these things to a large extent, not to make men more happy, not to make them more secure, but only to act as instruments of destruction and of suffering instead of the good purposes to which they might be used.

Today men are engaged in a real problem; they are struggling with the future of the atomic bomb, recognizing its awful destructibility and wishing and hoping that this newly discovered force might be turned into the ways of peace, to help men rather than to destroy men. They know not how to go about it, because as long as the heart of man is not regenerate, it can be nothing else but wicked. God says concerning the heart of man, that it is "deceitful above all things, and desperately wicked." In Romans 3:12 we are told, "They are all gone out of the way . . . there is none that doeth good, no, not one." Oh, the great need for the truth that only as Christ is received into the hearts of men can we ever solve the problem of world peace!

God's program is very clear, if we will abandon the ideologies of men and limit ourselves to the program as outlined in the Word of God. The Lord is going to allow man to prove that he cannot save himself, that man is an utter failure, that he is unable to bring in a man-made millennium, that the human heart is corrupt and deceitful and desperately wicked, and becomes only worse and worse as it becomes educated and trained. And when it seems that all is hopeless and that man will utterly destroy himself by the invention of his own hands instead of saving himself, then suddenly the Lord

will appear and call out the Church, the body of believers dead and living, and then after judging the
world for its wickedness and godlessness, the Lord Jesus
will return with His Church to set up His peaceful
global kingdom. He shall be King and the only King.
He shall rule the nations in righteousness, and prosperity
shall be the rule upon the earth. Wars will cease. The
nations shall beat their swords into plowshares and the
knowledge of the Lord shall cover the earth as the
waters cover the sea.

But this hopeful picture which we have presented is
only for those who have believed on the Lord Jesus
Christ, and refers only to those who have been saved,
for Paul places one condition on the hope of the Lord's
coming. He says, "If we believe that Jesus died and
rose again, even so them also which sleep in Jesus will
God bring with him." You must believe that Jesus died
and rose again. Then you can look through all the dark
clouds to that glad day when you will meet mother again,
and father, and when you, grieving mother, will be re-
united with that little blue-eyed, flaxen-haired darling
that was plucked from your bosom. Oh, if you have not
received Christ, in the light of all these imminent signs
of His return, will you not receive Him today? Then
amidst all the troubles and sorrows of life you can live
in peace as you hear Him say, "Let not your heart be
troubled . . . I will come again."

CHAPTER THIRTY-FOUR

The Signs of the Times, Part Two

And I heard the man clothed in linen, which was upon the waters of the river, when he held up his right hand and his left hand unto heaven, and sware by him that liveth for ever that it shall be for a time, times, and an half; and when he shall have accomplished to scatter the power of the holy people, all these things shall be finished. And I heard, but I understood not: then said I, O my lord, what shall be the end of these things? And he said, Go thy way, Daniel: for the words are closed up and sealed till the time of the end. Many shall be purified, and made white, and tried; but the wicked shall do wickedly: and none of the wicked shall understand; but the wise shall understand. And from the time that the daily sacrifice shall be taken away, and the abomination that maketh desolate set up, there shall be a thousand two hundred and ninety days. Blessed is he that waiteth, and cometh to the thousand three hundred and five and thirty days. But go thou thy way till the end be: for thou shalt rest, and stand in thy lot at the end of the days (Daniel 12:7-13).

These are the closing words of the book of the prophecy of Daniel, and record for us the final end and conclusion of the "times of the Gentiles," the age of Gentile domination which is man's rule of terror and confusion upon the earth in his effort to set up a man-made, man-governed kingdom and rule instead of the establishment of the kingdom of God upon the earth under His rightful King, the Lord Jesus Christ, who is called in Scripture the King of kings and the Lord of lords. Notice that the prophecy of Daniel ends with a promise. While Daniel contains much concerning judgment and God's revelation regarding the history of man upon the earth, yet consistent with the Word of God and the nature of God, this book ends with a precious and blessed promise to Daniel which by application includes all who like Daniel have placed their faith in the Lord Jesus Christ. The promise to Daniel is this: in the end of the days he shall stand in his lot, and in the meantime, he shall rest, that is, his body shall rest in the grave. The expression "end of the days," of course, refers to the days which are mentioned in the verses which we quoted at the beginning of this chapter. It is the promise that although Daniel will have to die and his body will be committed to the dust, at the conclusion of God's program in the ushering in of the Kingdom Age of the Millennial reign of Christ, Daniel will be resurrected from the grave and will stand in his lot, that is, he will receive the reward for his faithfulness and be restored to a place of reign and glory and power in the kingdom which Christ will set up when He comes again.

THE BEGINNING OF "THE DAYS"

You have probably noticed as you read these closing verses of Daniel that three definite periods of time are mentioned, all of which date from one event. These three periods of time begin with what Daniel calls the taking away of the daily sacrifice and the setting up of the abomination that maketh desolate. We have already repeatedly pointed out that the abomination of desolation will occur in the exact middle of the Tribulation Period, after a brief reign of peace under the false christ, the Antichrist. After the taking away of the Church of Jesus Christ, Satan, through his agent, the Man of Sin, will turn against the people of Israel, will take away the sacrifices which had been reinstituted in the Temple at Jerusalem, and instead of offering the Scripturally-enjoined sacrifices, he will set up an image of the beast which will be the fulfillment of the type of the image of Nebuchadnezzar which he set up in the plain of Dura and commanded all men to worship. We need not repeat again the reference from Revelation 13 as well as the other references in Daniel which present a description of the setting up of this image. The Antichrist will seek to bring into the world a universal religion and unite all men in one religious body. The center of this worship will be this image in the city of Jerusalem. This is the event from which the periods of time mentioned in the closing portion of Daniel are reckoned.

THREE PERIODS OF TIME

These three periods of time are called as follows: first, "a time," "times" and "a half" (Daniel 12:7); second "a thousand two hundred and ninety days" (Daniel 12:11); third, thirteen hundred and thirty-five days (Daniel 12:12). Because of the importance of these three periods of time we must remind you again and again that these times will begin in the middle of the Tribulation Period with the setting up of the abomination of desolation, spoken of by Daniel, by the Lord Jesus in Matthew 24, and again in Revelation 13, the **taking away of the daily sacrifice** which is the desecration of the Temple of Jehovah. Bear in mind that when the Lord Jesus Christ comes to take out His Church in the Rapture, the Tribulation, the day of Jacob's trouble, will be ushered in immediately. This Tribulation Period lasting seven years corresponds to the unfulfilled Seventieth Week of the prophecy of Daniel. This Tribulation Period is divided into two portions, or halves, and the entire period is called the Tribulation. The last half, or three and one-half years, is called the Great Tribulation. This second half of the Tribulation is ushered in by the setting up in the Temple at Jerusalm (which will then have been rebuilt under the rule of the Antichrist) of a gigantic image of the political head of the revived Roman Empire graphically described in Revelation 13.

This Antichrist, this Man of Sin, will command that all the inhabitants of the earth worship the image of this beast and, of course, the beast which it represents.

We have already noted carefully that the image of Nebuchadnezzar described in the third chapter of Daniel was a prophetic typical picture of this coming abomination. All those who will pledge allegiance to this beast, to the abomination of desolation, to this world organization, will be given a mark in their hands and in their foreheads which we believe will be the number "six, six, six," which will be their identification that they have aligned themselves with the enemies of Christ and have pledged obedience to the Antichrist and are willing to worship the image which has been set up in the Temple at Jerusalem. Remember in this connection that during the first three and one-half years of the Tribulation Period, Israel, the nation of Israel, will have returned to the literal land of Palestine under the promise of the Antichrist, the false Messiah, to rebuild their Temple, re-establish their Old Testament sacrifices and worship, and the promise of various favors to the now dispersed and scattered tribes of the nation of Israel.

However, all this apparent kindness will be only a ruse of the archdeceiver, Satan himself, and in the middle of this Tribulation Period he will suddenly turn against the nation of Israel, reveal his true color and identity, and one of his first acts, according to Scripture, will be to cause the sacrifices of the Temple to be outlawed. He will take away the daily sacrifice which has been re-established, and in their place will set up this image, a horrible image, which as we stated before and repeat without apology, will be the antitype and counterpart of the image of Nebuchadnezzar which was set up during his reign and which he commanded all the people to worship, and which was worshiped by all, with the exception of the few faithful Hebrews who were, as a result, cast into the fiery furnace. So too, in the end time, after the Church has been taken away, there will be a remnant of the nation of Israel, and an exact number of one hundred and forty-four thousand, who will again refuse, as did the three friends of Daniel, to worship the beast and to be disloyal to Jehovah, and as a result will be caused to pass through the fiery furnace of affliction, will be terribly persecuted, but again, like the three youths in the fiery furnace, the Lord will send His Son, the Lord Jesus Christ, the angel of the Lord, not only to preserve them, but to deliver and to exalt them.

Notice that the setting up of this image and the taking away of the daily sacrifice will occur in the middle of the Tribulation Period, and then, we are told, that a certain period of time will elapse after this, before the complete restoration of the Kingdom Age under the personal presence of the Lord Jesus Christ. It is important that one have a clear understanding of these three periods of time which are to follow. The first period of time which will elapse between the setting up of this image of abomination in the middle of the Tribulation and the personal public return of the Lord Jesus Christ upon the earth is called a period of "a time, times, and an half." This expression would perhaps be unintelligible if it were not for the abundance of Scripture which gives us in greater detail the exact length of this time. We are told in Revelation 13:5:

> And there was given unto him [that is, the Antichrist] a mouth speaking great things and blasphemies; and power was given unto him to continue forty and two months.

This reference mentions the definite period of time—three and one-half years, to be exact, which corresponds to the expression "a time, times, and an half." This is further identified as being exactly twelve hundred and sixty days. The testimony of the two witnesses mentioned in Revelation 11 corresponds to this period of time, the reign of the Antichrist, and is said in Revelation 11:3 to be forty-two months. In the third verse of Revelation 11 we are told:

> And I will give power unto my two witnesses, and they shall prophesy a thousand two hundred and threescore days, clothed in sackcloth.

This is the first division of the time which elapses between the revelation of the Antichrist and the setting up of the kingdom. Notice that this corresponds to the last half of the Tribulation to the coming of Christ in glory. In Revelation 19:11 we read:

> And I saw heaven opened, and behold a white horse; and he that sat upon him was called Faithful and True, and in righteousness he doth judge and make war.

We are told here that His coming will be public, and that He will be accompanied by the armies which are in heaven and will be seen by all men. In our next message we will consider the length of the time that Christ will be visible to the inhabitants of the earth before the day of Armageddon officially opens. The important question, however, before we conclude this chapter, is: *Are you ready for the revelation of the Lord Jesus Christ?* We believe that we are living in the very end-time age and the next event will be the calling away of the Church before God pours the vials of His wrath upon a disobedient world. Oh, how necessary, in the light of all these clear declarations of Scripture, that we should turn our eyes heavenward, away from the program of man, and prepare to meet the Lord Jesus Christ!

CHAPTER THIRTY-FIVE

The Signs of the Times, Part Three

And he said, Go thy way, Daniel: for the words are closed up and sealed till the time of the end. Many shall be purified, and made white, and tried; but the wicked shall do wickedly: and none of the wicked shall understand; but the wise shall understand. And from the time that the daily sacrifice shall be taken away, and the abomination that maketh desolate set up, there shall be a thousand two hundred and ninety days. Blessed is he that waiteth, and cometh to the thousand three hundred and five and thirty days. But go thy way till the end be: for thou shalt rest, and stand in thy lot at the end of the days (Daniel 12:9-13).

Before we conclude our study of the book of Daniel, we want to give you a picture of what lies in the immediate future. We believe, according to the signs of the times and the testimony in Scripture, that the next event in the program of God will be the return of the Lord Jesus Christ in the clouds of heaven to call out the believers, both dead and living, from the earth. Then, during the absence of the Church, He will usher in the Tribulation Period. After three and one-half years of false peace and prosperity under the mock messiah, the Antichrist, all hell will break loose upon this world.

This period will be ushered in by the setting up of a terrible image in the city of Jerusalem and an edict by the Man of Sin that all the world must worship this image. There will be, however, a company of people in Israel who will not submit themselves to this command, and as a result they will be terribly persecuted, but these one hundred and forty-four thousand faithful witnesses will be divinely and supernaturally spared and brought through the Tribulation Period. Exactly twelve hundred and sixty days after the setting up of the abomination of desolation in Jerusalem, the Lord Jesus Christ will return to this earth with His redeemed and glorified army consisting of the faithful who were resurrected at the Rapture. We find the record of this in Revelation 19, and we suggest that you study this chapter carefully in connection with the last chapter of Daniel. The Tribulation Period corresponding to the Seventieth Week of Daniel ends officially with the tenth verse of Revelation 19. Revelation 19:11 speaks of the visible personal return of the Lord Jesus Christ from heaven with His Bride. The account of the battle and its conclusion begins at verse 17 of Revelation 19. Chapter 20 of Revelation describes the establishment of the kingdom of Christ upon the earth with the binding of Satan and the reign of the saints. Note carefully John's declaration in Revelation 19:11:

> And I saw heaven opened, and behold a white horse; and
> he that sat upon him was called Faithful and True.

This verse speaks of the return of the Lord Jesus Christ, which is not an event that occurs in a moment of time, but is, rather, a series of events. We are told in verse 14, "The armies which were in heaven followed him." The fact that they followed Him indicates that a period of time will elapse between the Lord Jesus Christ's visible appearance and the beginning of the final Battle of Armageddon described in the last verse of this chapter. Daniel 12:11, as we have noticed, records this statement made by Daniel:

> And from the time that the daily sacrifice shall be taken away, and the abomination that maketh desolate set up, there shall be a thousand two hundred and ninety days.

We have already pointed out that from the setting up of the abomination to the personal coming of Christ was twelve hundred and sixty days. In this verse Daniel speaks of another period of time, twelve hundred and ninety days, or exactly thirty days more than the period mentioned in Revelation 11:3. The question is: What do these additional thirty days represent? We believe that they indicate the thirty days of grace which the Lord Jesus Christ will give to the nations between His personal appearing at the end of the Tribulation and the pouring out of His judgment in the Battle of Armageddon.

You will recall that in the days of Noah, which typified the second coming of Christ, the Lord granted the unrepentant a hundred and twenty years. Then Noah went into the Ark, but the judgment of the Flood did not fall until seven days after Noah had entered the Ark. During these seven days, after Noah had preached for one hundred and twenty years, the Ark was still open to any who might wish to repent and find refuge in the grace of God. The fact that none came does not take away the truth that the seven days before the Flood during which Noah was in the Ark represent the fact that God never sends judgment without a fair warning, without an opportunity to accept His grace.

When God comes to destroy the nations and to pour out His judgment in the Battle of Armageddon, He will again offer to man a period of grace, and this period between the personal return of Christ visibly with His Church and the beginning of His final judgment before the Millennium will be thirty days, the difference between twelve hundred and ninety (Daniel 12) and twelve hundred and sixty (Revelation 11). For a period of thirty days the Lord Jesus Christ will be visible to the nations of this earth gathered against Jerusalem and give them an opportunity to repent, but as we know from prophecy, they will not repent, but, instead, will join forces against the Lord and against His Christ. At the end of the thirty days the Lord Jesus Christ will begin His triumphal march from Jerusalem in order to destroy His enemies.

According to Daniel 12:12, this Battle of Armageddon will require an additional forty-five days:

> Blessed is he that waiteth, and cometh to the thousand three hundred and five and thirty days.

The period between the middle of the Tribulation and the return of Christ in glory will be twelve hundred and sixty days. Then will follow a thirty-day period of grace. After His visible return there will be a time in which the nations can repent if they will, but they will refuse. Consequently, at the end of the thousand two hundred and ninety days, Christ will usher in the Battle of Armageddon. This will require forty-five additional days and is described in detail in the nineteenth chapter of the book of the Revelation, beginning at verse 17.

> And I saw an angel standing in the sun; and he cried with a loud voice, saying to all the fowls that fly in the midst of heaven, Come and gather yourselves together

unto the supper of the great God: that ye may eat the
flesh of kings, and the flesh of captains, and the flesh of
mighty men, and the flesh of horses, and of them that
sit on them, and the flesh of all men, both free and bond,
both small and great. And I saw the beast, and the kings
of the earth, and their armies, gathered together to make
war against him that sat on the horse, and against his
army. And the beast was taken, and with him the false
prophet that wrought miracles before him, with which he
deceived them that had received the mark of the beast, and
them that worshipped his image. These both were cast
alive into a lake of fire burning with brimstone. And the
remnant were slain with the sword of him that sat upon
the horse, which sword proceeded out of his mouth: and
all the fowls were filled with their flesh (Revelation
19:17-21).

Although we realize that these closing verses of
Daniel have been subjected to many interpretations, and
despite the fact that they at first present a difficulty,
nevertheless we believe that this explanation is in
harmony with the remainder of the Word of God. Someone has said that the way to find the proper key is to
find the key which fits the lock. Therefore, after trying
all the interpretations of this closing passage of Daniel
we believe that this is the key which fits the lock
properly. Let us recapitulate briefly. From the time
of the return of the Lord for His Church to the middle
of the Tribulation will be three and one-half years. Then
Satan will reveal his Man of Sin and set up the abomination of desolation. After twelve hundred and sixty
days, three and one-half years, forty-two months, the
Lord will return. He will not judge the nations immediately but will permit them to have a period of respite,
during which they may still repent of their evil deeds.
After this thirty-day period of grace has ended, the Lord
Jesus Christ will pour out His judgment upon the wicked

nations so graphically described throughout the entire Prophetic Word. This will require a period of forty-five days, so that the time of the coming of Christ in His public appearing to the establishment of His kingdom upon the earth will be seventy-five days during which He will offer salvation and then pour out His judgment.

The Twenty-Three Hundred Days

We must, before we close, present a few additional facts about the twenty-three hundred days mentioned in Daniel 8:14. When we considered that chapter we reminded you that historically the two thousand and three hundred days constituted the exact period of time in literal days from the setting up of the image of Antiochus Epiphanes until the cleansing of the sanctuary by Judas Maccabeus. We have reminded you repeatedly that Scripture has not only a historic but a prophetic interpretation. We believe therefore that we are justified in saying that the twenty-three hundred days represent an additional period of time from the setting up of the abomination of desolation until the complete cleansing of Jerusalem and the ridding of the city and the land of Palestine of all the defiling rebellious nations. In Daniel 8:13-14 we read:

> Then I heard one saint speaking, and another saint said unto that certain saint which spake, How long shall be the vision concerning the daily sacrifice, and the transgression of desolation, to give both the sanctuary and the host to be trodden under foot? And he said unto me, Unto two thousand and three hundred days; then shall the sanctuary be cleansed.

Here, then, is the picture from the setting up of the abomination of desolation until the complete cleansing of the sanctuary, that is, the fulfillment of God's program in preparing for the kingdom of Christ would be twenty-three hundred days. This is an additional nine hundred and sixty-five days during which the land will be cleansed from the carnage of the recent Battle of Armageddon.

This, in briefest and barest outline, is the story of the days which lie ahead. Already we see the outline of the old Roman Empire being clearly drawn in Europe and throughout the world. We see the King of the North, the King of the East and the King of the South. It appears that everything is ready for the coming of the Lord Jesus Christ. It has been our purpose in these chapters to make God's people aware of the days in which we live in order that they may be encouraged in the face of discouragement, and, secondly, that we may warn those who are without Christ and who are still looking for a man-made millennium to turn away from all man's efforts and put their trust completely in the Lord Jesus. The most certain event is the coming again of Jesus Christ. The surest fact in the world is not death, but the return of the Lord Jesus Christ. When He comes again there will be a generation of people who will not see death. Jesus said, "He that believeth in me, though he were dead, yet shall he live: and whosoever liveth and believeth in me shall never die." We send this warning—it may be the last warning that we can give to a lost and dying world: *Jesus Christ is coming again.* This is today's message, not heard in many circles, to be sure, yet the most important message of this day: *Prepare to meet thy God.* May I ask you, therefore, are you ready for the return of Christ, and are you prepared to meet Him? Remember that the day of grace will be closed to you if you have heard the message and received the invitation but have deliberately failed to heed it. Remember that if you reject the offer of salvation, when the shout in the air calls God's people home—an event which may occur at any moment—it will be forever too late for you. The Bible says that then God will send upon those who have not believed the truth, strong delusion that they should believe the lie. You who have rejected the Lord Jesus Christ will then believe the Antichrist and with him not only pass through the Great Tribulation but finally be cast into the Lake of Fire forever. The door of mercy is still open. He is still pleading, "Come unto me, all ye that labour and are heavy laden, and I will give you rest." Receive Him now. Trust Him now. Be saved, and flee from the wrath to come. Let us close with the final verse of Daniel:

> But go thou thy way till the end be: for thou shalt rest, and stand in thy lot at the end of the days (Daniel 12:13).

Let us go our way and trust Him, resting in the promise that no matter how dark may be today, we have a blessed hope, and we can look beyond the clouds and human failure to that day when—

> Jesus shall reign where'er the sun
> Does his successive journeys run;
> His kingdom stretch from shore to shore,
> Till moons shall wax and wane no more.

The M. R. De Haan Classic Library

M. R. De Haan spoke to millions of listeners each week for some twenty-seven years on the *Radio Bible Class*. His academic training included a degree from Hope College, a medical degree from the University of Illinois Medical College, and further study at Western Theological Seminary. He was the author of more than nineteen books and countless daily devotionals in *Our Daily Bread*, published by RBC Ministries of Grand Rapids, Michigan.

Anyone interested in solid biblical studies for personal growth will find these titles to be rich sources of insight and inspiration.

Daniel the Prophet
ISBN 0-8254-2475-5   344 pp.   paperback

Portraits of Christ in Genesis
ISBN 0-8254-2476-3   192 pp.   paperback

Studies in First Corinthians
ISBN 0-8254-2478-x   192 pp.   paperback

Studies in Galatians
ISBN 0-8254-2477-1   192 pp.   paperback

Available from Christian bookstores or

kregel
PUBLICATIONS

P. O. Box 2607 • Grand Rapids, MI 49501-2607